Kitchen Cooks, Plate Twirlers & Troubadours

Writing Program Administrators Tell Their Stories

Edited by **DIANA GEORGE**

Foreword by Patricia Bizzell

New Perspectives in Rhetoric and Composition

CHARLES I. SCHUSTER, SERIES EDITOR

Boynton/Cook Publishers
HEINEMANN
Portsmouth, NH

Boynton/Cook Publishers, Inc.
A subsidiary of Reed Elsevier Inc.
361 Hanover Street
Portsmouth, NH 03801–3912
http://www.boyntoncook.com

Offices and agents throughout the world

Library of Congress Cataloging-in-Publication Data
Kitchen cooks, plate twirlers, and troubadours : writing program
administrators tell their stories / edited by Diana George.
     p.   cm.
   Includes bibliographical references.
   ISBN 0-86709-456-7 (alk. paper)
     1. Writing centers—Administration.   2. English language—
Rhetoric—Study and teaching.   I. George, Diana, 1948–
PE1404 .K56   1999
808'.042'068—dc21   98-54813
                                        CIP

Consulting editor: Charles I. Schuster
Production: Vicki Kasabian
Cover design: Darci Mehall
Manufacturing: Louise Richardson

Printed in the United States of America on acid-free paper
03 02 01 00 99 DA 1 2 3 4 5

*For Neva George, whose stories remain true
even as they change in my telling*

Contents

Foreword

On Good Administrators
Patricia Bizzell

"Oh no, not stories!" I moaned faintly, when Diana George told me about the collection on which she wanted me to comment. In theory, I admire writing that does serious intellectual work by combining the personal, the professional, and the political. Such writing might be called "loaded" stories. But in practice, I often find it hard to read, and even harder to write—my only venture in the genre being the introduction to *Academic Discourse and Critical Conscious-ness*, which David Bartholomae practically had to drag out of me one paragraph at a time. Why I shy away from this work would, no doubt, be a "loaded" story in itself, involving my strict Presbyterian upbringing, current political concerns, and more. But let's skip that for now.

What quickly became clear to me as I read *Kitchen Cooks, Plate Twirlers, and Troubadours*, however, is that there is a compelling reason for combining the personal, the professional, and the political in these essays. To understand his or her work as a writing program administrator, an author here might draw on knowledge gained as a parent, feminist theorist, poet, post-structuralist, or, in one case, commercial litigator. But such combinations are necessary because, to be a good administrator, as these essays show, you must draw on *everything* you know.

Can that be said of any academic position? I don't think so. Consider the traditionally trained and functioning tenured professor of literature. His or her job requires continuing to develop the specialized scholarship begun in graduate school—a task which literary scholars typically pursue alone—and conveying the fruits of this research to students—typically, my experience suggests, by traditional methods such as lecture or seminar discussion, while assigning a paper or two. This work demands a relatively limited number of skills and kinds of human interactions in the course of a day. One stays focused within a chosen discipline, and rarely interacts with anyone with whom one experiences a substantial power disadvantage. Interaction with professional peers in the department and in the larger professional world—e.g., as a journal reviewer—may also be required, and there may be more power imbalances here, to be sure, but basically once one is established in the profession, these interactions are among peers. At any rate, the key point here is that one is doing what one was trained to do in graduate school.

Administrative work, as the essays in this volume testify, requires a much greater multiplicity of tasks and interactions. The administrator may teach and do research in his or her area of graduate training, but this work constitutes only a small fraction of the job. The administrator must consider issues of budget, curriculum planning, personnel management, technological support, physical plant—a veritable host of issues—and must deal with a wide range of people, from students to professional subordinates and peers to power brokers in academic high places, to address these issues. Graduate training, as several contributors to this volume lament, does not—and perhaps cannot possibly—prepare a person for these demands. To succeed, even to survive, as I said before: you have to draw on everything you know. You have to draw on every inner resource for a wide variety of "people skills," you have to apply your training as a scholar and researcher to devising solutions to practical problems, you have to theorize the everyday—and often, you have to do these things unexpectedly, at top speed, for high stakes, higher than just your own professional well-being.

Perhaps this contrast between the tenured professor and the administrator is overdrawn; I admit it. Especially in disciplines other than English studies, collaborative scholarship is common and people have to manage grant budgets and numerous research assistants to get their work done. Other disciplines also have more opportunities for consultative work outside the academy, where an administrative-like multiplicity of concerns often enters into the problems being addressed. These may be some of the reasons why, as several contributors here note, faculty outside the English department often appreciate the work of the writing program administrator more than do those in her or his so-called home department.

Nevertheless, it has been my experience that good administrative work is not generally appreciated in the academy. Working on a committee that aimed to democratize faculty governance at my school several years ago, I was surprised to discover how many faculty wanted no part of governance—"Don't increase my role! I'm busy with my students and my research! Just let the deans do it. . . ." The work of the campus administrators seemed to be seen as a particularly onerous form of service that these people provided to the rest of the community, out of the goodness of their hearts or because they couldn't get out of it. There didn't seem to be any awareness that good administration requires special talents or offers special rewards. Rather the attitude seemed to be that any idiot could do it, but only an idiot would want to—an idiot, or someone exceptionally charitable. Odd, isn't it, how that's the same thing they often say about teaching writing: any idiot can do it, but only an idiot would want to, after the obligatory apprentice period is over?

In fact, as should be clear from the essays in this volume, being a good administrator does indeed require special talents. It is a much harder job than tending one's own garden in one's own academic specialty, fraught with toads though that garden may be, especially if one is untenured. Perhaps the most difficult administrative skill of all is the ability always to see the big picture, to keep the vision in mind of what your program and your college want to accomplish academically, even as you are bogged down in the daily trivia of memos, meetings, and the latest "crisis." But as these essays also make clear, good administration brings deep satisfaction to those who are able to keep the vision in view and to see it served, however partially. There is deep satisfaction in keeping things working reasonably well amid a host of constraints—indeed, working amid the constraints is the very condition that brings out the best efforts and creativity of really good administrators.

"A good administrator is concerned about the life people lead in the workplace," mused my husband, Bruce Herzberg, while we were discussing whether he would pursue an invitation to apply to become an academic dean at his school. I think this means something more than seeing to it that people do their work. A good administrator is not a supervisor. He or she is a person who thinks creatively about how to help people do their work better and enjoy it more. The good administrator notices minutiae of people's working lives that the people themselves take for granted—he or she can be like the person who finally fixes the dripping faucet that everyone else in the family has been ignoring while suppressing their annoyance at it. The good administrator maximizes everyone's access to their psychic strength.

Why is it so hard to accept that better administration means better teaching and learning? We firmly believe that better composition teaching produces better student writing, no matter how hard it is to document the improvement empirically. I believe the same can be said for writing program administration, and administration generally—when it's good, it produces better development for everybody. Truly, the contributors to this volume should be proud of their work. Above all, every contributor is concerned that the students and colleagues with whom he or she is working should grow and develop as writers, scholars, and as human beings. We all know, to our sorrow, what it's like to work under administrators who do not have these concerns at heart. What a great gift is given to students and colleagues by those who do.

Introduction

This is a book of stories, and so I begin with a story.

When I was a small child, my grandmother's kitchen was a mysterious world. No child was allowed in before or during meals. For hours before dinner, we could hear her banging pans—moving steadily from sink to table to stove—seriously tending to pot roast, potatoes, gravy, and bread. During dinner, she rarely stayed in her chair long enough to eat. She'd sit down and notice no salt. Then, she'd sit down and realize the baby needed a towel. Then she'd sit down and wonder who needed more milk. Finally, she'd settle in to taste a dinner she would glumly declare ruined. We children, absorbed in this wonderful food, happily ignored what we knew was false modesty. My mother's reaction was quite different from ours. My mother despaired. You see, my mother was no cook. Grandma had kept her locked out of that kitchen the same way she kept all of us out. As soon as my older sister and I could stand on a small chair and reach the stove, Mom put us to work in her own kitchen while she directed us from a chair in the next room. By the time Kathy and I were teenagers, Mom was deferring to our judgment in all matters culinary. We were Grandma, and Mom still remained outside the kitchen.

It may seem something of a stretch to say this, but I think Grandma would have made a classic, long suffering writing program administrator. She thought she had to do everything herself. She let others in under only the severest supervision. She was never satisfied with her own work, and she never complained about working too much. Of course, she also passed along none of her skills. My mother, even after ten children, never did quite get the hang of cooking. Kathy and I still try to guess at recipes that might have been Grandma's cinnamon coffee cake. We don't know. She left no directions. She told few stories, and those she did tell, she told briefly in a manner suggesting she couldn't see why we'd be interested in the first place.

As the title for this volume suggests, writing program administrators can be like the kitchen cook who works ceaselessly but jealously guards the secret of the great meal. Or, as Mary Pinard tells it in one of the contributions that first inspired this volume, WPAs are like those plate twirlers on *The Ed Sullivan Show*, deftly moving back and forth across the stage to keep all the plates going at once. Hers is an apt metaphor for the world of most WPAs—on stage, trying to sustain the illusion of perpetual motion, worried over how to end the show without losing control as those plates go crashing onto the stage floor.

I don't believe this was the volume I had in mind when Chuck Schuster first asked me if I would be interested in putting together a collection of essays in which WPAs tell their stories. I knew I didn't want war stories. And, Chuck and I were very sure we didn't want stories so tied to place and circumstance that readers might be entertained but not much more. To be honest, I had no idea what I would get, and for awhile I wasn't sure I'd get anything at all. Nearly every one of these writers has told me how very hard it was to write their articles. "I don't know what it is," Beth Daniell lamented one day over the phone, "Has anybody else had trouble writing this essay?"

Yes, Beth. Everyone has had trouble writing this essay. Meaningful stories, it turns out, are very hard to tell.

I do know that some of my colleagues would say that stories alone are simply not enough. Yet, some storytelling is necessary if we are to pass on more than theory and pedagogical or administrative tactics to those who come after us. And, I believe there are many stories worth telling, many that go far beyond the story alone. Today, the health of the writing program is crucial to the health of many departments. In addition to programs run from English departments, the writing across the curriculum program which is often placed outside academic departments, is in many places central to cross-curricular efforts throughout colleges and universities. WPAs make these programs possible, and their jobs are becoming, if anything, even more complicated as they encounter new technologies, tough political battles, the development of new and bigger graduate programs, labor rights issues, and the ongoing work of offering solid writing courses for their students.

As I read through this collection and note my own response to the stories here, I realize that it is not at all by mere chance that I wrote my dissertation on *Tristram Shandy*. At the time, I believed that Tristram knew more of the truth of human experience than Isabel Archer would ever guess at. But, of course, I didn't know much at all about human experience as James understood it. I knew much better the absurdity of human experience, and so I was drawn to Sterne and Faulkner and Welty and Swift and Fielding. By the time I finished college, I had learned to appreciate James, but I think I saw in him a heightened sensibility. Fielding and Sterne never reached such heights, yet somehow they got closer to what I believed was true of life: the absurd, the unexpected, the inability to tell one story without telling many (sometimes telling them all at once). So, what I have to offer in this collection is that kind of reality—the telling of one story through and around many. The world depicted in most of these stories is hardly one of heightened sensibilities, but it is one most WPAs will recognize. And, it is one that tracks the life of a profession in a very different way than ours has been tracked in most of our literature.

Our profession already has fine books that tell us about ourselves. Our shelves are packed hard with volumes and articles arguing theory, detailing pedagogy, analyzing curricula. We have collected essays on politics and the WPA, on the intellectual work of the WPA, on the WPA and interdisciplinary programs. Again and again, we seem to want to insist loudly that the work of administering a writing program goes far beyond seeking funding, fighting over scheduling, and fielding student complaints. This work comes, we argue, from our lives as teachers and scholars, writers and thinkers. The scholarship generated from these discussions has been important to what we do. And, yet, it may be even more important for us to understand that this is a job and that we are workers whose work lives are often not so very separate from the things that concern us in our home and our intellectual lives. It may be equally important to understand that what we do in these jobs is as figured by our cultural and social histories as by the institutional and economic restraints we confront daily in the workplace.

Although we have sometimes made it seem so, WPA work is hardly a world filled with selflessness and noble goals. That is certain. And, yet, it isn't the power trip some might have imagined, either. Many of these writers remind us—as they remind themselves—that they have little of the sort of power that makes others envious. The power they do have, though, might be what keeps them in the job: They have power to shape a curriculum. And what frustration, disappointment, and even sadness we see in some of these stories comes from not realizing that power to its fullest.

A good number of the administrators you will meet in this collection are what Jeannette Harris has called herself: "accidental." Before they found themselves running programs, very few had ever even considered working as an *administrator*—a word that calls up not even Dilbert but his clueless boss. And, yet, it is clear from what they write that they do love this work. More than one write about the trauma of turning the position over, even when they chose to. Many (and I'm one of these) gave up the position once only to be lured back into it a few years later. We said it took up too much of our lives, but we apparently liked that part of our lives more than we were willing to admit. And, many (I am also one of these) went on leave the year they gave up their positions. We all said we needed the break. That is probably true, but I suspect we also didn't want to watch someone else rearrange our kitchens.

In my family, there is one great grandfather my mother used to describe as a "song and dance man," which she said meant he was probably in Vaudeville. That may be. I do have a picture of two young girls—stage name The Locket Sisters—who my grandmother claimed were the "theatrical cousins." So, perhaps the theater is really what that great grandfather did. My own guess is that he might just as easily have been what most of us mean today when we call someone a "Song and Dance Man." He might have been good at a story—not so good at putting things into practice but very good at setting up the illusion.

More than one WPA has certainly felt like a Song and Dance Man (or Woman), though few I know meant simply to create a good illusion. Still, we've run programs that had little or no funding, created live curricula against the painted flat of the undergraduate catalogue, tapped cleanly across the polished stage wondering who picked that music, and some have made promises they knew they could never keep. The writers in this volume are good storytellers, and many have created much out of very little, but they are not just doing a song and a dance. Through stories like Richard Miller's and Marguerite Helmers', they are able to show us the political realities of writing program administration. Or, like Mara Holt and Nancy Grimm, they examine how we have grown to understand ourselves and our work through the theory and pedagogical practice important to the curricula we create and enact.

I suppose what I had in mind for this collection was a kind of workhorse document. What I got was something much beyond workhorse prose. I got a portrait of people in a profession. And, in that portrait, I got a portrait of a profession.

Like many good stories this collection opens with origins. In Part 1, "Who We Are; What We Would Be," the writers tell of personal histories that intersect with their professional lives and that help them define the job of writing program administrator. Part 2, "WPAs at Work," presents the writing program within the context of institutional realities—first-year student orientation, TA rebellions, programs expected but unfunded. In Part 3, "WPAs in Collaboration," WPAs tell of projects that are interdisciplinary, of programs developed over time and in the spirit of collaboration, and of the changing demands that technology is placing on writing instruction. I conclude this collection with a coda and with Jeanette Harris on the importance of mentoring in our profession. We are, she reminds us, always teachers and mentors to our students and to each other. If anything, I'd say this is actually a mentoring collection, a place to learn of and from each other.

A good story does more than hold us in its world as it unfolds. A good story tells us something of ourselves. For WPAs, a good story ought to send us back to the scholarship and the institutional realities with yet another important piece to the puzzle of this work. And, that, in the end, is what these stories are meant to do.

Part I

Who We Are; What We Would Be

In the summer of 1988 Newport, Rhode Island, was having an uncommonly hot and humid spell just in time for the first WPA Summer Conference I attended. I had to be talked into going because, even though I liked the work I was doing in our writing program, I couldn't imagine anything less interesting than an entire conference on administration. That summer conference remains one of the best professional experiences I have had, but it is also worth mentioning here because it was the first time I had ever heard a graduate student frame a question with these words: "As someone who hopes to be directing a writing program one day, I wonder if you could tell me . . . ?"

Actually, I don't even know the rest of the question. I have only recently come across my notes from that conference, but I do remember why I recorded only the first part of what this student asked. The rest of the question didn't matter much to me. I was astounded at how much the profession had changed since I had finished graduate school and had begun my own work as a writing program administrator. Most of my fellow graduate students had wanted to get as far away from teaching writing as quickly as they could. They surely didn't ever want to be condemned to running a writing program. I could tell them what energized me about that work, but I knew they couldn't hear that. One had even written to tell me that teaching composition was turning his brain into cream of mushroom soup. He had meant to be a scholar.

The stories in this first section are from scholars and writers who might also call themselves reluctant administrators, at least in the beginning. They narrate a kind of coming of age tale in which their personal histories merge with their intellectual histories to help them make sense of what they do now and how they understand the job of running a writing program. Within stories of family matters and private wishes, they address questions of gender politics, of class background and expectation, and of institutional and economic realities. It is within these contexts that the writers here tell their stories of becoming WPAs.

Critique's the Easy Part

Choice and the Scale of Relative Oppression

Richard Miller

This work. The teaching of writing. The training of teachers. And most of all this business of assisting in the administration of a large writing program. Especially, this work and everything it entails: handling complaints, making policy decisions, ranking applicants, mediating between warring parties, shuffling paper, writing reports, serving as a link in a chain of command that extends over the horizon, catching flack, attending meeting after meeting after meeting. This work, its activities and its states of being. This was not what I originally wanted to do with my life. It was not my first choice.

Like so many people who end up in this profession, I, too, had other plans. Indeed, when I was preparing to graduate from college in 1983, I had devoted myself to fashioning the persona of someone resolutely anti-professional. So, while my peers were getting ready to move on to law school or med school or business school, I was entertaining myself with tales about the writer's life. Looking into the future, I could see quite clearly that, when my peers were off satisfying their venal lusts in some corner office, I was going to be hard at work perfecting my craft, nurturing that cold gemlike flame. Seduced by the romantic allure of suffering in the garret and the poet's noble quest to create beauty in an otherwise indifferent world, I saw my days taken up with casting about for inspiration, composing, revising, reading, perhaps even sitting in a café distributing equal doses of wisdom and disdain to those within earshot. I knew such a life would require discipline, solitude, and patience. I knew, as well, that there would be years spent anxiously hovering over the mailbox, waiting for news from the editor of this or that small journal. Years where, if I was to keep going, I would have to find in every letter of rejection confirmation that the world was still lagging behind, still blind to the truths it was my job to reveal. This was sure to be disappointing work but, because I had been so thoroughly schooled in the virtues of persistence, I was certain I had what it took to hold out for that great day of discovery. And so, at one point in time, if you'd asked me—and perhaps even if you hadn't—I would have said that my first choice was the writer's life and everything I imagined it to be.

It's easy enough to say, now, that the young man I've described was deluded: about the pleasures and rewards of writing, about the importance of poetry, about his commitment to such work, about his own talents. However satisfying it is, though, to make such judgments, I have resurrected this previous incarnation of myself not to indulge in the modest pleasures that autocritique affords but rather to foreground, as a problem, the activity that lies at the center of any life. That is, given an array of possible courses of action, a set of possible lives, how does one choose what to do?

I can put this problem another way. After years of schooling, analysis and critique become one's second nature. So much so, in fact, that looking at the world and determining its shortcomings ceases to require any effort at all. And, perhaps because those of us who go on to enter the teaching profession are paid to extol the virtues of critical thinking, we lose sight of the fact that unleashing this automatic response on the social text of one's life (or on the culture at large or on departmental policy) is, in itself, no more challenging — or useful — than shooting ducks in a barrel. For, as we all know, after the flurry of noise and feathers, there's never anyone around to clean up the mess. That is, it's easy enough to know when things are going wrong and to rail away at a world gone mad. The hard part comes in the wake of critique, because it is here that one must choose a course of action, invent solutions, and then fabricate the conditions that generate the life-sustaining sensation of forward movement.

I am on intimate terms with the limits of critique and the complex demands of social agency now, but I knew nothing of these matters when I was just out of college. Back then, I could talk the talk about choosing one's own destiny, but in the event, my fervent convictions about my place in the world actually left me with no options. For reasons that aren't worth pursuing here, I felt at the time that writing was what I had to do, that it was my destiny. I would write my poems, my short stories, my pithy observations about peculiar local mannerisms. I thought this would be sufficient to my needs.

I was, in fact, surprised by how precipitously the creature comforts fell away. In a matter of months, I had relocated to Vermont, moved into an apartment directly above a college bar, settled into the writer's life. My roommates got the bedrooms; I chose the two oversized closets: one for my mattress and the cardboard box that held my clothes; the other for my desk, my typewriter, my books. I waited for inspiration. I bit the end of my pencil. I wrote about feelings I wished I had, about experiences I had read about.

I went on public assistance.

Young, healthy, newly possessed of a college degree. Buying cheese curls and ice cream with food stamps. Floating.

This rapid downward spiral was one of many final outrages. This was another: my roommates and I went up to the neighboring college to listen to an end-of-semester poetry reading. A nice gallery, lots of exposed wood, student work gracing the walls. An earnest young man who read the following one-line poem:

My penis is the ripcord of the universe.

According to generic conventions, the turning point in a literacy narrative is supposed to occur when the protagonist catches a glimpse of the power of reading and writing and this glimpse, in turn, sets in motion the machinery of critical reevaluation that in turn changes the course of the protagonist's life. Usually, the protagonist feels that he or she is in the presence of an extraordinary power—literacy itself—or an extraordinary book—the Bible—or an extraordinary mind—you choose the example. In this instance, though, I felt none of these things. Rather, this ridiculous poem with its foolish, stumbling sense of self-importance, captured only too well my dawning awareness that I had grossly over-valued the act of writing. One could even say that "the poem" didn't stop at critiquing the very notion I held most dear—namely, that writing matters more than anything, but that it went on to expose "the writer" to be a social-isolate who mistakenly believes that the salvation of the world depends on his actions alone.

This critique did not lift me out of myself. Nor did it give rise to a transcendent experience that revealed to me the necessity of my continuing to spend hours in my closet penning poems even I could hardly bear reading. Quite to the contrary, I began to see with an almost unavoidable clarity that I had made a terrible, perhaps uncorrectable, mistake in heading down this path. I looked into the future and saw a lifetime spent attending readings where the authors shared their thinly veiled masturbatory fantasies, their recollections of violations—both real and imagined—their outrage at the world, and their plaintive longings for a sense of connection. I saw, as well, a lifetime spent producing similar material and I wanted to put a gun to my head.

I knew I had to get out. But when the going gets tough, the clueless get to floating. So, I floated. I worked in a bookstore. I spent some time as a secretary, a world traveler, and, in my darkest hour, a technical writer. Years passed.

The enabling myth of career counseling books like *What Color Is Your Parachute?* is that, at some point in everyone's life, all career options are open. All you need do is spend some time checking out the lay of the land. Do an internal inventory, some soul searching, a check of differing geographic locales and differing salary levels. What kind of life do you want to live? What are you good at? What do you enjoy doing?

Make a choice.

Go for the informational interview. Find a way in the backdoor. Get in on the ground floor. Build a network. Make some connections. Move up whatever ladder it is you've climbed on to. Go for it!

I spent an afternoon punching in answers to these questions, getting career counseling from a computer. At the end of the day, my destiny was clear: all roads led to podiatry.

This record of my floating could go on interminably, but I've told enough to foreground the problematic nature of the concept I believe must occupy the center of any writing program administrator's professional life: choice. Now, from a certain vantage point, linking writing programs and choice must seem a willful act of self-deception since, as we all know, first-year composition carves out a province in the academic empire where choice is a privilege accorded only to the very few. The students, we must remember, take the courses we oversee because they are required to, not because they choose to. And, on the other side of the lectern, many of those who teach our courses do so because these assignments are the only ones available to them, not because they are committed to this work or because they have a particular talent for it. For example, here at Rutgers, the writing program employs over one hundred teaching assistants from the English department and another fifty from other disciplines across the university. Most all of these teachers would rather be providing instruction in their major fields of study—this would be their first choice. But, because the first-year writing requirement produces a demand for instruction that is felt nowhere else in the curriculum, our teaching assistants, adjuncts, and part-timers are given the responsibility of handling a course where endless amounts of student writing must be read, assessed, and responded to. To put the bleakest face on it, then, WPAs are in charge of a course taught by a reluctant labor force to a conscripted audience. And, while various managerial decisions can serve to alleviate this problem, creating converts among students and teachers alike, no amount of tinkering with the system is going to alter the fact that the vast majority of students and teachers look forward to putting first-year composition behind them as quickly as possible.

These are hardly working conditions that evoke images of choice, of free individuals freely choosing their destinies. It is rather a line of work where one is all too likely to encounter what Susan Miller has called "the sad women in the basement"—those exhausted, abandoned laborers who, like the cleaning staff, perform a service others would prefer not to think about. And given this fact about work in composition, it is little wonder—we must admit—that few would say they had always dreamed of becoming a writing program administrator. That this life was their first choice.

And, though it may seem paradoxical, it is precisely for this reason that I think it so important that we think about what role choice can play in the administration of a writing program. As it turns out, I actually feel extraordinarily lucky to have ended up in composition and luckier still to have been hired into a program where the director has shielded me from most of the administrative work in the years leading up to my tenure vote. In other words, I feel quite fortunate that I *didn't* get my first choice and that I was able to escape what was, for me, the unbearable loneliness of writing for and to myself. When I gave up on the writer's life and began casting about with increasing desperation for something to do with myself, I fell into a job as a "learning skills specialist," was sent, by chance, to CCCC the year it was in New Orleans, and suddenly found there what I didn't know I was looking for—a community of teachers committed to thinking about writing as a social act. What appeared, in the moment, to be a series of random acts and aimless decisions has since assumed, in retrospect, the shape of a coherent plan. This is the power of narrative at work, which can erase both the contingent nature and the unintended consequences of any given act of choice.

My point, then, is this: While I consider myself quite fortunate to have ended up in composition studies, I didn't always feel this way. I had wanted the writer's life, or at least so I had thought. And, when that door closed, I didn't know what to do. Luckily, I was forced to contend with a world that was unresponsive to my personal desires, a *social* world where I had to place my needs and interests in dialogue with the needs and interests of others. Luckily, the contingent nature of this same social world *made* me see that "free choice" is an illusion and that all we ever have at any given moment is "constrained choice"—choice among a handful of options, those few made visible to us by the indeterminate interplay of our historical moment and our personal predispositions and predilections. This is the space of creativity and imagination, this is where one learns to make the best of what's at hand.

Thus, I've begun by describing the mismatch between my own desires at a given moment and the consequences of pursuing those desires not to shake my fist at a cruel world that refused to nurture the artistic ventures of one of its denizens. Rather, I have meant to illustrate the importance of cultivating what might be called "the arts of contending with disappointment" for, surely, there is nothing so dependable in this line of work as disappointment, rejection, defeat. Or, to put this the way I think it must be put if one is going to find pleasure and satisfaction in the business of overseeing the labor of others, the life of a writing program administrator affords one endless opportunities for innovation, negotiation, and collaboration. This shift in terminology may well seem a handy bit of doublespeak born of necessity or, worse yet, a serving of chicken soup for the soul—that anecdotal office technology designed to instill in the disenfranchised the belief that, when the world spirit has handed them lemons, it is their job to figure out how to make lemonade. Perhaps because I, too, find loathsome the mandatory optimism of corporate culture and its chief promulgators—the new army of change managers who all intone, in unison, the necessity of seeing that the glass is not half-empty, I can only defend the lexical substitutions I have suggested here by saying that they have helped me the most in fending off the constant companions of institutional life—cynicism and despair. Acknowledging these constraints lets me know what I'm working with.

Of course, the fact that institutional life gives rise to a general feeling of hopelessness and powerlessness is obvious to us all: indeed, the very

pervasiveness of these sentiments in the academy guarantees that anyone involved in this business can easily be prodded into sharing his or her vision of
some better world where the work wouldn't be so alienating, the bureaucratic
structure so enfeebled, the administration so indifferent. With regards to the
administration of writing programs, these dreams tend to take one of three
forms: utopian plans for writing communities comprised of fully-intending,
free willed subjects happily engaged in the composing process; collaborative
projects that lead faculty members across the university to share the responsibility for providing sustained writing instruction; or resolutions for creating
working conditions where writing teachers are accorded the respect and the
salaries they deserve. And, when such plans for revolutionizing the world of social relations fail—as they must—to be fully realized, the nearly irrepressible
urge that everyone feels is to blame the failure on bureaucratic malfeasance and
the other ills that are imagined to plague higher education: a "weak" student
body, a conservative faculty uninterested in teaching, an unsupportive administration, a reactionary public, state governments committed to the quick fixes,
etc. Get disappointed enough times, see two or three carefully thought out plans
go down the drain and cynicism and despair seem like the only reasonable responses to have. And, once one has fallen into that mindset, all that's left to look
forward to in the long walk to retirement is a life spent letting everyone else
know that everything in the system works together to prevent innovation. That
change isn't possible. That hope is for the young, the naive, the foolish.

I have come to believe that composition's love affair with the writing process has, in its own way, actually helped to perpetuate this cyclic, institutional
production of cynicism and despair. Our disciplinary predisposition to cast the
world of social relations in terms of the writing process (Freire and Macedo's
Reading the Word, Reading the World being the locus classicus) has worked,
perhaps inadvertently, in combination with the post-structural project of textu-
alizing all experience to promote the sense that what awaits us all is a world
ready and willing to be "revised." This analogy is not entirely without merit,
so long as it is understood that "revision" is a highly constrained, largely uncertain activity. As writers and as writing teachers, we all know that the blank
screen is not a free space, but one overrun by a host of shaping concerns that
determine what can be said aloud. We know, in other words, that it simply isn't
the case that *anything can happen* during the revision process. And we know
as well that quite frequently almost nothing does: what change occurs is often
slight, almost imperceptible, and even occasionally regressive, when the writer's
awareness of new possibilities sends the ever recursive writing process spiral-
ing into retrograde.

We know this as writers and teachers and yet, as I've said, there's an almost
irresistible temptation, when thinking or speaking of "revising" institutional
relations or pedagogical practice or the social sphere more generally, to con-
ceive of an absolutely compliant world ready to be rewritten in whatever way
we see fit. Now, for the sake of argument, we can entertain the hypothesis that,

in the privacy of one's study, it is possible to hold off the pressures of all potential audiences for one's writing and to begin to revise freely, deleting unsatisfactory paragraphs, typing over lines, tightening the cadence, getting everything, however briefly, to make sense. But, as important as this private scribbling is to the writing process, it is impossible to know the significance of such work until one moves one's newly revised product from the study to the mailbox, submits it for publication, and puts it into circulation in the heterogeneous world of possible readers. Once one's writing has moved into the social world—the world of feedback and assessment, it becomes clear that revising in the study isn't the free activity one might have imagined it to be. To begin with, if the writing is going to be read by anyone besides the author, there are all the obvious problems involving real audiences: there are the available journals, the available readers; there are the prevailing concerns and the required citations; there are the shifting codes and conventions—written and unwritten—for presenting an academic mind at work on a problem. Then there's the inescapable fact that what makes sense in the study just won't and can't ever make the same kind of sense to other readers out in the world. And, finally, there are the consequences of this fact—namely, that what has now become the "proto-article" will have to be changed, often in substantial and unanticipated ways, if it is ever to see the light of day. In revisionary work of this kind, one never gets one's "first" choice. One gets, instead, what the world and the profession happen to offer at any given moment. One is, in effect, compelled by circumstance to innovate, negotiate, and collaborate.

There are a number of ways to describe the options a writer has under these circumstances. On the one hand, there's compliance, complicity, toeing the party line, selling-out, kissing butt; on the other, there's fidelity, artistic integrity, staying true to one's vision, speaking truth to power. Cast in these terms, it's not hard to know which choice one is supposed to make. But, calling on another set of terms can muddy this simple decision. On the one hand, there's learning how to gain a hearing; on the other, there's the solitary pleasure of a good rant. Or, reversing the poles completely, one could say: on the one hand, there's work; on the other, food stamps.

How do you choose?

As long as the world of choice is schematized along such starkly dichotomized lines, there is little hope that the work of revising for publication—or of the business of writing program administration—can be understood or experienced as anything other than a process of corruption, whereby what is pure and good is sacrificed to what is venal and expedient. Obviously, this is a handy way to make sense of the world, since it guarantees that the success of others can be dismissed as mere pandering to the lowest common denominator, while one's own failures can be infused with a kind of quixotic heroism. This, at any rate, is how I deployed this critical frame while I was trying to decide where to go once I stepped off the commencement stage with my bachelor's degree: the pure life of writing over the compromised life of the professional. This way of understanding the choices that lay before me didn't serve me particularly well on that occasion and, were I to have continued to rely on this rhetoric of moral superiority while serving as Acting Director of the Writing Program, I would have been blind to all the options that exist between the poles of purity and corruption. I would, in short, not have been able to function effectively in the pragmatic, compromised world of administration.

I realize that defining the job of writing program administration in such mundane terms opens me to the charge that I'm a manager, not a teacher, and that, as such, I must have the interests of management closer to my heart than those of the teachers or the students. Indeed, I was not long in my office before a teacher informed me that my hiring policies were "arbitrary" and "neoconservative," a student labeled my thinking "archaic" and "bureaucratic," and an editor derided my manuscript on the politics of educational reform as "reactionary." Critique is, as any administrator knows, the easy part. The hard part is navigating the murky, morally ambiguous problems that arise whenever anyone is entrusted with the task of overseeing the labor of others. And so, however useful it may be to dissect the processes by which surplus value is extracted during the labor process, we must admit that such analyses do not, in themselves, provide a clue as to how one might serve as a humane manager within the constraints of a capitalist system. Attempting to find an inhabitable solution to *that* problem has absorbed more of my creative energy and required more of my critical thinking than any other project I've been involved with. And, for this very reason, this has been the most rewarding and most intellectually stimulating job I've ever had.

The rewards and the challenges are not what I had expected, though. In order to explain how working under such seemingly constrained and compromised circumstances can be construed as intellectually reinvigorating, I want to conclude by describing a few of the problems that were awaiting me when I became the Acting Director of the Writing Program. Because these problems are specific examples of conflicts generic to the work of managing the labor of others, thinking through these problems will not only make clear how restricted one's choices are within any specific institutional arena at any given time, it will demonstrate, as well, why it is imperative that we reconceive these restrictions as the very ground upon which meaningful social action can be constructed. One way to launch such a reconsideration is to present the challenges involved in administering a writing program as a set of test questions for, surely, the experience of running a writing program feels, at times, a great deal like the experience of being tested by an impatient examiner with a remarkable talent for demanding immediate solutions to unresolvable problems on material one has only briefly studied.

So, you're sitting there in your office, trying to figure out how the phone works, when the following problems make themselves known to you. Obviously, you don't have much to go on, but that's part of the point. Given what you do know, how would you choose to respond?

1. It has been brought to your attention that one of your instructors has been coming to school intoxicated. None of the instructor's students has complained.

2. A number of assistant directors help you run the writing program. They all perform nearly identical duties. This was not always the case, though: in the distant past, the work loads were quite different. The pay scale continues to reflect the previous workload differential with the result that some assistants receive substantially lower salaries than their peers. The Director has tried repeatedly to have this problem corrected. When you bring the problem to the attention of the dean, you are told that there is no money available to address this imbalance.

3. In order to staff your courses, you draw on teaching assistants, full-time instructors, and part-time lecturers. Instructors receive three year, non-renewable contracts and teach a 4/3 work load. Part-timers receive no benefits and a flat fee of $2700 a course. Your reliance on this flexible, migratory labor force increases each year. When you bring this to the attention of the administration, the problem is acknowledged, but you are told that hiring permanent faculty to teach these courses is out of the question for fiscal reasons. You are also told that it costs substantially more to have an instructor teach a course than to have a part-timer do so.

4. Each year, admissions increases the size of the entering class in order to address budgetary shortfalls. Your program is stretched to the limit: you have had to hire inexperienced teachers; your writing centers cannot handle all the students who need extra help; your administrative staff cannot provide support to everyone who needs it. When you bring this to the attention of the administration, they are sympathetic, but insist that their hands are tied.

When I presented these problems to a group of graduate students in a seminar I taught this past summer, one of the students had no trouble completing the task: she simply wrote "need more information" after each question. While I continue to harbor a deep admiration for such refusals to play the game of education, I have come to recognize the profound costs of such symbolic acts of disengagement. In a certain sense, one always "needs more information"—about the teachers, the students, the administrators, budgetary allocations, the local government, the economy, the revolution of work and the creation of a migratory, underemployed knowledge class, globalization, the future. But the truth is that we are all regularly called upon to act in the absence of such information for the simple reason that collecting all the relevant data and interpreting it in the fullness of time is a luxury extended to no social agent at work in the world.

In making this observation, I'm not arguing for willed ignorance or for the virtues of impetuousness. Rather, I wish to foreground the fact that no amount of additional information is going to make it *unambiguously* clear which response to the problems described above is best. Take, for instance, the matter of the gross pay inequities among the assistant directors. It certainly helps to know the following details: two of the assistant directors make $9,000 a year less than their peers. Besides being unfair, this salary differential creates the illusion of a difference in quality among the directors, which produces in turn any number of managerial problems. While the obvious solution is to raise the salaries of the two underpaid directors, this solution is not on the table. At this point, the faculty has been working without a contract for more than two years, its union locked in a bitter and, to date, utterly futile dispute with an increasingly hostile administration. Our governor was elected on the basis of her promise to cut state income taxes by 30 percent in three years and she has fulfilled this promise by dramatically reducing allocations to the state university. And, as this money has dried up, faculty lines, vacated through retirement or resignations, have gone unfilled, leaving fewer teachers to handle more students. The economic injustices here are manifest and manifold. The problem, though, is that a writing program administrator doesn't have the power to advance contract negotiations, get the governor's ear, replenish the funding of faculty lines. The only possible site for intervention is the salary level of those employed by the writing program, but the only fair solution isn't available.

Satisfying though it may be to voice one's moral indignation about injustices of this kind, doing so doesn't change anything: letting it be known that you think workers performing comparable duties should receive comparable pay may be personally satisfying, but it doesn't alter the affected workers' salaries. And, for this reason, I would argue that the first step in becoming an effective WPA involves recognizing the fact that openly expressing moral outrage about working conditions is actually counterproductive, since this discourse exercises almost no rhetorical or institutional power in the academy at this historical moment. And from this it follows that, if the writing program administrator is to succeed in addressing inequities of the kind described above, the administrator must learn to speak in some other register to those in control of the purse—a register that translates moral problems into economic ones. That is, instead of simply celebrating polyphony, multivocality, and heteroglossia, the effective WPA must develop a fluency in those discursive practices that do exercise rhetorical force in the academy at present—statistics, accounting, standardized testing—and acquire a deep knowledge of the local political scene.

Of course, a magisterially well-intended document like the Wyoming Resolution doesn't make this argument for the necessity of developing an arsenal of locally effective strategies. Rather, it merely advises what *should* happen in this instance: the directors' salaries should be equalized; the nonrenewable appointments should become tenure-track jobs, with administrative expertise and teaching accomplishments given the same weight as research; and all our part-time and adjunct teachers should be moved on to the tenure track as well. The problem, though, is that debating whether or not such things should occur draws attention away from the fact that none of these options is available at this moment at my institution. In fact, the more information one collects, the more it appears that one's options are so restricted that recasting the problem as a multiple choice question would better represent the resident forces of constraint. Thus, given the known salary disparity and the additional information about the surrounding institutional context, would you choose to:

a.   Leave things as they are.

b.   Equalize everyone's salary by lowering some and raising others.

c.   Radically reduce the workloads of the underpaid directors, effectively compensating them in the form of time what you can't produce in the form of money.

d.   File a grievance with the union, knowing that by the time the grievance is resolved, the affected parties will have completed their appointments and have moved on to work elsewhere.

e.   Reduce your own salary to make up the difference.

f.   None of the above.

Each option has its merits, each also potentially exposes the administrator to a good deal of criticism. So how do you choose? How do you know if this is a fight worth waging?

We can continue to work through the calculations, slide figures and fantasies up and down the scale of relative oppression, but the truth is we have no way of knowing for sure whether or not we've made the right choice at any given moment. So here the analogy to a test breaks down, for there is no right answer. We have only the information at our disposal, our guiding principles and, perhaps, some inexplicable intuition about which way to turn. What remains is to decide and to act and then make the best of whatever ends up happening.

> This work. Learning from others. Traveling to conferences. Making contact. Solving problems. Especially this business of solving problems and all that it entails: talking to students, teachers, and administrators, studying the known parameters, imagining alternatives, pushing back against necessity, finding a way out, joining the discussion, learning again and again that there are other ways of thinking. This work, with its frustrations and its rewards, has turned out to be much better suited to my needs and my abilities than my first choice. This work. It sure beats writing in isolation hoping to be heard.

"The Way the Rich People Does It"

Reflections on Writing Center Administration and the Search for Status

Nancy Barbara Conroy Maloney Grimm

> But, while they lived inside middle-class American homes, Irish maids were still outsiders, made conscious of the border within the household. Their relationship to the family was a hierarchical one of upstairs and downstairs, masters and servants. They were present but invisible in a very intimate setting.
>
> —Ronald Takaki,
> *A Different Mirror*

Writing center directors often seem to find themselves in positions similar to Irish maids of the early part of this century—very much aware of what sorts of writing and teaching of writing goes on in their university and very intimately involved in that work, yet regularly reminded that they are in service roles, marginalized and excluded from decisions that have direct impact on their work. In the daily exchanges on WCenter, an on-line discussion list, one routinely finds requests for advice on status issues: an attempted raid on the writing center space, another department's interference with the way tutors are hired and trained, a faculty member's unilateral decision to require students to have writing center tutors "sign off" on papers before they are submitted. As I add another story to the already large collection of status stories, I want to offer something more than what Joyce Kinkead warns against–another "celebration of marginality," a story whose message focuses on "what is being done to us . . . rather than what we do well" (139). To take a proactive rather than a reactive approach, I will examine patterns in stories about status, including stories of cultural assimilation. History offers no lessons at all if we focus only on accomplishments and ignore the negative patterns which we are destined to repeat if they remain unidentified.

From his study of writing center histories, Peter Carino identifies two patterns that writing center people are especially fond of: the progressive model and the dialectic model, both of which tend to valorize the director and legitimate the current program (37–39). The progressive model stresses the pattern of "increasing knowledge and professionalism" and the dialectic model adopts another common cultural pattern, the "heroic tale of resistance" (39). Carino acknowledges the political purposes of these patterns, but he suggests a cultural model of history-telling, one that offers thicker descriptions of context, a model elaborating "the multiple forces in play at various moments and demonstrating that writing centers and those who work in them are always imbricated in the history of writing programs, higher education, and public debates as well as in local and even personal imperatives" (39). Following Kinkead's warning and Carino's advice, I plan to weave my story about professional status in writing center work into stories of cultural assimilation lived by my grandmothers, both of whom were immigrants, both of whom led lives influenced by status issues. Their stories allow me to identify the hidden transferences in my own life story, the ways that their tacit lessons influence my approach to decision making, revealing the personal imperatives that Carino suggests are just as much at play in our work as the academic and theoretical imperatives. Their stories also reveal cultural assumptions about gender and about service work, assumptions that strongly impact writing center status issues. More important, their stories, because they offer historical perspective on status issues, allow me to see beyond local and personal issues, to begin theorizing about status—to ask why status is desired, why it is denied, how it influences choices, what it costs, whom it benefits, who decides.

The relationship between gender and status in writing center administration is not simply imagined but empirically documented in the pages of *WPA*. In 1988, for example, Gary Olson and Evelyn Ashton-Jones reported on a survey of writing program directors who seemed to expect writing center directors to be a "kind of wife," an "idealized support-mate." To substantiate this use of the wife metaphor, Olson and Ashton-Jones illustrate with comments taken from the surveys. Writing program directors described the qualities of the writing center director using the "generic" she. She is supposed to be "nice," to "know her place in the chain of command and respect it," to be "friendly cooperative, and have lots of personality," to be "personable and flexible," "supportive but not critical," "sensitive to the needs of others," and to "provide chocolate chip cookies to writing center clients" (23). Seven years later, in 1995, Dave Healy reports in *WPA* on a survey of writing center directors that he designed and conducted. His survey results confirm common perceptions: writing center directors "are disproportionately female, they work long hours for not a lot of money, many lack the academy's ultimate validation (tenure), and they struggle with inadequate resources" (37). In fact, nearly half of Healy's total respondents indicated that their official title was not writing center director or writing center assistant director. Healy quotes a sample of official job titles, some of which include "staff coordinator," "writing lab coordinator," "writing center manager," "writing center advisor," "Instructional Program Manager," "College Lab Assistant I" (29). These official titles indicate that writing center administration is still often imagined as supervisory rather than academic. Both

Healy's and Olson and Ashton-Jones's surveys confirm an impression of writing center work as linked to historical perceptions of woman's work: clean-up and household management that is dependent on external decision making.

Assumptions about gender roles and responsibilities are carried and performed tacitly in ways that become patterned until someone questions them. Barbara Conroy, my maternal grandmother, died three months before I was born, but she was very much alive in the tacit beliefs and values that informed my mother's child-rearing practices and in the stories told by her sisters, my Aunt Nan and Aunt Julia. Barbara was the oldest of these sisters who left Ireland in their late teens to find jobs as maids for wealthy families in Pittsburgh. A quick learner and hard worker, Barbara was often the person who found jobs for younger family members. She used their temporary residence in her home as an opportunity to address their rough rural habits, teaching them how to behave in respectable ways. To an extent, she foreshadowed an early writing center in her kitchen, where she corrected and commented on language, habits, and attitudes, explaining what would lead to success and what wouldn't. From stories I've been told, Barbara was a very directive tutor, and because she was a woman, she was called "bossy" rather than "strong."

For Barbara, success in America translated into doing things "the right way," a way determined, as she and her sisters frequently put it, by "how the rich people does it." The straight lines of their thin lips, the set of their chins when they invoked this reasoning made it law in the household. Family protocol—like never putting the milk carton on the table and always using a tablecloth, no matter how faded and worn—was determined by the importance of imitating the habits of the rich, which as maids they had ample opportunities to observe. The Conroy sisters were lace-curtain Irish, determined at any cost to create the appearance of prosperity. True to her upbringing, my mother kept a mirror and lipstick in the kitchen drawer so she could check her face before answering the doorbell, believing, it seemed, that even one unkempt appearance could reduce the family's status in the neighborhood. Before Easter Sundays, First Communions, Confirmations, and family weddings, she spent many late nights in the basement at the sewing machine to insure that she and her daughters created a respectable appearance in our parish church, which was attended mostly by families much "better off" than ours. For lace-curtain Irish, projecting the appearance of prosperity was the necessary prerequisite to achieving it. For the Conroy women, a "critical" approach to the habits of the rich people meant careful attention to the details that mattered to them and a critical eye to the family members whose habits fell short of "how the rich people does it." This approach is one I inherited and one that has proved useful in learning to run a writing center, paying attention, for example, to the things that matter to the people in funding positions in the university.

The Irish, who arrived poor in this country carrying a history of colonization, adopted a strategy of assimilation at any cost. I don't believe they had choices: for them, there were no alternative jobs; there was not the option of returning to the country of origin; they could not live more simply than they already did. The sad part of their story of assimilation was the bigotry they developed, the long-term ethical and moral cost of keeping African Americans and the immigrants who followed the Irish "in their place." In his book entitled *How the Irish Became White*, Noel Ignatiev observes that "In the early years Irish were frequently referred to as 'niggers turned inside out'; the Negroes, for their part, were sometimes called 'smoked Irish,' an appellation they must have found no more flattering than it was intended to be" (41). Ignatiev argues, in agreement with Du Bois, that whiteness is not a natural attribute but manifests itself as social action observable in labor movements, political parties, and churches (183–85). This was not benign social action. With emigration to the United States, the Irish adopted strategies that changed them from victims of racial oppression to upholders of white supremacy. The habitual pattern of looking to the rich people in order to make decisions about what counts as status became so strong that they lost contact with the history they had lived in Ireland.

The pattern that my grandmother and her sisters followed in this country had been culturally established for Irish immigrants for more than fifty years. According to cultural historian Ronald Takaki, in the 1850s, 80 percent of all female household laborers in New York City were Irish immigrants. Domestic service provided an intimate glimpse of the practices of middle-class America (rich people to the Conroy sisters), practices many of these women brought home and drilled into their families. Not surprisingly, the daughters of many of these women entered white-collar employment. By 1910, second generation Irish-American women constituted one-fifth of all public school teachers in northern cities; and in Chicago, one-third of the school teachers were second generation Irish. Clearly, the drive for status benefited the children of Irish immigrants. The costs were transferred to other groups: African Americans, Italians, Eastern Europeans.

Traces of the assimilation pattern can be found even in the third generation. I was the first in my family to graduate from college, and true to the historical trend, I became a high school teacher. When I moved in 1978 with my husband and our two young children to the Upper Peninsula of Michigan, the job market for public school teachers was closed. After a few months, I took a job as a temporary part-time tutor in the university's new Language Skills Lab, the earliest version of the writing center that I now direct. My "temporary" status lasted seven years. In addition to tutoring during that time, I taught composition courses, becoming one of about fifteen stigmatized part-time laborers, most of us spouses of faculty, who were hired from term to term as needed. In 1985, as a result of the university's effort to address "the part-time problem," I was offered a professional staff position as the writing center coordinator at a salary less than I had made the previous two years in part-time positions. I was told to focus on the consolation of having a yearly contract and offered the backhanded compliment that I would "never be paid what I was worth."

Patterns of working conditions were reaching into the third generation. Research on the working conditions of Irish maids tells of the round-the-clock beck-and-call schedule and the mandatory wearing of apron and caps that were badges of inferiority. I remember the sharp snap that Aunt Nan gave the apron as she removed it and how she seemed to smack the kitchen drawer shut on those rare days when the rich people were out of town and she invited my mother to bring us for a visit. We part-timers didn't wear aprons to work, but there were other reminders of our status, like not having access to campus parking lots, having our mailboxes in the bottom row, and receiving the letter that came every April bearing the university's logo, the letter reminding us that our contract expired at the end of the term and that there were no guarantees of employment the following year. These letters seemed to arrive on the days we felt most worn down from teaching four sections of composition every term. Because so many of us lacked "terminal" degrees, the badge of status in higher education, we found it difficult to argue with our yearly terminations.

Takaki quotes a maid who wrote how "a smart girl keeps on her feet all the time to prove she isn't lazy" (157), and I remember the slits Aunt Nan cut in her daytime shoes to accommodate the swollen joints in her feet. I recall, also, the run-down housing project where she retired and the three bolts she locked on the door. Aunt Nan didn't have children, so her search for status ended in the poverty it began with. Takaki quotes the daughter of a maid who protested: "I hate the word service . . . now I tell every girl I know, 'Whatever you do, don't go into service'" (158). In my family, the costs of service, of respectability, of assimilation were not often counted. Getting ahead, doing things like the rich people, mattered the most. The family theme of earning respectability in the neighborhood, in the church, in the community motivated much of my personal life. Between 1978 and 1995 I mothered children, rehabbed an old house, taught religious education, and served on the parish council, earning status in the community and church. Augmenting that family theme was professional advice about status issues in writing center circles: Olson and Ashton-Jones, for example, concluded that essay reporting on the status of the writing center director by recommending that writing center directors should be required to be rhetoric and composition specialists and that they should hold tenure-track appointments. Like other workaholic program directors, I kept careful records, read theory, planned training, determined schedules, figured out financial reports, pursued additional funding sources, promoted and developed the other learning center programs on campus. Imitating the values of professional "rich people" in the department, I became active professionally. With good colleagues, I coedited *The Writing Center Journal*, and served as executive secretary of the National Writing Centers Association. In addition, I started graduate school, believing I had no claim to status without the credentials that "the rich people" had. With the support of family members, colleagues, and friends, I earned the professional credentials (MA and PhD) that I was lacking.

In addition to the family pattern of the search for status, there are traces in my story of the good daughter's search for endlessly delayed patriarchal approval. I was part of the first wave of feminist baby boomers who transferred their unspoken desire for fulfillment (approval) from the home to the workplace. I am not the only female baby-boomer to earn a PhD late in life who is involved in writing center administration. There are also traces of an economic pattern motivating my story. The inflation of the last thirty years requires that middle-class families have two wage earners, even if one of the two has a low salary. Quitting work wasn't an option I considered. Half of my earnings kept the extra car running, dressed the family for work and school, paid for summer sports and music camps; the other half went into savings for our children's college tuition.

In 1995 I thought I had overcome the final obstacle in the way of having a "respectable" position in the academy as a writing center director. After seventeen years of work in the department, I completed my dissertation and successfully competed for a tenure-track position which included the responsibilities of directing the writing center. But with my new credentials, I earned a salary less than what I had made the previous three years and through the routine protocols of the university, I was regularly reminded that I had been admitted to that prolonged period of apprenticeship as an untenured assistant professor. Well-intentioned people who wanted to acknowledge my changed status in the department greeted me with, "Welcome to the department!" Being "welcomed" into a department in which I had already worked ten years in a full-time staff position and seven years in part-time positions was evidence that the status story had not come to a happy ending; in fact, it had circled around to a new beginning. I was over fifty, I had spent most of my working life in higher education, and I was still the new kid on the block.

It was at about this time that my paternal grandmother, Catherine (Milunas) Maloney, began to appear in my dreams. In her late teens, Catherine had immigrated to the United States from the politically and economically ravaged country of Lithuania. She had worked as a seamstress, her specialty being the bound buttonholes on hand-tailored suits. Unlike my maternal grandmother, she married young, and her husband, in order to obtain and keep his status as a steelworker, changed their family name and nationality from the Lithuanian *Milunas* to the Irish *Maloney*. True to Ignatiev's history, the Irish had control of the labor unions in Pittsburgh and were loath to admit anyone but "their own kind," so Alexander Milunas became Al Maloney and worked as a ladle-liner in the mill. Status issues enacted an expensive price in this family. Although Catherine was alive throughout my childhood and adolescence, I barely knew her because my family visited her only in yearly rituals of obligation. She rarely spoke but often smiled at me, particularly when she took me outside while she watered her garden and enjoyed the sanctuary she had created for the birds.

When she became "senile" (the word used then to explain bizarre behavior of old folks), Catherine reclaimed her language, speaking to her visitors only in Lithuanian, a language my father knew but refused to acknowledge or to translate because of how fully he had bought into the identity of the name Maloney. He was not a bad son but a man deeply conflicted about his identity.

His "Irish" father had died when he was eleven; his "Irishness" had made him a respectable match in my mother's family (where "marrying your own kind" was regularly preached), and he was the only son in his large family whose "Irish" name had already been passed along to children. Becoming Lithuanian in his middle-age was not an attractive option, and he was torn among loyalty to the family he had married into, the family he and my mother created, and the family who had raised him. Catherine and her grandchildren lost out in the process; we barely knew each other because my father avoided contact with his unresolved identity issues. Catherine had taken a less assertive approach to assimilation than Barbara. She was known for her talent with skilled needlework in the neighborhood, but the fine gentlemen who bought the suits either never gave it a thought or else attributed the excellent detail work to the tailor. She grew old in the spare bedrooms in her daughters' homes. When I encounter Alzheimer's victims today, I wonder if in the ravages of the disease, some of them are reclaiming emotions, languages, attitudes, developmental stages, identities that they earlier suppressed.

In the way I construct their stories, my grandmothers represent two extremes in cultural assimilation. For Barbara, status meant disciplining the self to become the other. Because she was bilingual when she arrived in the United States, language mattered less than values, habits, attitudes, practices. For Catherine, status was determined by others, first a stern father and then a determined husband. Still, status decisions made for her profoundly affected her relationships, her identity, and her language use.

The professional and personal ambivalence of my former position as a professional staff person is echoed in the pattern of the Irish maid who is inside but not "of" the household, "present but invisible in a very intimate setting" (Takaki, 157). The reality of my current position as an untenured assistant professor is echoed in the conflicted identity of my father. I "married" into an institution, into its ranking and merit system, but in middle age I find myself facing the first step in a much longer status story, regularly warned by friends and colleagues that going up for early tenure is always a big mistake. I think of Jerome Bruner who writes that cultural ways of telling stories "become so habitual that they finally become recipes for structuring experience itself, for laying down routes into memory, for not only guiding the life narrative up to the present, but for directing it into the future" (36). The assimilation-at-any-cost story of Barbara and her sisters very nearly became the recipe for my life. The conflicted identities in my father's family offer an alternative recipe but not one more attractive.

When I move outside family to understand the patterns of status stories, I find that stories about status issues are so common in writing center circles that we now have stories that offer meta-level commentary on them. I turn now to three of those commentaries to locate some middle ground in the extremes. Stephen North, who gained renown in the writing center by offering idealism in exchange for low status, recently reexamined his early offer, for its "less desirable legacies, particularly the issues that idealism concealed" (10). North took himself to task for telling a story about writing centers (in his 1984 *College English* essay, "The Idea of a Writing Center") that failed to contextualize student writers within school culture, for leaving out the "seaminess" of the perspective on teaching that writing center work sometimes provides, for creating a vision of a writing center that absolved and insulated the institution from the differences that literacy work exposes (12–15). North's revisionary argument asks us to stop telling romantic, idealized versions of writing center work, stories that lead to "institutionalized martyrdom" (18), and instead to take a good look at the system that structures what we do with literacy in higher education. The hidden issues that North exposes echo the themes in my grandmothers' stories which are themselves nested in an American bootstraps narrative with its relentless focus on the individual and its habit of ignoring the social and personal costs of status quests.

Terrance Riley, in an essay juxtaposed to North's called "The Unpromising Future of Writing Centers," locates his argument about professional status in a romantic celebration of "happy amateurism" (32). Using stories of professional status achieved by the disciplines of American literature, literary theory, and composition studies, Riley argues that professionalization establishes an in-group, "close[s] the intellectual borders and develop[s] a rhetoric designed at once to distinguish and to exclude" (27). He cautions that playing the professional game in writing centers will lead us "into commitments that we will end up regretting" (29). He concludes with advice based on the "hard lessons" of history: "Fall out of love with permanence; embrace transience. Stake your reputation on service rather than on publication. Acknowledge that directing a writing center does not involve the difficulties for which advanced degree preparation is necessary" (32). Riley's advice came at an odd time in my life. I had directed a writing center without an advanced degree; but now I had one. I had focused on service; now I focused on publication. Was I contributing to an unpromising future for writing centers? Would my dissertation, a critical examination of the ways writing centers are theorized, be something I would regret writing? Was I driven by something that would be good for me rather than something that would benefit writing centers? Would my attention to personal tenure concerns compromise my attention to local writing center concerns? North and Riley, while they structure their arguments to provide some answers, actually lead us more deeply into contradictions.

Lisa Ede, in an essay responding to North's and Riley's, suggests we "turn toward" the difficult questions that they raise in order "to complicate our understanding of the story of writing centers" (113). Reminding us that writing centers "currently narrate a variety of acutely situated stories," Ede suggests that for some, "professionalization may indeed represent a threat to a writing center's integrity and vitality" while for others "such hallmarks of professionalization as an adequate budget and full-time director might be necessary grounding for their very development" (117). The arguments we make and the ways we make them will be defined by the politics of our location, just as the stories we tell are motivated by often unconscious need. Whether that need is to entertain, to gain the sympathetic attention of one's friends and colleagues, to problem-solve, or to project an image of competence, stories can sometimes betray us by revealing more of our needy selves than we intended. Learning to move into contradiction rather than into narratives that are cultural recipes for structuring experience is necessary if we want to challenge that which structures what we do, if we want to define status in ways that benefit more than one individual and his or her progeny, if we want to challenge "the way the rich people does it," if we want to write a different kind of story about cultural assimilation. The recipes that fill the cookbooks in my kitchen speak more of good intentions than of actual great meals. The great meals that do come together in my kitchen are often unplanned potlucks with people who shared unexpected stories around the kitchen table.

The stories that students tell us in writing centers are often stories about the conflict between the search for status and respectability (better grades in English) and the search for self identity. We would be wrong to read these conflicts with an inflexible notion of identity, and we would be unwise to dismiss these conflicts as the price we pay for success. I think of two students I worked with last term, one who told me stories of the bombs he built and detonated in his backyard and another who told me stories about going to the Promise Keepers' convention in Washington, DC, and the evangelization work that interferes with his intentions to study on weekends. Both students have stories to tell that exceed the subjectivity created by the practices of the composition program, stories that aren't quite respectable. In spite of some gentle urging from me to explore these stories as possible essay topics, both decided not to share these "kitchen" stories in written essays. They instead tell stories that fit more neatly into coherent form, that conform to the genre offered to them, stories that raise fewer questions, stories that leave no messy questions behind. Even though their kitchen stories were left unpublished, they were told to me at a writing center table, perhaps as a way to say "there is more to me than you see here, even though it looks like I have assimilated."

The parlor stories, the public grand narratives with the scripts already written, are difficult to change, and if I didn't work in a writing center, I would not know that those kitchen stories existed. I would feel, as sometimes I do after a so-called good teaching experience, that I had succeeded in unifying the world in my own image. It seems to me that one primary function of a writing center is to keep the profession in contact with those kitchen stories, to remind them that those neat narratives they collect for grading are not all there is to students. By sharing kitchen stories, writing centers can make it difficult for teachers to blame students for lack of ingenuity or lack of initiative. The kitchen stories can turn the mirror back on the profession of composition studies (in which I include writing centers), revealing the work that remains to be done to create approaches to literacy education that do more than reproduce the status quo. The kitchen stories remind us that status issues in the profession are ulti-mately status issues about students. How much does it matter whether the cul-tural forms and recipes we offer to students are suited to the stories they have to tell? How adequate is the cultural assimilation story told three or four gen-erations ago to the cultural issues we face today?

Literacy is the banner people wave when they are concerned about status. We worry, for example, about the status of the department if the administrative aide speaks "nonstandard" English on the phone and about the status of the writing center if a writing coach says "he don't" in casual conversation. Re-gardless of the qualifications and competence of individuals, their language is still used to make decisions about status and respectability. J. Elspeth Stuckey refers to this as the "violence" of literacy, the ease with which literacy is used as a weapon, a tool to separate and exclude individuals. Because writing cen-ters are often imagined as places that teach people the "right" way to use lan-guage (or the way the rich people use language), we are implicated in this violence as long as we never question these judgments. Questioning social judgments made under the disguise of literacy is a problematic activity for the weakly positioned, the part-timers, the untenured, the staff people, yet in the process of achieving status, we might become "white," implicated in actions that justify unjust uses of literacy, out of contact with the stories that remind us of the paradoxes of literacy, writing about ourselves as if our positions are something we achieve because of natural attributes rather than a result of social forces that shape us and deform others.

The survival lessons that Barbara taught to new immigrants in her kitchen, lessons that ended when she rolled up the carpets for music and dancing, and the beauty Catherine caught in her needlework and gardening, those are the legacies for which they are respected, their routes to respectability notwith-standing. The location of the Irish maid, neither inside nor outside but both, may be the position of agency for writing centers in the academy, provided that writing center administrators learn to transform the vertigo of multiple per-spectives and unstable positions into administrative actions that do not simply resolve tensions by assimilating to the status quo. Opportunities for agency are more likely to come from the ability to sustain the tension between our institu-tional selves and our private selves, from attaining the meta-level vision in which we can freeze-frame dilemmas long enough to imagine alternative pos-sibilities. The politics of our locations, personally and professionally, are re-plete with paradox and contradiction. Historical perspective on status, the ways our stories are told two generations from now, might ultimately hinge on what we do with these contradictions. Do we move into them, stay in contact and in advocacy and call attention to the social structures that attempt to limit our choices, or do we avoid the unresolveable, the discomfort?

There are occasional days when the faculty parking lot gate fails to re-spond to the swipe of my ID, and the momentary resistance of the gate takes me back to when I didn't have a guaranteed spot in the lot, reminds me of the backs I stand on, the backs that are sometimes broken in the structuring of respectability and status. The car I drive into that lot is a more reliable one than I had as a part-timer, but getting in and having a job depends on people like Barbara and Catherine who cleared the family path as well as plow drivers who rose earlier than I did to clear the snow from the lot as well as the new admissions clerk who lends me her ID with a smile when mine fails as well as the students who wait in the writing center. That network of relationships can too easily disappear in the ways we achieve and measure academic status.

Traditional notions of service can be transformed in the scholarship of writing center administration but only if we remember those relationships and take the risk of creating new patterns rather than reproducing familiar ones. Writing centers can serve students well by focusing attention on the tensions students negotiate as they learn to perform academic discourse; by teaching the profession to read writing they "are not prepared to read" (Bartholomae, 12); by highlighting the accumulated layers (Brandt) of literacy in the academy; by calling attention to the ways that literacy is used in even backgrounded ways (Barton) to construct relationships of power. This notion of service keeps an eye on the rich people while at the same time keeping the imagination open so that new patterns can emerge.

Works Cited

Bartholomae, David. 1993. "The Tidy House: Basic Writing in the American Curriculum." *Journal of Basic Writing* 12 (1): 4–21.

Barton, Ellen L. 1997. "Literacy in (Inter)action." *College English* 59: 408–37.

Brandt, Deborah. 1995. "Learning Literacy: Writing and Learning to Write in the Twentieth Century." *College English* 57: 649–68.

Bruner, Jerome. 1994. "Life as Narrative." In *The Need for Story: Cultural Diversity in Classroom and Community,* edited by Anne Haas Dyson and Celia Genishi, 28–37. Urbana, IL: NCTE.

Carino, Peter. 1996. "Open Admissions and the Construction of Writing Center History: A Tale of Three Models." *The Writing Center Journal* 17 (1): 30–43.

Ede, Lisa. 1996. "Writing Centers and the Politics of Location: A Response to Terrance Riley and Stephen M. North." *The Writing Center Journal* 16 (2): 111–30.

Healy, Dave. 1995. "Writing Center Directors: An Emerging Portrait of the Profession." *WPA: Writing Program Administration* 18 (3): 26–43.

Kinkead, Joyce. 1996. "The National Writing Centers Association as Mooring: A Personal History of the First Decade." *The Writing Center Journal* 16 (2): 131–43.

Ignatiev, Noel. 1995. *How the Irish Became White.* New York: Routledge.

North, Stephen M. 1994. "Revising 'The Idea of a Writing Center.'" *The Writing Center Journal* 15 (1): 7–19.

Olson, Gary A., and Evelyn Ashton-Jones. 1988. "Writing Center Directors: The Search for Professional Status." *WPA: Writing Program Administration* 12 (1–2): 19–28.

Riley, Terrance. 1994. "The Unpromising Future of Writing Centers." *The Writing Center Journal"* 15 (1): 20–34.

Stuckey, J. Elspeth. 1990. *The Violence of Literacy.* Portsmouth, NH: Boynton/Cook.

Takaki, Ronald. 1993. *A Different Mirror: A History of Multicultural America.* Boston: Little, Brown.

On Coming to Voice[1]

Mara Holt

> When democracy is taken seriously with its end of individuality to
> flourish and flower, it makes every set of elites tremble in their
> boots.
>
> —Cornel West
>
> A way comes into being through our walking upon it.
>
> —Chuang Tzu

I started this piece two years ago during a sojourn at the beach, shortly after
receiving tenure at Ohio University. Peter Elbow had sent me Mary Rose
O'Reilley's *A Peaceable Classroom*. While I read, I wrote O'Reilley a letter. "I
am writing to you," I began, "because your book has touched me, and touched
off an exploration of my personal history in the profession." I wrote her about
how some of her experiences at "Black Hole School" (a school for emotionally
disturbed children) helped me rethink my early experience teaching. Reading
her words I felt relief that mine hadn't been the only left/liberal assumptions
that were tested, and I shared her guilt and sorrow about not having known
more then. O'Reilley spoke of wrestling with a student over a grade—her student's issue was the Vietnam War; in a similar situation, my student had said
that my grade was sending him back to work in a factory. It's hard to look back
at those experiences. O'Reilley's confessions started me thinking.

I had been going through a professional crisis. Although I had been con-
scientious in a job that had required an unusual amount of administrative work
for six years (compared to literature faculty, anyway),[2] I felt neglected by my
chair during my tenure year. My chair had appreciated my work, at least verbally,
so I was surprised that he paid so little attention to my tenure case. He dele-
gated the preparation of my case to the overworked WPA, who was left to do it
in a last-minute rush, causing problems for both of us. I think of the title of this
book: *Kitchen Cooks, Plate Twirlers, and Troubadours*. I think of Wendy
Bishop's metaphor of "juggling" and of another WPA's metaphor of writing program administration as a "high wire act." I wonder why a WPA was expected
to do a chair's work. Because the tenure case was in composition studies?

My tenure case was successful, and the WPA, who by that time was running for chair of the department, asked me to be Director of Composition if she

were elected chair. I stalled. For the six years that I had been there, I had seen her work in the position she was asking me to take. She worked long hours day after day, doing multiple and apparently ceaseless tasks. I rarely heard her say anything positive about her job. I needed some time to research the conditions I would need to have in place before I accepted the position.

Further, I was exhausted from the tenure process. Wounded. Crazy from having kept my mouth shut for the previous year and a half, just in case I might inadvertently plant some malice where it could unconsciously sabotage me. I was developing physical symptoms of stress that I'd never seen any sign of before. I was more angry than I ever remember being, and frightened to act. In thinking about the cost of my silence, I remembered Audre's Lorde's "The Transformation of Silence into Language and Action." Lorde speaks of the consequences of not speaking what you feel: "What are the words you do not yet have? What do you need to say? What are the tyrannies you swallow day by day and attempt to make your own, until you will sicken and die of them, still in silence?" (41). She speaks of her own fear of revealing herself and its apparent danger. Her daughter counters:

> Tell them about how you're never really a whole person if you remain silent, because there's always that one little piece inside you that wants to be spoken out, and if you keep ignoring it, it gets madder and madder and hotter and hotter, and if you don't speak it out one day it will just up and punch you in the mouth from inside. (42)

Since I am not easily silenced, I was experiencing more profoundly than I had ever before the dis-ease that Lorde and her daughter talk about. I was amazed at the physical and emotional effects. Further, I kept questioning myself about the validity of my "oppression." Surely Lorde's words don't apply to white assistant professors.

More deeply rooted was a kind of deadness I felt about my work, especially my writing. Reading Lorde's work helped explain it. In "Uses of the Erotic: The Erotic as Power" she writes of the connection between work and pleasure, and how, if we suppress our feelings, our motivation for work becomes problematic. And she speaks of the value of anger. I had suppressed my feelings, my motivation for work had become problematic, and I was angry.

I had accepted a position as an assistant professor six years before, after earning my PhD in rhetoric and composition. My spouse and I were fortunate to have secured tenure-track academic positions at the same university in different fields, and by coincidence. What I didn't realize until years later (at a workshop for new WPAs) was that from the first day in my new job I was an unofficial associate director of composition—without released time, without clerical support. The chair had relinquished his power over the composition program, graduate and undergraduate, to the WPA. I found myself overwhelmed and supervised by another overwhelmed person who was just trying to do her job, and probably trying to meet the expectations of the chair. With no help and before tenure, she had overhauled the writing program and created a substantial MA program in composition. I imagine she expected no less of me.

Within a week of my move to Athens, I was teaching the TA training course, a five-credit hour theory/practice course with a hefty set of responsibilities. After that, I was on rotation, teaching the course every other year. This meant that for half the TAs at any given time, I was a teaching advisor, often attempting to explain and justify policies that I had had no voice in creating. The WPA, who also held the WAC position, had me do workshops for campus-wide and regional campus faculty, supervise a faculty mentoring program for TAs, select textbooks, revise the curriculum, defend the writing program, and fulfill a relentless series of other tasks, a situation no doubt familiar to many untenured rhetoric/composition faculty members. Before my arrival all of this, I imagine, had been up to the WPA.

During those six years I received an NEH summer stipend to write a book that I never finished, even after taking two quarters of unpaid leave to make up the time I had lost. I had come to Ohio University as a scholar with promise. My dissertation had received an award from my graduate program. I had been offered more interviews than I could fit into three days at MLA (in the best job market in years) and multiple job offers. For a relative beginner, I had a decent start in the national community. I had been taught in graduate school that one acquired a professional voice through research and publication. My experience as an assistant professor, however, was that I was expected to do an inordinate amount of "service," which took time and energy away from my "professional voice" and perhaps suggested that if I were to find voice in my situation, it must include "service."[3]

I had gone to Texas five years earlier to study collaborative learning, a term that in 1983 wasn't well-understood. I had had a tough time at Texas trying to do the work I wanted to do. I wanted to study collaborative learning theory, but for a long time (until Jim Berlin came for a year as a visiting professor) I ran into barriers at Texas against talking about practice theoretically, or talking about theory practically. I went to Texas, I wrote in a piece later published in PRE/TEXT,

> believing in social construction, almost like a religion—or, more accurately, a science. I believed that I had a right—more than that, a responsibility—to speak that followed directly from my belief that knowledge is socially constructed. I believed, in short, that the non-foundationalist implications of post-structuralist theory were implicitly and inevitably liberating, that once people realized that knowledge is socially created a socialist democratic state would just fall into place. (Holt and Trimbur 1990, 49)

Theory had freed me to speak more unselfconsciously than I had ever spoken in an academic setting. It also had made sense of my worldview gleaned from my childhood in the Air Force, always on the move. I had always seen the world as composed of overlapping and mutable discourse communities, but I had never had the language for it before. One of my peers in graduate school, now an accomplished scholar and theorist in the field, said at dinner one night a few years ago that part of theory's importance to her was that she had come to political activism through theory. My first experience with theory was more like bell hooks' argument in "Theory as Liberatory Practice." It provided me with a way to make sense of my life, my experiences with political activism, and a vision of the possibilities for change.

Well, as you can imagine (as I can imagine, now that I'm a professor of graduate students), no one in graduate school was impressed. I can see now how I went about it wrong, how I probably came across as arrogant. My professors and I were talking about many of the same things, but I had read different books and had had different experiences. I should have listened, read their bibliographies, and learned from them. My introduction to social construction had failed to teach me about power.

I learned a big lesson in power at Texas, because the English department fought a civil war over the role of rhetoric in a department of mostly literature faculty. Rhetoric lost the war, the mission in the department changed, and, of course, this didn't happen democratically. Overnight, certain dissertation topics became unfashionable. A disdainful attitude toward pedagogy developed even among rhetoric/composition graduate students. I began to feel less free to speak or write, certainly about collaborative learning. And I became increasingly uncertain about my value in the field and about the value of the field for me. I see this disjuncture now partly in feminist terms, but I had no way to theorize it then. My experience with social construction hadn't taught me about gender politics either.

"A Community of Knowledgeable Peers"

I date my interest in "the field" from my first day at Kenneth Bruffee's 1980 Brooklyn College Summer Institute in Training Peer Tutors. I was a Writing Center Director in the Basic Studies Program at Alabama State University, an historically black university in Montgomery. Alabama State had received a federal grant for the writing center to work with each of its 1500 first-year students, but the grant had provided for no tutors. My supervisor brought to my notice an ad in the Chronicle for a summer institute in training peer tutors funded by FIPSE and taught by Kenneth Bruffee. I applied, I was accepted, and Alabama State agreed to meet FIPSE's conditions. In the summer of 1980, then, I found myself going to New York, an experience I faced with (incredible as I think back) mixed feelings.

In Montgomery I had been an environmental activist. And I was living in the South, where rural life enjoys a hip status. I had no reason to think that I would like New York, home (in my mind) of big corporations and toxic waste. To my surprise (and no one else's) I was hooked on the City even before the cab dropped me off at the NYU dorm near Washington Square Park where I was to spend the next six weeks. During the first few weeks, Bruffee took fifteen of us—writing center directors from across the country—through a whirlwind version of the course he had developed for peer tutors. We wrote short papers, read them aloud, and exchanged them with each other for various peer critiques, creating a professional community in the process, much as I imagine the National Writing Project functions locally. Bruffee introduced us to his ideas on peer tutoring and intellectual development (see "Brooklyn Plan") and to the resources on peer tutoring available in the New York area. Those of us who had PhDs exclaimed how different the spirit of this institute was from graduate school. Those of us who were MAs took out of the institute a sense that graduate school—even the profession—could be like this.

We were a motley crew. Marcia Silver, who was administrating the FIPSE grant with Bruffee, was working on her PhD in linguistics at CUNY. Harvey Kail had recently returned from Papua, New Guinea, where he had started a writing lab, and then accepted a position as assistant professor of English at the University of Maine, Orono. Bene Scanlon (later Cox), with whom I had coincidentally gone to graduate school during my MA, held a tenure-line position at Middle Tennessee State University. John Trimbur was an adjunct at Baltimore Community College, Carol Stanger an adjunct in a community college in Enfield, CT. There were several other community college faculty members, as I remember, from Cincinnati (Marv Garrett), Albuquerque, and Laramie, Wyoming.[4] It was 1980 in a bad job market, and we were a marginalized and disenfranchised lot, meeting three years before what some would later term the beginning of the discipline of Composition Studies.

We were enacting a vision of teaching writing and of the profession that would soon become what people might call a "paradigm shift." We were collaborating with each other, and not just in the harmonious, cooperative way that Joe Harris and others would later critique (see Harris' "The Idea"), but in agonistic ways as well. We confronted, tested, and supported each other, played out dysfunction and resolved some of it. We reflected on what we were doing, individually and as a group, through our logs and our discussions and with the help of Columbia University social work professor Alex Gitterman.

In the short run, we were practicing for the kinds of reactions we might expect from our students. In the long run, we were together creating knowledge that would join with other voices (Patricia Bizzell and David Bartholomae, to name two) to become a movement in the field. Further, we were enacting an alternative definition of what it means to be an academic professional, a definition I would later understand as feminist in Marcia Dickson's "situational" sense.[5] Ken was a wonderful nondefensive leader in this experiment. He didn't come with an agenda, although he came with plenty of authority.[6] He brought us together for his own benefit as well as for ours, to see what happened when a group of WPAs from a diversity of environments talked, worked, and lived together. I can't overemphasize the importance of play to our creativity—hanging out in New York, listening to jazz, riding subways, going to the theater, talking about Rorty and Vygotsky and Geertz in coffeehouses and bars and on stoops. Many of us were drawn to collaborative learning out of a personal history of social action. We were enticed by the dialectic of theory and practice that we not only read about in Ken's bibliography (we were given a copy of Dewey's *Experience and Education* before we got there), but that we lived every day.

Supercharged by the experience, and helped along by the FIPSE grant's dictates that our respective institutions create a course for training peer tutors, many of us returned to our institutions with the enthusiasm of the newly converted. After instituting a peer tutor training course at Alabama State, I quickly found another tenure-track job at Embry-Riddle Aeronautical University in Florida and impulsively took it (I'd always wanted to live at the beach, among equally questionable motives). Soon I petitioned the Provost to start a Writing Center at Embry-Riddle. Bruffee's summer institute had given me the tools to do at Embry-Riddle what I had done at Alabama State. It involved teaching a peer-tutor training class which doubled as an honors writing class, and which could be registered for by invitation only. At Embry-Riddle this class filled a need for students interested in the humanities in an otherwise scientific/technological environment.

The creation of the writing center and its concomitant peer tutor training class resulted in an environment in which students could do meaningful work, get to know each other, and help other students. My work with these students helped me to understand better connections between collaborative learning and social construction while I kept in touch with my institute colleagues. Near the end of my first year at Embry-Riddle, I heard from Ken Bruffee that FIPSE had funded a follow-up two-week workshop for summer, 1982, and the "ticket in" was a paper. My preparation for that paper came to mind as I was reading Mary Rose O'Reilley's *A Peaceable Classroom* many years later. O'Reilley writes: "I simply wrote. No negotiations. Good, bad? None of my business. I wasn't doing it. By resigning as the self-conscious author, I wrote freely" (xv). I was grading the exams of 125 students and the paper was due. At the same time I was ambivalent about participating in the follow-up workshop. My instincts told me that I was at a fork in the road, that the second workshop might lead me to a PhD program, which was more of an investment in the academy than I had been willing to make. I wasn't sure (and as it turned out, my anxieties were well-founded) that the unbridled ambition and competition of the academy were what I wanted for my life.

I wrote the "ticket in" without investment in the consequences, and therefore it was a pleasure to write. I remember working very hard, but without urgency or fear. I interviewed two former students about their experiences with collaborative learning. One talked about how collaborative learning had transformed his experience of competition. "In a course like this where you've got people working together trying to improve their writing, if someone gets an A, you're happy, because you helped him get that A," he said. This amazed me in a school full of males competing for a couple of Air Force flight slots a year. I remember piecing this paper together on a typewriter and just making the deadline, every breath a kind of prayer. The decision came in, and I returned to New York. Ken divided us into working groups by categorizing our papers. Unlike the 1980 Institute procedure where the small-group composition had changed from day to day, during the two-week workshops we subdivided ourselves into interest groups in an attempt to produce some publishable papers. Continuing to combine profession with play, we again took full advantage of a temporary life in Greenwich Village and Soho.

We were not, however, the Brady Bunch. It was easy to shift unexamined assumptions of academic hierarchy onto a group whose mission was to question that hierarchy. We found ourselves at times scapegoating and excluding people, being excluded ourselves, and talking through and intellectualizing our concerns about issues of exclusion with social work professor (later Dean at Columbia) Alex Gitterman, whom Ken astutely brought in to help us understand group dynamics and who framed what was happening in terms of unresolved and mutable issues of "intimacy and authority" (see Bennis and Shepard). In retrospect I think most of us would agree that we would have done well to examine our own material and ideological situations more thoroughly. Several of us were Jewish; one of us was Mormon. At least one of us was gay. All of us were white. We ranged from politically conservative to Communist, from adjunct to tenured faculty. Certainly issues of race, class, gender, ethnicity, ideology, and sexual orientation were as crucial to understanding our "group dynamics" as anything we did discuss.

On the whole, however, I felt that the collaborative dynamics worked to prove in the end that everyone was important to the project. In the 1982 session, for instance, when the groups were scheduled to report to each other, they challenged each other seriously. The theory group challenged the basic writing group for not being theoretically informed. And the basic writing group challenged the theory group for excluding basic writing issues. We took home not only a new and concretized respect for the importance of a theory/practice dialectic, but also a respect for the practice of collaboration in providing a forum for challenging this binary. Marcia Dickson notes that

> many 'collaborative' projects can be the results of one person putting pressure on a number of others to take part in programs they do not believe in or trust. No matter how often this group meets to discuss the theory behind the practice, if all the participants don't feel that they have the freedom to say, 'This isn't working for me. What if we did this instead?' then the project will not encourage growth. (147)

We were learning the importance of what Walter Lippmann called "the indispensable opposition."

The confidence I gleaned from these institute experiences catapulted me into activities that I previously had not thought to pursue. I applied for jobs and to graduate schools, receiving multiple opportunities. Richard Enos and Peter Elbow (who had been an FIPSE evaluator during the second institute) called personally to try to talk me into coming to Carnegie-Mellon and SUNY Stony-brook respectively. In the end I went to Texas.

Hook 'em 'Horns

In 1983, my first semester at the University of Texas, I gave a talk at a graduate student brown bag, from the paper that had been my "ticket" into the 1982 NY institute, and which had received an enthusiastic reception. Although I am embarrassed now to think of my presumptuousness then, I asked a faculty member who was a friend of one of the institute members to come to my talk. I had hoped she and the others could give me advice for revising the piece for publication. In attempting to revise the paper after the institute, I had had trouble broadening my audience beyond the institute members, and I wanted help. I remember hearing some arguments against the premise of my paper from a creative writing student, and then the faculty member asked me how many drafts of this paper I had done. When I answered "Seven," she replied, "If it's not ready by now, it's not going to be. Some things just don't need to be published." That was the first in a series of discouragements I experienced in graduate school about sending anything out for publication. It wasn't until I became a reviewer of articles that I realized how wrong-headed and stultifying that advice can be.

The brown bag, then, was my entree into a different facet of the rhetoric/composition national community, one with assumptions and practices much closer to the academic norm. I had entered graduate school with a vision of graduate education based on what I would later understand as feminist, collaborative principles: that my teachers would help initiate me into the field. Because of the continuing support of my "collaborative learning" community, it took a while to lose my confidence (or brashness?). I was caught in a theoretical loop—I believed in social construction; therefore if the Texas community didn't assent to my work as being worthy of "the conversation," what could I do as an individual graduate student? In the anti-expressivist dichotomy that I then adhered to, I had cut myself off from a discourse which could have encouraged me to stick to my guns, to seek credibility within myself, to believe in myself even without what Bruffee calls "a community of knowledgeable peers." I was experiencing one of the problems with social construction as conceived by Bruffee, the courage it takes to speak what Richard Rorty calls "abnormal discourse." John Trimbur would later analyze this problem from the perspective of "Consensus and Difference." Sherrie Gradin would attempt to resolve it (differently) with her analysis of "social expressivism."

In addition to the standard graduate school socialization, I was soon situated in the department's rhetoric/literature civil war, which ultimately put rhetoric in a defensive and compensatory position in relation to literature (at least for the time I was there). I survived it, as many of us did, with the merciful help of Jim Berlin, who swooped in like a visiting professorial angel and took care of the graduate students while the other rhetoric faculty had their hands full with department politics, a situation with which I can now empathize. But I left graduate school a much more timid scholar, easily shamed, walking on professional eggshells. I left puzzled by memories of male peers treated differently for asking questions similar to mine. It wouldn't be long before I had an explanation for that professional behavior. I left graduate school having yet to position myself as a feminist.

Every word I wrote I questioned. I wondered about the nature of the attack I would endure, and I tried to defend myself from it, but I didn't know enough, could never know enough to defend myself against it all. In this competitive academic model, learning from one's critics didn't seem to be an option; one was required constantly to defend oneself, and frankly, I didn't have the academic street smarts. I kept reliving Elaine Showalter standing at a podium in Texas, badgered by assistant professors and graduate students about whom she had omitted, what political sins she had committed with her words. No one who stood at that podium was spared. In a dissertation study group, I participated in the unconstructive criticism of a peer's work, modeling perhaps unconsciously the behavior I had observed among the faculty.

I don't mean to downgrade my education at Texas. It was a superb schooling in rhetoric and in politics. I had entered naive, and as violent as the education sometimes felt, it was useful in preparing me for department life. The rhetoric faculty, and some of the literature faculty, were good to graduate students, even as their own professional lives were under siege. I can more easily imagine now what kind of energy their attention cost them. Many of my peers at Texas (who have their own different perspectives about graduate school) have become lifelong professional and personal friends. But had I not also experienced an alternative, nearly feminist model of academic politics, I'm not sure I would have found a place for myself in the academy. Oddly, the New York experience both ill-prepared me for graduate school and provided me with an alternative that sustained me.

Certainly the support of my New York community continued. Carol Stanger and John Trimbur put together a conference at Yale in 1984 with Stanley Fish and Peter Elbow. In 1990, some of us led a special week-long workshop at Bard College, during which we made everyone justifiably angry by not respecting the knowledge they already had about collaborative learning. Ken Bruffee, Carol Stanger, John Trimbur, and I conducted a collaborative learning demonstration with Harvey Weiner for the CUNY system in 1991. But that support wasn't without its fissures. Issues of exclusion continued, as some of us participated in events and others did not. I used my privilege sometimes well, sometimes poorly, when I had it. I was beginning to see the inevitable cracks in our version of collaborative learning at about the time Johanna Atwood, who wrote the first MA thesis I directed, introduced me to feminist pedagogy, which I discovered to be a huge piece missing from the puzzle of collaborative learning as I knew it.[7]

At the same time that we were, I suppose, experiencing differently the ambivalences woven through any such set of academic relationships, our careers were moving in different directions. Carol Stanger moved to New York to become the Writing Center Director at John Jay. Harvey Kail became a department chair, using what he had learned about collaboration to deal expertly with faculty relations. Bene Scanlon Cox became, briefly, an administrator, and she used her position to create successful collaboration among the state university faculty in Tennessee. Marcia Silver left New York to take a position as Director of the Writing Center at Portland State University in Oregon. Peter Hawkes moved to a tenure-track position at East Stroudsburg University in Pennsylvania, where he became writing director, then chair. Ron Maxwell redesigned the curriculum of the Writing Center at Penn State. And John Trimbur's reputation skyrocketed as he published prolifically and worked for reform within composition studies. Ken Bruffee had two more children and became director of an honors program at Brooklyn College. And I was overwhelmed with the contradictory demands of being a new assistant professor. We had started out in 1980 as a group of mostly marginalized WPAs, and we had taken what we had learned with us to different arenas.

On the Tenure Track

Despite a promising dissertation, I was getting nowhere fast trying to write a book, given a relatively heavy teaching load and the "invisible" WPA service. Meanwhile, the field of rhetoric was moving toward a more standard "male" academic model, emphasis on "research," narrowly defined. I remember telling John Schilb at a 1988 conference in Miami, OH, that when I had entered graduate school in 1983 I had promoted theory in rhetoric/composition, and now a few years later I was promoting practice. I hadn't changed, but the discipline had. "Rhetoric" and "composition" had begun to be thought of as a binary, with "rhetoric" as primary and having little to do with writing instruction (see Calderonello). I remember going with Sue Simmons to a History of Rhetoric conference in Miami and trying to make a case for the inclusion of "writing instruction" as rhetoric. We faced many blank faces and Jim Berlin's (later reconsidered) silence, which perplexed and worried me.

I had lost much of my confidence. I had such faith in the appropriateness of my insecurity in the unpredictable world of English Studies that even my successes made me suspicious. (What were the real reasons for my winning a departmental dissertation award?) I found myself at CCCC suffering from an inability to speak during the question and answers periods after sessions. A speech by Peter Elbow at the 1989 CCCC enabled me to begin breaking through that barrier. I was moved by his vulnerability, his courage to risk attack (having been one of those who had attacked him in my paper at that conference).

Upon returning home I wrote him a letter. "Participating in a feminist theory group at Texas," I said,

> I watched women falter over their speech, in fear of saying something politically incorrect. As it turned out, the word 'I' was politically incorrect, along with 'sympathy' and 'identification.' As I watch rhetoric and composition go from social construction to politics, I see more exclusion, more fear of speaking. Somehow the political implications of social construction, at least the ones I saw, have turned into their opposite. All this has made me rethink expressionism, made me remember the inarguable value in enfranchising a single voice. If people are afraid to speak until they know the 'right' vocabulary, we don't have democratic participation, we have totalitarianism. It was your talk, your model that helped give me the courage to speak again, to ask a question, to challenge an interpretation at the conference, something I hadn't been able to do for a while. It was your focus on the validity of the self that gave me the impetus to participate in a 'democratic' way.

A year or so later I struggled with embarrassment (revealed in the text itself) to write an expressive/academic piece in a special issue of PRE/TEXT. This was my first attempt to reclaim my voice after the academic socialization of graduate school, and I have struggled ever since. The national community, however, hasn't been the only arena in which speaking has been a struggle.

When I entered my current department I was one of only two untenured faculty members. The department had had a stable faculty for so long that its operating assumptions were tacit. Part of the legacy of this situation is that there is little debate. Sometimes women who speak passionately (or men who speak violently) are discredited in whispers in the halls. My sense of the value of solving problems by rhetorical means—the need to persuade a group of people of the merits of an argument—is not shared by many. Nevertheless, I have chosen to speak, respectfully and carefully, and invite response, hoping to help create the environment I want to work in. After eight years my patience is wearing thin and I am afraid of becoming one of the "passionate" women. If I "get a reputation" will that disable my voice?

In my department it "goes against every tradition the department has!" to hold a department meeting for prospective department chairs to speak to the faculty before the election, or so the then-chair responded harshly to me when I made the suggestion. "You're trying to blindside [one of the candidates]," he continued. I got a similar reaction from both candidates for chair when they found out what I had suggested. One called my suggestion an act of betrayal (but later reconsidered). Assuming that such discussion is crucial to self-governance in a department, I couldn't fathom how my merely making a civic-minded suggestion could provoke such anger. I felt confused about the extreme reactions to my suggestion. In a daze of wonder about what kind of history could produce those kinds of reactions, I went to hear Cornel West speak about how important it is for people to have a say in the conditions of their lives.

What Kind of Organization Would Have Chuck Schuster as President?

In 1994 the former WPA was elected chair of the department and asked me to be Director of Composition. After some difficult negotiating that resulted in a year's delay, I accepted the position. The chair had already begun the process, however, of requesting a WPA consultant-evaluator review for our writing program without, as far as I know, discussing it with anyone. I felt that an evaluation was a good idea, but that the timing was wrong. I wanted a chance to learn the job, make the changes I could make on my own, and then invite WPA to evaluate. I had long respected the WPA consultant-evaluator program. Ken Bruffee, as one of the founders of WPA, had engaged John Trimbur and Harvey Kail as evaluators early on. I knew about their training process and their philosophy of situating their evaluations in terms of the goals of the writing program they were reviewing.

Because it was a last-minute operation, however, the chair was unable to hire the evaluators whose assumptions fit best with our program. The composition committee hastily prepared our self-study in a frenzy of crisis, the committee members learning about the program as they went along. The visitation schedule gave me very little time with the evaluators, whose whirlwind tour was confusing to everyone. The visitors came, left, and sent the report. Although my chair was satisfied with the report, I felt that it was in part inaccurate, offered few constructive suggestions, and weakened our position in the tenuous political web of university politics. Rattled by the WPA review and other incidents in which I felt that my professional opinions had been unsought or disrespected, I went to the WPA Workshop for new WPAs in Bellingham, Washington, a workshop which my chair suggested herself, and which she was happy to fund.

I roomed with my friend Beth Daniell, whose strong and clear voice has inspired me since graduate school. Soon we sat eating ice cream sundaes in a cozy, dark-paneled restaurant in Bellingham, catching up on each other's stories. After hearing mine, Beth said, "You've got to talk to Chuck Schuster [at that time President of WPA and one of the workshop leaders]." I looked at Beth incredulously. I couldn't imagine what she was thinking.

"What stake does Chuck Schuster—whom I do not even know—have in me? He'd have much more of a stake in protecting WPA," I told Beth.

"What reason do you have not to trust Chuck Schuster?" she persevered.

"What reason does he have to trust me?" I shot back. "The default is not to trust, Beth. Trusting is not the default."

"You're a shell of your former self," she said, looking at me sternly. "You can't possibly get through a year of being a WPA in the shape you're in."

Chuck and I sat on a couch next to a white grand piano in a dormitory lounge with a view of the Bellingham Bay out the window and other new WPAs lined up outside the room waiting for their turn with Chuck. He listened to every word, stayed still while I cried, expressed sympathetic outrage, and at the end said, "How can WPA help you in these egregious circumstances?" He urged me to speak, to fight for myself, even in matters that would involve a critique of the organization he was then president of. That's the part I'm most grateful for. To find that not everyone is a cover-up artist these days was so liberating. He supported me wholeheartedly in a way so healing that it brings tears to my eyes as I write. Together we explored some alternative approaches to my situation, and he asked me to keep in touch.

I wrote a letter voicing my concerns to the Consultant-Evaluators who had visited my campus. One of them has since apologized to me. WPA has offered another visit to my campus, free of charge. Kathy Yancey has visited my campus as an assessment consultant. I have had phone and e-mail and listserv support from members of my WPA workshop group and others. Finally, once again, I feel I have found a context in which open dialogue is encouraged and valued. I have been on leave for a year, gathering data for a research project on writing program administration, for which Leon Anderson and I received a WPA grant. Last summer at the WPA annual conference and again at NCTE in the fall, WPAs participated in focus group interviews for our project. The beauty of focus groups is that they are a dynamic, dialogic process—particularly amenable to feminist research (Reinharz, 222–23). To work well they must provide each participant with the opportunity (as well as convey a sense of responsibility) to speak—much as in collaborative learning. Consistent with what social theorist Norman Denzin has referred to as a "feminist communitarian ethical system," this interactive research "employs a communicative, care-based ethic that presumes a dialogical view of the self" as well as the social construction of knowledge. Based in an "ethic of caring" as developed by Patricia Hill Collins, it celebrates the expression of personal voice, cherishing "each person's invisible dignity, quiet grace, and unstated courage" (276). Focus groups have provided for me a new way to do research, consistent with the practical and theoretical stances that interest me.

My struggle for voice remains. WPA couldn't remake workplace culture in the United States to make my life easier. I still get angry reactions from people for merely speaking my opinion. It sometimes makes me doubt myself, stealing my energy. Some people in power over me continue to abuse that power, regardless of my opinions on the subject. I must stay aware that sometimes, without knowing it, I may do the same. Others, thank God, use their power and privilege in ways that inspire me, heal me, teach me, give me the energy and courage to continue. These include my colleagues in the NY summer institute, in the WPA summer workshop, former teachers, Texas-exes, scholars I've never met, people in my local community, the Poor Clares, students, strangers. The bottom line is this: The democratically minded voices in my head most of the time outnumber the harsh voices of hierarchy-by-fiat trying to shut me up. They have helped me embrace my role as a "warrior" in Audre Lorde's sense. They have helped me to fight for myself, to be on my own side. Further, when I am able to use my own power well, in the service of myself and others,

I am energized. My work with writing teachers, for instance, gives me a chance every year to reinvent my own (fractured) feminist vision. More often than not, it has worked well enough, and it has been a joy, providing a contrast to the conditions sometimes imposed on me.

Creating Dialogue, Reclaiming Voice

When I look over this narrative, when I consider my career as a rhetorician and WPA, I am struck by the parallels between my personal struggles to achieve professional voice and the efforts of myself and other WPAs around the country to develop democratic contexts in writing programs. Many of the barriers and setbacks I've faced, of course, are reflected in the literature and lore of composition studies and writing program administration, as well as in WPAs' comments in our focus groups. Many, if not most, of us have had our confidence undermined as we have worked to define a place for ourselves in the academy. While I've been writing this paper, I've had to ask myself: Aren't such conditions the price one pays for doing any kind of meaningful work in this culture?

What my deepening affiliation with other WPAs has given me is validation of—and partnership in—the broader social agenda in which my personal struggle has been embedded: the effort to promote a radical democracy of open and responsive dialogue. As most of us know all too well, this liberatory praxis cuts against the grain of market-dominated hierarchical American institutions, including education. And as Cornel West has cautioned, "[I]t takes a tremendous act of faith, in the long run a tremendous act of courage to cut against the American grain in a serious way" (62). Along with the feminist and African American critiques of the academy I have read, my connections with other WPAs have helped me revive that faith.

In the focus groups Leon Anderson and I have conducted, many WPAs have said that the work they're able to do with various people is one of the best parts of their jobs. "There is a transforming experience working with students [and new teachers] in this way," said one WPA. Another echoed the sentiments of many others when he said "I like being in a position where I can make a difference. . . . Our positions allow us to find out a lot more about how institutions operate." Nearly all the WPAs we interviewed emphasized, however, that the fostering of community among the writing teachers they supervise is not enough. WPAs need to find a supportive peer environment, and the Council of Writing Program Administrators provides many of us with that support. "My first piece of advice to new WPAs," many of those we interviewed said, "is to join WPA."

My own experience with WPA as an organization has shown me an activist community full of diversity and honesty and support and fighting and nurturing and engaging difference among the variety of voices that find their way into the conversations. WPA as an organization and the WPAs in individual institutions are crucial, not only to us as WPAs, but to higher education in that they often provide democratic, feminist academic models to counter exclusionary academic practices. Like much of what has been said about "women's work," WPAs (women or men) must confront daily the practical issues of pedagogy and of other people's lives as they interact with the institution. Theory, then, is in constant dialectic with lived experience, however malleable and shifting. The composition community in general and writing program administration in particular have widely embraced a dialogic, feminist ethic that assumes "the irreducibility of individuality within participatory communities" (West 32). This democratic ethos, although regularly contested, has pervaded the field partly because writing instructors are forced to face the practical consequences of their theories and partly because our current manifestation of rhetoric in the academy is historically related to the civil rights movement.

Our democratic ethos, however, is always under siege—from within and from without. Theresa Enos, Susan Miller, and Eileen Schell, among others, have been candid about the problems with the "second class citizenship" that often comes with teaching and administering composition. Some of us react to such critiques by "identifying with the oppressor," attempting to gain mainstream status by identifying primarily as scholars, exploiting the rest of us who value teaching and service as scholarship's equal. The relatively recent tendency to dichotomize "rhetoric" and "composition" reveals such a fissure in the profession. Others of us, those who feel "at home" in composition studies, may neglect the necessary examination of the exclusions we perpetuate in order to maintain that sense of belonging (see Martin and Mohanty).

To be sure, WPA labor can be thankless, marginalized work, and we must be careful not to participate in our own oppression and in the oppression of others. We must rather continue to fight for better material conditions and higher status for writing teachers in the academic workplace. Rather than judge ourselves and the significance of our work by mainstream academic standards, however, we can support each other in acting as forces of positive change in our universities, as Mary Trachsel argues. We must find ways to keep faith, while recognizing that we are struggling against the grain. WPA work provides an opportunity for an engaged, feminist work ethos in the profession, a place where many of us can speak about what we care about and then become stronger voices for change in the academy.

Notes

1. I'd like to thank Mary Trachsel, Leon Anderson, Jim McIntosh, Beth Daniell, Nancy Peterson, and Kenneth Bruffee for responding to various drafts of this paper. And I would like to absolve them from any responsibility for its contents, since I was stubborn enough not to take all their suggestions. I would also like to thank John Trimbur for his integrity and his generous way of living in the world. In the years since I met him in 1980 he has supported my work (and the work of countless others) and provided for

me a model of professionalism that combines genuine political commitment with ethical strength. He also has great taste in music.

2. Theresa Enos writes that "all writing faculty spend a large percentage of their time on administration: research faculty, 33 percent; four-year, 25 percent; liberal arts, 18 percent; and two-year, 18 percent" (71).

3. Shelley M. Park makes a persuasive argument against the largely unchallenged hierarchy of research, teaching, and service. The MLA Commission on Professional Service recently came out with a document that attempts to unsettle this hierarchy.

4. Ron Maxwell—tenured at Penn State—joined the group in 1981. And Peter Hawkes—then a lecturer at Columbia—joined us in 1982.

5. Dickson states that "a feminist administrative structure is faculty-centered and privileges the personal" (148), although her argument is much more complicated than that, and you should definitely read it. I liken our group to Dickson's definition in the sense that we were faculty-centered and we took into consideration our different institutional structures and their diverse needs. We fell somewhat short of Dickson's emphasis on personal, individual differences among people. Although Bruffee told me years later that he had been influenced by women's consciousness-raising groups in the 1970s, our group did not attend to the feminist literature that could have informed and strengthened our work.

6. Ken's perception is different than mine. Reading a draft of this paper, he responded: "I think it may be more than somewhat inaccurate to say that I 'didn't come with an agenda, although [I] came with plenty of authority.' I certainly did have an agenda. But it felt to me that (at that time, anyhow) I didn't have much authority at all. You guys, responding so wonderfully as you all did, constructed whatever authority I emerged from the experience with. Except for the most practical part—the peer-tutor training procedure—I was making most of it up as I went along. That's why I wanted Alex [Gitterman] there. And he turned out to be successful in all kinds of ways far beyond my expectations."

7. Johanna introduced me to Nancy Schneidewind's and Carolyn Shrewsbury's work on feminist process, which I subsequently used in T.A. training classes to show the parallel movements of feminist pedagogy and collaborative learning.

Works Cited

Bennis, Warren G., and Herbert A. Shepard. 1956. "A Theory of Group Development." *Human Relations* 9: 415–37.

Bishop, Wendy. 1993. "Doing the Hokey Pokey? Why Writing Program Administrators' Job Conditions Don't Seem to Be Improving." *WPA: Writing Program Administration* 21 (Spring): 46–59.

Bruffee, Kenneth A. 1978. "The Brooklyn Plan: Attaining Intellectual Growth Through Peer-Group Tutoring." *Liberal Education* 64: 447–68.

———. 1997. E-mail to Mara Holt. 6 July.

Calderonello, Alice. 1995. "Women in the Academy: Can a Feminist Agenda Transform the Illusion of Equity into Reality?" (Feminist workshop). Conference on College Composition and Communication, Washington, DC.

Denzin, Norman. 1996. *Interpretive Ethnography: Ethnographic Practices for the Twenty-First Century.* Thousand Oaks, CA: Sage.

Dickson, Marcia. 1993. "Directing Without Power: Adventures in Constructing a Model of Feminist Writing Programs Administration." In *Writing Ourselves into the Story: Unheard Voices from Composition Studies,* edited by Sheryl I. Fontaine and Susan Hunter. Carbondale, IL: Southern Illinois University Press.

Enos, Theresa. 1996. *Gender Roles and Faculty Lives in Rhetoric and Composition.* Carbondale, IL: Southern Illinois University Press.

Gradin, Sherrie L. 1995. *Romancing Rhetorics: Social Expressivist Perspectives on the Teaching of Writing.* Portsmouth, NH: Boynton/Cook.

Harris, Joseph. 1989. "The Idea of Community in the Study of Writing." *College Composition and Communication* 40: 11–22.

Holt, Mara, and John Trimbur. 1990. "Subjectivity and Sociality: An Exchange." *PRE/TEXT* 11 (1&2): 47–56.

hooks, bell. 1991. "Theory as Liberatory Practice." *Yale Journal of Law and Feminism* 4 (1): 1–12.

Lippmann, Walter. 1993. "The Indispensable Opposition." In *A Short Course in Writing: Composition, Collaborative Learning, and Constructive Reading.* 4th ed. Edited by Kenneth Bruffee. New York: HarperCollins.

Lorde, Audre. 1984a. "The Transformation of Silence into Language and Action." *Sister Outsider.* Freedom, CA: The Crossing Press.

———. 1984b. "Uses of the Erotic: The Erotic as Power." *Sister Outsider.* Freedom, CA: The Crossing Press.

Martin, Biddy, and Chandra Talpade Mohanty. 1986. "Feminist Politics: What's Home Got to Do with It?" In *Feminist Studies/Critical Studies,* edited by Teresa de Lauretis. Bloomington: Indiana University Press.

Miller, Susan. 1991. *Textual Carnivals: The Politics of Composition.* Carbondale, IL: Southern Illinois University Press.

MLA Commission on Professional Service. 1996. "Making Faculty Work Visible: Reinterpreting Professional Service, Teaching, and Research in the Fields of Language and Literature." *Profession:* 161–216.

O'Reilley, Mary Rose. 1993. *The Peaceable Classroom.* Portsmouth, NH: Boynton/Cook.

Park, Shelley M. 1996. "Research, Teaching, and Service: Why Shouldn't Women's Work Count?" *Journal of Higher Education* 67 (1): 46–67.

Reinharz, Shulamit. 1992. *Feminist Methods in Social Research.* New York: Oxford University Press.

Schell, Eileen E. 1992. "The Feminization of Composition: Questioning the Metaphors that Bind Women Teachers." *Composition Studies/Freshman English News* 20: 55–61.

Schneidewind, Nancy. 1993. "Teaching Feminist Process in the 1990s." *Women's Studies Quarterly* 21: 17–30.

Shrewsbury, Carolyn M. 1993. "What Is Feminist Pedagogy?" *Women's Studies Quarterly* 21: 8–16.

Trachsel, Mary. 1995. "Nurturant Ethics and Academic Ideals: Convergence in the Writing Center." *The Writing Center Journal* 16 (1): 24–45.

Trimbur, John. 1989. "Consensus and Difference in Collaborative Learning." *College English* 51: 602–16.

West, Cornel. 1993. *Prophetic Thought in Postmodern Times.* Volume 1 of *Beyond Eurocentrism and Multiculturalism.* Monroe, ME: Common Courage.

The WPA as Father, Husband, Ex

Doug Hesse

When I was ten or eleven, going out to eat meant going once a month or so to a drive-in. It was the mid 1960s, and I was the oldest of six kids. On a Sunday night, Mom and Dad would put us in the car to drive twenty miles to Davenport, Iowa, to the MacDonald's on Brady Street, built well before indoor seating or playlands. In the parking lot Dad kept track of orders in his head. One or two of us might help carry sacks back to the car. Sometimes Dad got only coffee, sometimes nothing. Not hungry tonight.

Only years later did I learn that Dad knew to the penny how much money he had in his pocket. He subtracted prices and taxes from that total and ordered for himself from what was left. The difference between a shake and a pop or a cheeseburger and a hamburger governed what he got for himself, if anything. But of course this was a mental spreadsheet we kids never saw.

When Dad got home from Korea, he threw away everything touched by the army—uniforms, decorations, letters explaining the GI Bill. He worked briefly at the Alcoa Aluminum plant in Bettendorf, quit that to drive endloaders and graders for the county, quit that to buy his father-in-law's Shell fuel delivery business, about the time I was born.

But the natural gas pipelines reached eastern Iowa in the early 1960s. People converted furnaces and pulled fuel oil tanks from basements, and Dad tried to staunch the losses by selling fishing bait and tackle. My sister, Joellyn, and I picked nightcrawlers by flashlight for a penny a worm. When I was ten I started running the store several days a week, riding my bike across town at dawn to unlock the door and scoop dead minnows out of the tanks. Mom would bring a lunch at noon, and in the afternoons I'd listen to the Cubs, still with Ernie Banks and Billy Williams. Dad took on a second job (or third, depending on how you counted), working third shift at Caterpillar in Mt. Joy, painting tractors. Finally, in 1970, he and a partner bought a trash truck and bid for the town's garbage business. I moved from picking worms to pitching trash every summer until I graduated from The University of Iowa.

My model for directing a writing program—for work generally—was my father, as was my model for being a husband and father myself, to degrees I've only recently realized. It is a model driven by a sense of providership, characterized by stoicism and sacrifice, continually gnawed by the pessimistic belief

44

that economic circumstances are more likely to get worse than better, that the circumstances of one's working life are fragile and only hard work can stave off disaster. Such a model has rewards: despite or, rather probably, because of becoming WPA my second year as an assistant professor, I made full professor by my eighth year at Illinois State University. And yet, however noble our culture may make forbearance and stoic sacrifice—the equivalent of telling colleagues and teaching assistants that you're just not hungry today—it ultimately costs its practitioner an awful lot. Last year I had to deal with life as a half-time parent, following a reasonably congenial but numbing divorce.

The professional literature has commented astutely on the feminized position of writing teachers generally and WPAs specifically. Most particularly, Lynn Bloom has modified Judy Seyfer's venerable essay "I Want a Wife" to "I Want a Writing Director," listing the countless chores and hidden tasks, usually unappreciated and unrewarded, that writing directors perform, for programs that are frequently themselves "weaker sex" partners to powerful and agent-full literature programs. I want to explain a different subject position that at least some WPAs inhabit: that of father and husband, in both real and metaphorical terms. Conventional depictions of the patriarchy don't nearly reflect the complexity of that subject position, assuming a kind of agency, power, and freedom that I've experienced only in the most vexed of circumstances.

Michael Messner notes that "men share very unequally in the fruits of patriarchy." In "The Men We Carry in Our Minds," Scott Russell Sanders narrates a surprising revelation at leaving his working class family for the university:

> Here I met for the first time young men who had assumed from birth that they would lead lives of comfort and power. And for the first time I met women who told me that men were guilty of having kept all the joys and privileges of the earth for themselves. I was baffled. What privileges? What joys? I thought about the maimed, dismal lives of most of the men back home. What had they stolen from their wives and daughters? The right to go five days a week, twelve months a year, for thirty or forty years to a steel mill or a coal mine? The right to drop bombs and die in war? The right to feel every leak in the roof, every gap in the fence, every cough in the engine, as a wound they must mend? The right to feel, when the lay-off comes or the plant shuts down, not only afraid but ashamed? (115)

He goes on, then, to acknowledge the lives of women he knew, maimed and dismal in a different fashion, his point being that pronouncements about gender must be tempered by understandings of class. My own past amplifies Sanders' questions. I'm someone who feels every student complaint as a leak in the roof, every criticism of the writing program as a cough in the engine. I have only come recently to understand that these burdens of responsibility, institutionally but also self-imposed, are not permanent, even if they are hugely complex and resistant. The working-class men that Sanders describes, those men that constituted my own sense of what it is to work, play, and be a parent, did not create the conditions under which they simultaneously benefited and suffered. My father did not start the Korean War, whose horrors, embodied for him in having to bulldoze a building held by renegade POW's while soldiers shot those who fled, held no glory. No sense of patriotic duty or manliness presented itself to him in Korea but rather a cultural and economic trap. Of course, the educated and reflective man should resist, should decline participating in whatever patriarchy that exists, but to imagine this as easy and obvious is to trivialize both the density of acculturation and the intractability of personal histories. So it is that certain work and personal practices persist even when most men that I know understand, focally and viscerally, that "men tend to pay heavy costs—in the form of shallow relationships, poor health, and early death—for conformity with the narrow definitions of masculinity that promise to bring them status and privilege" (Messner 1997, 6).

I came to Illinois State University in 1986, three weeks after defending my dissertation. In my second year, I was asked to coordinate a modest WAC program. In May 1988, the department chair asked me to become director of writing programs, a new position that combined Director of Composition, Assistant Director of Writing, and WAC Coordinator. Each of these positions had one-third time reassigned from teaching; obviously, I didn't want to stop teaching completely, so I was offered a one-course teaching load each semester and in the summer, plus two month's salary in the summer. My children, Monica and Andrew, were seven and four, and my wife had decided not to teach after finishing an education degree so that she could be home with them. I remember sitting in the backyard with Dawn discussing whether or not to take the position. Undoubtedly even by the late 1980s there were published warnings against untenured faculty taking administrative positions, but I hadn't seen them. Besides, I had a naive faith that I'd make tenure. Instead, I worried about the magnitude of the position and how it would affect my writing. I really liked to write.

As meager as it may sound now, one of the deciding factors in my accepting the position was that our car, a 1981 Plymouth Horizon, was getting old and too small for the family. I had been hired at $2600 a month for nine months ($23,400 a year), and in 1988 I was making $2800 ($25,700). Eleven months' salary was better than nine. I told the chair yes, and the next week we bought a station wagon. It's unseemly in higher education generally and in the humanities especially to admit that motives for a particular career decision might be at least partly financial. When we do talk about money, it's usually in regard to the reprehensible circumstances in which too many adjunct and graduate student teachers find themselves. Perhaps in light of their situations, those of us with tenure-line positions find it petty to talk about money matters and pressures. However, I increasingly think our failure to talk openly (if not obsessively) about pay and its implications helps keep the work and private worlds divorced from one another. Especially for new assistant professors in competitive situations, there is already great pressure to define one's life narrowly as the pursuit of tenure. Our reticence about discussing things like salary only contributes to the tendency for academics to define themselves and their colleagues one-dimensionally, as academics. In any case, for me becoming a WPA didn't mean nice vacations or season tickets; it meant replacing an old car and having to worry less about the mortgage and the summer health insurance premiums.

It also meant a certain kind of recognition and way of being needed. Part of this may be some kind of primal male desire to serve as leader of the pack. But for me it also grew from a working class childhood of spending lots of time by myself, selling bait in my father's store, climbing on and off a garbage truck. I participated in all sorts of extracurricular music and sports in school, but never had or made time for doing things with the guys. I was always welcome but rarely comfortable with them because I always felt I was imposing; on the afternoon of my graduation from high school, while many of my classmates went to a county park, I wrote thank-you cards. Until I went to college I never felt worthy to be with people in certain kinds of professions or what seemed like leisured lifestyles. Becoming a professor and, later, a WPA meant access to people that I long had a yearning to join.

But this was—and still remains for me—a provisional access, my worth constantly needing to be justified, legitimate only so far as my last publication, curriculum revision, or bureaucratic victory, subject to my being discovered as the interloper in the academic world that I irrationally know myself to be. I'd constructed myself as responsible caretaker who cast himself in a certain social level and role, much like the Anthony Hopkins character in *Remains of the Day*. This self-revelation is paranoid and nearly pathological, I know. The role of WPA-as-father, as I lived it, is destructive to the extent one fails to recognize or discuss such motivations.

In retrospect, I see how my combined motives of being provider and being prover governed my work as WPA. My first big task was to revise the undergraduate writing curriculum. Illinois State had a two-semester sequence driven by a "high process" pedagogy. The first course was organized by the aims of discourse, with students writing an expressive, analytic, and persuasive paper, each taken through several rounds of drafting and revision. The second course emphasized a research paper and students learning ways to write about readings and use sources. My colleagues and I were concerned that both courses lacked an appropriate rhetorical focus, that they were highly formalistic despite their process methodology.

In response I revised the goals and requirements for each of the two courses, making English 101 a course in popular persuasive discourse and English 145 a course in academic discourse, both classes heavily informed by theories of intertextuality, forum analysis, and discourse communities. The key phrase is "I revised," for I did this work on my own, proposing it to the writing committee for ratification once it was drafted. There were other ways I could and probably should have worked.

In the late 1980s and early 1990s, Illinois State was probably one of the best handful of places in the country to be in rhetoric and composition. Gail Hawisher had been hired the same year I was. We joined Ron Fortune, Jan Neuleib, Maurice Scharton, and others, on a tenure-line rhetoric/composition faculty that usually stood around seven people in a forty-member department that also included three people in technical writing and four in creative writing. We had a solid critical mass, plenty of undergraduate and graduate courses, a writing minor, a masters in writing, and several doctoral students in rhetoric and composition, every one of whom was getting a tenure line job. Even more important, we were full-fledged members of the department, our field accepted and respected, the department chair and graduate director, Charlie Harris and Bill Woodson, well-convinced of the legitimacy of rhetoric and writing. At a time when the professional literature and the hallways of the 4Cs conferences were filled with reports of writing faculty struggling against fiendish literature colleagues, I had little grasp of such fights because it was so foreign to my direct experience. Additionally, we had just gotten funding for ten classrooms worth of computers, becoming the largest writing program to teach every meeting of every writing class in computer environments. Most of what was true then of the Illinois State English department remains true now, although good faculty colleagues have come and gone, and other programs around the country enjoy similar or better numbers of faculty, courses, graduate students, and so on.

The point is that there were plenty of people here with expertise and interest in composition pedagogy. I needn't have revised the curriculum by myself, but I did and for two main reasons. First, I knew it would be more efficient. Developing a curriculum through collaborative work would be a long process of meetings, drafting, and revision. I was confident (aren't we all?) that my sense of theory, research, and pedagogy positioned me to develop state of the art courses, and I was confident, further, that my colleagues shared enough of my view that they would agree to the types of courses I drafted. When I shared the courses with the Writing Committee for comment and revision, my assumptions seemed to be born out. Obviously, I knew that the process of developing a curriculum, however tedious the collaboration might be, had advantages beyond the mere having of the curriculum.

But this line of thinking was trumped by a second reason for going it alone: I didn't want to trouble my colleagues. After all, they were busy people working toward tenure and promotion, teaching their own classes. Coordinating the writing program was my job, my responsibility. I was the one reassigned from courses to do it. I was the one getting paid during the summer. In short, I was the father. I'll explain, further, the shortcomings of this way of thinking; I know them now painfully well. But I don't want one point to get lost. I considered my reasons to be fairly altruistic, not colonially paternalistic in the ways that men's actions are often described, but rather practicing good fathering and husbanding as I knew it: self-reliant and taking care of others. It is true that my being willing to handle most of the writing program business enabled my colleagues and graduate students to teach and publish probably more freely than they might have been able.

I'm not saying these twin reasons for doing such projects mostly alone—efficiency and a sense of responsibility—are entirely good or bad ones. Rather they were and to some extent still are part of my motivations. They manifested themselves in other administrative practices. One day during my first year as WPA, I visited the classroom of a first year doctoral student from the People's Republic of China. As she patiently explained a new writing assignment, one of the class members mimicked back her sentences in a parody of Chinese pronunciation. This continued for several minutes until I finally asked the student to show some respect for his classmates and the teacher and to be quiet. I suppose I actually said, "Shut up." He told me, loudly, to go fuck myself, and the room shot still. I told him to join me in the hallway. The outcome was my taking him before the Student Judicial Board, where he was eventually censured. I still think I did the right thing, though I'm less confident now than I once was. The student was abusive, the classroom and teacher abused, and I had the position, experience, and responsibility to end at least the outward manifestations of the action. But did my action help the teacher in the shortish term of that class or the longer term of her teaching career? By flexing agency I modeled it for her; given the cultural differences, she likely wouldn't have taken such an action on her own. Working with her outside of class, we could have developed some strategies, over time, but just not as efficiently. Was efficiency the highest goal in this case?

Anyone who has been a WPA knows that dealing with conflicts between students and teachers happens more often than any of us would like, whether over attendance, late work, grades, personalities, or politics. I tried to address them by developing policies, everything from statements on "free speech" and its limitations in writing courses to portfolio scoring rubrics. Eventually, I compiled a Course Guide that reached 150 pages, which I edited and controlled. I developed an extensive multiple measures, formative teaching supervision program and chose a few advanced doctoral students each year to help mentor the thirty-five new teaching assistants. There was a step in every phase of that mentoring process, from teaching journal to classroom observation to final teaching portfolio, where I reviewed and commented on every piece of writing, giving advice not only to the teaching assistant but also to the program assistant.

There was a strong controlling dimension to my actions, a belief in my own perspective and rightness. But, too, there was that sense of responsibility. At the first WPA summer meeting I ever attended, at Miami University, in 1990,

David Bartholomae spoke of the WPA as icon for writing on campus, and I surely felt that. But I was more struck by the figure he chose, of Michael Keaton's Batman, standing high over a dark Gotham City, protecting and responsible yet also brooding, the aptly named Dark Knight.

All of this may sound—in fact, is—in the tradition of what Hildy Miller has characterized as masculinist administration or what Jeanne Gunner would view as "centered" WPA. But there are other dimensions of WPA as father beyond authority and judge. Elizabeth and Joseph Pleck's historical survey of ideals of fatherhood in the United States traces the rise and fall of various archetypes, from the stern patriarch of colonial America, to the distant breadwinner of the nineteenth century, to the "dad" of the middle three-fifths of the twentieth century, who was depicted as "playmate" and "chum" of his children. With their leisure time spent in good part creating environments for and interacting with their children, such dads, Pleck and Pleck contend, were "a symbol of the bourgeoisie and, thus, a marker dividing the middle from the working class" (41), functioning as what M. Haralovich termed "the Genial Dad."

I organized a regular Friday afternoon coffee with the TAs at a local shop. When we had a colloquium or visiting speaker, more often than not I baked the cookies we served and made sure we had apples and bananas, not just sweets. Much of our daylong annual symposium on teaching writing I would spend in the kitchen, like Martha (the Biblical, not the Stewart), making coffee and filling trays for between sessions. I kept boxes of Kleenex in my office for frustrated and hurt teachers and students.

I did this. I did that. There's a point to this egocentric display, and I'll get to it eventually. It's not that I was noble, and it's certainly not that I'm unique among WPAs, alas. Like me, others have served on numerous university committees, have directed a couple dozen theses and dissertations, have published themselves through tenure and promotions, have performed national leadership and service. Like me, others have had spouses and children.

I was, after all, husband and father in a traditional, not just metaphorical sense. As I am writing this, Monica and Andrew are 16 and 13. I've missed a scant handful of all the plays, swimming meets, ball games, and concerts they've ever been in—and most of those misses were due to CCCC and WPA Summer Conferences. I have changed diapers, packed lunches, cooked dinners, done laundry, coached teams, announced swimming meets, run the fish pond at PTO carnivals, the whole soccer dadding line, but I will say that for the first ten years of their life my emotional investment in my children's lives was always shadowed by my physical concerns. I was a willing and involved father—within certain limits, those limits usually dictated by how much work there was to do; while I may not have missed an inning of a baseball game, neither did I join many picnics afterwards.

As I noted earlier, my wife and I had decided she would stay home with the kids until they were old enough for both of us to work, a decision we still think made sense. However, the arrangement had several costs. Getting by on a single income made the extra summer pay as WPA first a luxury and then a necessity. Any number of times I would have resigned the position to become "just" a professor, except that we couldn't afford it, and I felt trapped. Having Dawn always there to take care of the kids enabled me to work stupidly long hours, nearly every night and one day per weekend for six or seven years. And while I'd like to think we had a collaborative marriage and that I was liberal and open in ways more meaningful than sharing household chores, the truth of the matter was that my opinion always counted more. By weight of my having the job, I could always invoke the specters, sometimes real and sometimes self-puffed, of tenure and promotion. The style with which I ran the writing program (and I intentionally use this strong and unsightly verb) reinforced and was reinforced by my role as husband and father, in a dynamic that got less and less healthy.

When Dawn became a full-time graduate student, I took on more of the "routine" child and home care. By this time established in my career and experienced in the routines of being WPA, I was able to spend less time at work: occasional evenings, very rare weekend days. Finally, all the promised payoffs of graduate school and tenure seemed to be here. We began traveling as a family to conferences, and after spending days interviewing candidates in Toronto and San Diego, no, I didn't go to sessions. We took a three-week vacation, camping in the mountains. The entire family was cast in the community theatre production of *Oliver* (tellingly, I was Mr. Brownlow, the solid merchant who turns out to be Oliver's grandfather). Yet relative seniority and experience brought new demands: chairing university committees, rather than serving on them, editing the WPA journal, getting frequent invitations to publish, to advise on tenure and promotion at other institutions, senior consulting. I've not held white collar jobs outside the academy and so can't say that professors are unique. But a debilitating fact of life in higher education is that one's work is never done. Autonomy has a price. There is always a better way to teach a class, always another article that could be written. In one of the most sensible appraisals of WPA life that I've ever heard, Kathleen Yancey once told me that she knew she was too busy when she was so fragmented she couldn't reassemble herself. I was there.

In July 1995, my wife told me she wanted to separate. Then, on a Sunday night in August, the day before I was to begin an orientation for new GTAs, she returned from a trip and announced that she wanted to divorce. Several months later we were divorced. Two weeks after the divorce she remarried. We have a joint parenting arrangement, the kids spending half each week with each of us. I miss my former sense of family, even as I treasure the new one. This essay is not the place to rehearse what happened in the marriage and why. Divorce is hard for the one leaving as well as the one left, and any story I told would necessarily be one-sided. I had taken the marriage for granted, had spent not nearly the time and energy on those areas of life beyond work, had failed in ways I confess abjectly to help sustain the emotional relationship she and I needed. She contributed to the demise of things, too.

I spent the fall semester crying and finally sought counseling, which I grudgingly found extremely helpful. (When my father cut his palm with a chain saw, he went to Jack Scott's drugstore and bought a bottle of iodine and a bunch of butterfly bandages, and that was that.) My professional life went to a maintenance level. I deferred hugely to Eric Martin, then the assistant WPA, and I discovered, to line this funnel cloud with silver, something so obvious as the fact that work was part of life, not life. In certain ways, I became a better father as a result of the divorce, and a better WPA, too, someone who had no choice but to rely on others, who had been smacked by the limits of his energy and efforts.

It would be reductive to say that being my kind of WPA cost me a marriage, for to do so would be to deny my agency and complicity. But it would also be reductive to say my motives were wholly of my own making. Because of my own background, I elevated breadwinning and caretaking roles over relationship building ones, and those roles justified, in my mind, a dynamic of efficiency and responsibility. I maintained that dynamic even despite obvious evidence that my current circumstances were hardly those in which going to MacDonald's was a rare treat. Being a good provider in a world I construed as hostile to people like me had to come first, relationships later, even taking care of themselves. One source of tension in my marriage stemmed from this vestige of class; as the daughter of a physician, Dawn had grown up in a different environment than I had, and while she was sympathetic, she saw as silly my degree of fretting about work. From my present, outside vantage point, she was mostly right. I constantly sought to prove myself in ways that seemed selfish and yes, were to an extent—but that I viewed as appropriately defensive. Whatever the cause, the effect was unhealthy.

In her fine essay "The Feminization of Composition," Susan Miller analyzes the complex ways in which composition functions as women's work, the writing teacher inhabiting a split identity as nurturer but also disciplinarian, in a "soft" subject matter that, nonetheless, is expected to "initiate students into 'essential' cultural knowledge" (48). Miller notes that one construction of the female as "mother" is "a person who will sacrifice her 'personal separateness' to attend to the frequent and private bodily needs of young children—elimination, cleanliness, and nurturance" (40). The professional literature is replete with tales of WPAs whose attention to the bodily needs of their programs and institutions sacrifice their personal separateness of publishing, with dire consequences (for example, Chuck Schuster's "The Politics of Promotion"). Part of what I experienced as a WPA and the way the position demands time and energy, seemingly without bound, can be explained in terms of the feminized, in Miller's terms, nature of this kind of work. But there are two questions I don't think have been fully explored.

1. What about the life beyond work? The professional literature has mostly focused on the work-related dimensions of feminized composition. To put it plainly: how does mothering or being wife to a composition program (and I am invoking a nonessentialized sense of these terms, focusing on aspects of the role and not the sex of the role holder) compete with being a wife or mother in life beyond work? The question is most profoundly extended beyond the sheer physical competition of time and energy to the psychological and social dimensions. Our professional literature is almost entirely devoid of discussions of our work set in the context of the life beyond work. We represent ourselves to one another in one dimension: professors or WPAs. Even when our scholarship "goes personal" it tends to go historically autobiographical, revealing our past selves, as does Mike Rose's *Lives on the Boundary*, but not the complexities of our current situations. (The happy exception may be the other chapters in this volume.) One of the reasons I've come to enjoy the WPA summer conferences so much are those languorous times spent eating catfish at a bar in Oxford, Mississippi, or dancing reggae on the shores of Lake Superior, or riding a boat in Bellingham Bay, seeing other WPAs as people.

2. How do the feminized dimensions of being a WPA, those dimensions that Lynn Bloom so neatly evoked, mutate in combination with certain class-bound masculine outlooks and practices? If it's the case that the WPA-as-mother sacrifices personal separateness to attend to others' needs, what are the consequences for the WPA-as-father who does much the same, but who additionally is socially constructed to devalue relationship building? One result, I think, is a crippling kind of alienation from both self and those others (wife, children, colleagues, friends) who might ameliorate the separation.

In the summer of 1997, I divorced the writing program. This time I was the one leaving—and for another suitor, if you'll forgive the corrupt analogy. I became Director of Graduate Studies in English, still at Illinois State. It was a lateral move in my opinion, and a step back in the opinion of my salary. After nine years of being WPA, I hadn't exactly burnt out, but I felt it was healthier for both of us, the program and me, to move on. It was hard to go, even sad leaving one identity for another. A fresh start in a new relationship.

Being WPA had gotten bitter in the last year, partly due to the changing politics and demands of institutional administration, partly due to my recognizing more fully the limitations of my style of fathering and husbanding. For the first time in my academic career I lost an administrative fight. The institution was revising general education. The process had gone on five years, and I'd been an integral it, as writing director, as a member of the academic senate, as drafter of the university's piloting and implementation plan. But I'd fairly much left the process in the spring of 1996, convinced that it was on a good trajectory. I was tired, and due to the divorce I was reassembling my life.

One aspect of the very ambitious program we'd crafted was a two-semester writing sequence whose development I'd coordinated. Suddenly, late in the eleventh hour, in December when the program was due for a final vote in February, a senate committee decided that humanities wasn't well enough represented in the program. It recommended that the second writing course become, essentially, a course in writing about literature. I protested.

So did the English department, all forty of us unanimous in passing a resolution decrying the assumptions that writing about literature, especially in this newly proposed New Critical/Arnoldian fashion, even remotely shared intellectual terrain with the "rhetorics of the academy" course we proposed. As I noted earlier, ours is an English Studies department, with savvy and enlightened literature faculty. No one from English was on the senate committee. I wrote white papers and attended hearings; I had some blind faith in logos buttressed by my ethos, faith that my authority and right reasoning would convince the academic senate. I lost. While my colleagues and I succeeded in having the course slightly modified, the end result bore little resemblance to any course I would happily teach as a writing course.

I was convinced the senate had heard our arguments in bad faith; I realized they had probably seen my arguments as made in bad faith. I hadn't done the relationship-building it takes to fashion coalitions in academic politics. In nine years a university faculty can change quite a bit. People I'd known from years earlier, when I done lots of WAC workshops had retired or gone, replaced by faculty who didn't much know me, faculty whom I hadn't tried to know myself. I suppose in becoming graduate director I took the "easy" way out, deciding that I was too tired to work on the marriage with the writing program.

My work as a graduate director will benefit from my work as a WPA. I've certainly learned that the job is not the life, and I hope I've learned that efficiency and protective responsibility aren't superordinate. Maybe I'm less worried about proving myself, but probably not. Each week the department chair, the undergraduate advisor, the new WPA, and I meet for an hour to discuss not only administrative matters but broader issues of concern about the job, and that simple interaction makes this position less lonely than I used to feel at work.

Becoming graduate director meant changing offices. I spent a week going through drawers and boxes, trying to decide what to keep and what to pitch. How about all those 5¼ inch floppy disks, written with WordStar 3.3? How about those minutes from 1989, printed with that whizzbang daisy-wheel printer, in 10-point Courier? Much I kept for archival reasons, much I kept for nostalgia.

Divorce demands cleaning and rearranging, too. Dividing the furniture is easy. But there are kids' pictures and Christmas ornaments, decisions about not only who gets what but whether some things get kept at all. The wedding album? (I kept it for my kids.) Last July, my former wife telephoned. She was putting together a scrapbook for Monica's sixteenth birthday, and would I look in the garage for the boxes of old school papers and art? I did, which led to an afternoon of reading old poems and looking at old fingerpaintings, perhaps the most bittersweet thing a parent can do. The one that broke my heart (there is no better figure) was a picture of me my son had drawn in preschool, on construction paper, now laminated. The printing on the picture was the teacher's; obviously he had dictated. It read

My Dad

My dad stays at his office until nighttime.

Sometimes he takes me with him. I love my dad.

Andrew Hesse

The picture is more poignant and painful for me than any other artifact of my professional life. I keep it where I can see it often.

Works Cited

Bartholomae, David. 1989. Plenary speech given at the Annual Conference of the Council of Writing Program Administrators, Oxford, Ohio, July.

Bloom, Lynn Z. 1992. "I Want a Writing Director." *CCC* 43 (2): 176–78.

Gunner, Jeanne. 1994. "Decentering the WPA." *WPA: Writing Program Administration* 18 (1/2): 8–15.

Haralovich, M. B. 1992. "Sitcoms and Suburbs: Positioning the 1950s Homemaker." In *Private Screenings: Television and the Female Consumer,* edited by L. Spigel and D. Mann, 111–42. Minneapolis: University of Minnesota Press.

Messner, Michael A. 1997. *Politics of Masculinities.* Thousand Oaks, CA: Sage.

Miller, Hildy. 1996. "Postmasculinist Directions in Writing Program Administration." *WPA: Writing Program Administration* 20 (1/2): 49–65.

Miller, Susan. 1991. "The Feminization of Composition." *The Politics of Writing Instruction: Postsecondary,* edited by Richard Bullock and John Trimbur, 39–54. Portsmouth, NH: Boynton/Cook.

Pleck, Elizabeth H., and Joseph H. Pleck. 1997. "Fatherhood Ideals in the United States: Historical Dimensions." *The Role of the Father in Child Development.* 3d ed. Edited by Michael E. Lamb. New York: John Wiley.

Rose, Mike. 1992. *Lives on the Boundary.* New York: Penguin.

Sanders, Scott Russell. 1987. "The Men We Carry in Our Minds." *The Paradise of Bombs,* 111–17. Athens, GA: University of Georgia Press.

Schuster, Charles I. 1991. "The Politics of Promotion." In *The Politics of Writing Instruction: Postsecondary,* edited by Richard Bullock and John Trimbur, 85–96. Portsmouth, NH: Boynton/Cook.

Surviving the Honeymoon

Bliss and Anxiety in a WPA's First Year, or
Appreciating the Plate Twirler's Art

Mary Pinard

> Plate twirling is a kind of gyroscopic juggling, wherein the
> performer spins, twirls, or otherwise rotates an inanimate object . . . .
> Some other variations of gyroscopic juggling include devil sticks,
> diabolo, rope spinning, knife throwing, and yo-yo.
> —Burgess, *Circus Techniques*

In a chance meeting last June, three months before I began my first year as the WPA at Babson College, a colleague said to me, "Good luck, and by the way, be sure to use your honeymoon." Honeymoon. I'd always thought of that as the necessary trip newly married couples take in order to recover from planning and staging their own wedding. For a WPA, it takes on less romantic, or shall I say less recuperative connotations. But it is, nonetheless, a crucial time that can make or break a relationship.

Now that I've survived the first year, I've learned that a new WPA's honeymoon—let's call it the early months of the first year—is precious for its novelty and trust, and at the same time precarious for its novelty and trust. What makes it wonderful—the power, permission, potential—also threatens to make it killing. Its guile is beguiling. Its shifting ground is its stability. Its lies are its truths. Its no yes, its bliss anxiety.

Somehow, though, the new WPA must negotiate this confusion to survive and prevail in her program, whether or not the ground after the honeymoon continues to shift. And by way of reporting on my own survival, I'd like to offer three suggestions for the new WPA: (1) recognize skills you bring to your job that may seem, on the surface, unrelated; (2) embrace luck; and (3) seek balance. Such feats of great courage and risk are regularly accomplished by part-time college teachers, poets, and plate twirlers. Let me explain.

My professional relationship this past year has been informed—and deformed, to be sure—by my own history as a very seasoned part-timer and a poet, as well as by the specific history and identity of the institution where I work. So, let me tell you about us individually.

56

Babson College was founded in 1919 by Roger W. Babson, a graduate of MIT who is perhaps most famous for predicting the stock market crash of 1929, and so his name is synonymous with business forecasting. His legacy is apparent at Babson today, where the commitment to being an international leader in management education is strong. The college enrolls about 1600 undergraduates and grants the Bachelor of Science degree. The curriculum's focus is on the management disciplines, but emphasis is also placed in science and liberal arts through an integrated approach known as the "40-40-20 program." A student's coursework includes 40 percent management courses, 40 percent liberal arts courses, and 20 percent electives (from either area). Of the 52 credits necessary in liberal arts, four represent Composition, the only required writing course. Typically, students who come to Babson are practical, privileged, and driven to become managers, if not CEOs. This population can be alien and alienating for someone from a liberal arts background; learning to be successful in the writing classroom at Babson is challenging for both student and teacher.

Babson also offers the MBA degree. It is consistently ranked among the best independent business schools in the country; recently, such magazines as *US News & World Report* and *Success* have named Babson the #1 business school in the United States for entrepreneurship.

Entrepreneurship? What could such a term mean to someone like me: a 1978 graduate with a BA in Theater and English from a small, Catholic, all-women's liberal arts college in the Midwest; with a MA in English; and with a MFA in poetry? What could the attraction be? How did I end up as the WPA at a business college?

It was a circuitous and accidental path, to say the least. I'd been college teaching, part-time, for ten years, and on some levels, I thought I might always be so engaged. I'd taught every imaginable permutation of writing and literature courses, a number of which I inherited from someone else who'd gotten a job, a grant, pregnant, or fired, and in almost every kind of college or university—public, private, community, communication, junior, secretarial. To put it gently, I'd really dated around.

Then, in 1990, the same year I decided to return to school to get my MFA in poetry, I answered an ad for yet another part-time position at a place called Babson. After teaching two sections of composition each semester there for four years, the WPA position opened up and I was asked if I wanted to consider applying.

I'd never anticipated this, nor can I remember ever imagining myself in such a job. Part-timers, depending of course on how long they've been part-timing and on the market, start believing they'll always be such. And poets who teach in academia are, generally, just happy to be employed. Not thrilled, perhaps, but happy. I'd long since given up the idea of a PhD in English; I knew I wanted to make poems, not scholarly articles. Since 1979 when I was in graduate school for my MA, the field of composition and rhetoric had developed and grown so that there was a new generation of scholars trained in these areas. And my passions were elsewhere engaged in my efforts at making poems, giving readings, and studying the craft.

Also, I had been able to make financial ends meet by keeping a number of part-time gigs active around me. I was like one of those plate twirlers who used to perform on *The Ed Sullivan Show*; remember how they'd keep all those plates twirling atop long, wobbly rods, running gingerly between them, lightly spinning each plate's edge, just enough to keep them from slipping and crashing? As those know who have done it, making part-time teaching a full-time job is a lot like this, only the rods aren't all on the same stage. My situation was less dire than for some in my position since I happened to be married to someone who had a good job.

In any case, I've come to understand that the roller-coaster experiences of my part-time tenure and what it demanded—flexibility, endless energy, tolerance of both ambiguity and rut, jack-of-all-tradism, marginality—as well as my life as a poet, with its intrinsic itineracy, risk, and imaginative core, prepared me surprisingly well for the plate-twirling bliss and anxiety of my first year.

The Bliss. New identity. Apparent special treatment. Much, much better pay. Benefits. Recognition. Collegiality. My *own* office, a name plaque on *my* door, business cards with raised letters. Like most anyone shifting from part- to full-time status, I felt blissful. True, the poet in me worried about how I would keep my writer's life functional in my new life of new commitments—would I be able to use and conserve my creative energy? I told my poet self I could, and I believed that—at least in the beginning.

I accepted the position in May 1994, and for me, that's when the honeymoon began. While my contract didn't officially begin until September, I decided—and was encouraged, I might add—to get a head start during the intervening summer; I was paid a pre-contract stipend that amounted to just slightly less than I'd been paid to teach a section of Composition. I couldn't believe what I felt was my own good fortune, nor could I judge how much work was enough—two very dangerous kinds of ignorant bliss, nonetheless.

Since I'd been part-time at Babson for four years, I had specific and very useful knowledge—albeit somewhat cursory—about the Writing Program there, its faculty, and my predecessor. It was as if we'd all been on a long, long pretty good date, only maybe in different cars. This familiarity gave me the confidence to do some investigating. I spent time visiting individually all of my five full-time, senior writing faculty colleagues; among other questions, I asked each one, "How would you define or describe the Writing Program at Babson?" After I got five significantly different replies, and after I panicked, I realized I had the opportunity to do some defining of my own.

In addition, I knew from my predecessor, who had been my immediate supervisor while I was part-time, that over his six years as director, pockets of resistance had formed to some of his initiatives, as well as to his management style; over time, these had grown larger and had taken on the character of inactivity and drift. He was very generous in his counsel, but he was too soon gone to his new position elsewhere, and I realized that I was, truly, on my own with perhaps much more power than I knew what do with.

And what I didn't know at that point, didn't hurt me; in fact, it probably helped, particularly in terms of power and politics, the p-words of any WPA's existence. Unburdened with this kind of sensitive wisdom, I could blunder around long-standing feuds, blithely knock on doors of deans and comptrollers, vice presidents and chairs, and bother staff innocently for basic information on everything from purchase orders to water coolers.

I felt powerful, even if at that point I really wasn't, and there was a surprising sense of invincibility: I was full-time, I was new at this job (which by the way, makes the job new too), people were welcoming, it was summer. What did I have to lose?

For no other reason than instinct, and perhaps a little imagination, I think, I decided to focus my attention on the Writing Center. I knew some of its problems, since over the years I'd sent my composition students there: poor location (3rd floor of the library in a tiny study room); no visibility, image of remediation, directoral power struggle. What if I could move it to the large, largely unused twenty-four-hour study room next to the main entrance of the library, and in time for fall semester? I think I figured such an undertaking wouldn't be too great a risk since the Center had been neglected—any progress would probably be perceived as success, and on the other hand, if nothing happened, no one might notice.

In retrospect, I realize that since I had to start from scratch to make this move work—from securing permission from the library director, deans, and security, to installing outlets for computers and phone lines—I came into contact with virtually every office on campus. It allowed me to introduce myself to a number of key figures on campus, to talk with them about the Writing Program, writing center pedagogy, and future plans. Even though it was summer—or perhaps because it was summer—people were amenable and cooperative. Did I know I was learning something here about luck, change, and the true nature of the WPA honeymoon?

By midsummer, it seemed the move would in fact go forward, but not until the first week of school. No problem! I scurried around anyway, making myself visible, making myself extremely available, making myself thin.

Luckily, I'd already registered for the WPA Workshop in Oxford, Mississippi, scheduled for late July. I'd learned about it from a concerned colleague who, upon hearing about my new position, urged me VERY strongly to attend. "They can help you prepare," she said emphatically.

And they did. After three days of intense discussions, readings, wonderful small group work, even homework, my eyes were opened. Wide.

The Anxiety. Naked power. Power games. Broken promises. Funding cuts. Professional denigration. Slippery slopes. Fickle review standards. ESL, WIC, WAC, RAC, WC, PC. Burn out.

I returned from my own Oxford having read, among other fine, but for me harrowing articles: Edward White's "Use It or Lose It: Power and the WPA," (even the subheadings in this article are telling: "The Enemies of Writing Programs" and "Wielding Power"); Sue Ellen Holbrook's "Women's Work: The Feminizing of Composition"; Thomas Recchio and Lynn Z. Bloom's "Initiation Rites, Initiation Rights"; and Chuck Schuster's "Climbing the Slippery Slope of Assessment: The Programmatic Use of Writing Portfolios." These articles gave names to issues and analyzed situations I'd intuited, but their delicate application to a WPA's experience was new to me.

I returned from my own Oxford startled by how similar my new anxieties and awarenesses felt to my old anxieties as a part-time teacher and poet. Did I know more than I thought about the true nature of my job? About what could happen after the honeymoon?

I hadn't thought so before the WPA workshop, but I could see in the profile of the WPA the ghostly but recognizable profile of the part-timer—and for me too, certain elements of a poet's professional experience—at least in a general sense. What does this mean? For WPA's, it means their job, like part-timers' work, can be devalued, marginalized, underpaid, disempowered; it can also surprise, resist, rankle, and remind institutions about their vulnerabilities, blindspots, and professional responsibilities. It seems to me it could be informative for WPA's to consider these similarities, and what the part-time experience has to offer that's both cautionary and useful.

For me personally, the connections between the WPA and the part-timer mean that I'm more prepared than I could have imagined for what's ahead. From my finely tuned part-time vantage point, I'd certainly seen through the thin veils of naked power, felt the sting of broken promises, and the dislocation of funding cuts; and what part-timer hasn't known professional denigration? And especially as a poet, there is always the specter of review standards if you're working in any traditional English department—what exactly is a creative writer anyway? Certainly not one of the chosen, the enlightened scholars of worthy texts.

Of course, what's different for me now, a year later, is the means with which I have to address these anxieties. Those of you who are very experienced WPA's, could I'm sure see in my description of the summer honeymoon before I officially began my job, the sizable hole I was digging for myself before I knew any better. You noted the way I spread my enthusiasm around campus, taking on anything, promising everything, setting no limits for myself. You shook your heads, knowingly.

After Oxford, though, heavy with cautionary tales and some fear that I'd already gone too far, I still had to follow through with the Writing Center move and all the work it entailed. Luckily, and because my timing was right for a change, it turned out to be a successful gamble: in the new space, computer and phone were installed, bookshelves, tables and furniture scrounged, handouts designed, a database designed for record keeping, peer consultants trained, PR developed and expanded across campus. The results? Increased visibility, use, and satisfaction with Writing Center services, and the number of writers visiting the center more than quadrupled over the entire year, from approximately 250 students the year before to over 1000 students this past year. And more and more faculty members call to ask advice about writing and writers.

That was the bliss of success. The anxiety of it is that I myself took on too much, defining most of the tasks as mine. After all, I'd set myself up to be the nice girl, eager to please, especially during the honeymoon.

But I became overextended, exhausted, and worried about the expectations I'd set everywhere, like traps, for myself. In part, this was due to my insecurity in the job and my desire to be worthy of it, a particular legacy, I think, of my part-time life. Ironically, what made me feel insecure was also what gave me the confidence I needed to move forward. In any case, all this set me up for a kind of plate twirler's nightmare: too many plates spinning and at different speeds. And I've been running, well at least jogging, ever since.

And so, what about my advice for honeymoon survival? Let me reiterate.

1. Recognize the skills you bring to your new WPA job that seem, on the surface, unrelated, especially during the honeymoon. For me, discovering similarities between my years as a part-timer and my WPA position helped me to understand the tricky nature of a WPA's job and to feel confidence even on its shifting ground.

   My training and experience as a poet prepared me to take risks and to tolerate ambiguity. I came to this job a patient observer of detail—poets are known for their ability to stare something, anything, into meaning. I came to this job ready to use my imagination without apology. I've learned all these skills are put to prompt, if not profound use in the WPA's world.

2. Embrace luck, or be flexible enough to design new goals when fortuitous situations arise. Had I not acted to move the Writing Center when I did, the opportunity would have passed. I might have been less frazzled, but I'd be much less savvy about my program, and the Writing Center would still be tucked away, a dot on the map of remediation.

3. Seek balance amongst the many, often swirling issues in your program, but expect discombobulation: a slow wobbling on the one hand, and a blurring speed on the other. Of course, extremes are necessary at times; they can shake up the status quo, reveal weakness (or strength), signal imminent disaster (or triumph).

Early last summer, I was in high gear—almost a blur—preparing the ground for the Writing Center relocation. When I arrived at the WPA Workshop in late July, I had to slow down, take note of the issues I was encountering, and without much awareness. Yes, it was like a kind of whiplash. By the time the school year actually began in early September, I felt at least partially on balance—an equilibrium, if fleeting—having spun in the direction of both extremes. What I want to suggest here is that in addition to whatever the new WPA brings to her job, she could benefit from considering the predictive, dexterous, delicate skill of a plate twirler, the essence of which is balance and cool.

What the WPA honeymoon lacks in duration, it makes up for in tolerance and a kind of elasticity—it will expand and contract to accommodate discovery and distraction, all those opportunities a new WPA needs to test extremes and to envision a balanced future.

Works Cited

Burgess, Hovey. 1976. *Circus Techniques.* New York: Drama Book Specialists.

Holbrook, Sue Ellen. 1991. "Women's Work: The Feminizing of Composition." *Rhetoric Review* 9 (2): 201–29.

Recchio, Thomas, and Lynn Z. Bloom. 1991. "Initiation Rites, Initiation Rights." *WPA: Writing Program Administration* 14 (3): 21–26.

Schuster, Charles I. 1994. "Climbing the Slippery Slope of Assessment: The Programmatic Use of Writing Portfolios." *New Directions in Portfolio Assessment: Reflective Practice, Critical Thinking, and Large-Scale Scoring,* edited by Laurel Black, Donald A. Daiker, Jeffrey Sommers, and Gail Stygall. Portsmouth, NH: Boynton/Cook.

White, Edmund M. 1991. "Use It or Lose It: Power and the WPA." *WPA: Writing Program Administration* 15 (1–2): 3–12.

Part II

WPAs at Work

Very early in my career I interviewed for a job as the Director of Composition at a large state university. At some point during the interview, the all-literature faculty gathered to question me admitted that this was the department's only position in writing. The previous director had quit. The man currently directing the technical writing courses wanted to go back to the literature faculty. They needed someone who could direct the first-year composition program, train teaching assistants, teach undergraduate writing courses and graduate courses in rhetoric, administer the technical writing courses, correct problems in the writing center, design and run a new writing across the curriculum program that had yet to be funded or approved, create and administer an outcomes assessment exam that had been mandated by a faculty senate not at all sold on writing across the curriculum, *and, I found myself thinking, coach the volleyball team?* It was the old joke. Plate twirling all over again.

Fortunately for me, they never offered the job. It must have been something I said. Just as fortunately for them, the woman they did hire to fill the position had sense enough to manage all of those tasks taking each one separately, over a period of several years. She even convinced this department eventually to hire additional faculty for what has become a writing program, not simply a loose collection of courses staffed by one faculty member and a gathering of disgruntled teaching assistants. Years later, I asked her how she had found the courage to accept that position, and she told me that she knew what the department did not know: The position they wanted filled was actually four or five positions. She would just take it slowly and carefully and build her own faculty along the way. Very wise.

When asked to tell a story, many WPAs will certainly tell the story of their own coming of age in the profession as a way of getting at what this job is. Others, however, will tell workplace stories because it is only through actually running a program that WPAs begin to understand the many dimensions of that work. At a WPA Conference in Bellingham, Washington, Keith Rhodes opened the paper reprinted in this section with his guitar as he sang the ballad of its opening lines. You can try it yourself if you remember the tune of *The House of the Rising Sun*, though this version warns new WPAs of the "sin and misery" that awaits them if they go unprepared to that dark place—the place of the untenured program director. Keith also reminds us of the power and powerlessness of national organizations. The Wyoming and Portland resolutions are important, but resolutions do not make for action. And the action called for by resolutions may look good for a discipline, but it isn't always the kind of action needed in specific places for specific people whose jobs have sometimes been threatened by the very resolutions meant to protect them.

The essays that follow provide us with much beyond the "war stories" Chuck Schuster and I feared we might get for a collection like this, but many of them do begin with moments when the WPA can certainly feel embattled. Over the years, I have counseled friends and colleagues who came to work one day only to discover the program they had labored on for months or years had been canceled—no notice. Or, the writing center they directed had been closed. Door locked. Room dark. Writing center staff dismissed. Again, no notice. Just gone.

These are not isolated events. WPAs, more often than they would like to think about, have had to explain again and again what they do and why they do it. My guess is that a part of any collection of WPA stories will always address those moments when the WPA must explain to others what it is we do and why. That is where the scholarship and the research in this profession come into the workplace. Sexual politics, disciplinary lines drawn in the sand, accountability—these are real and important concerns in the life of WPAs. Or, as Keith Rhodes crooned to those gathered in a small classroom in Bellingham:

> *Oh rhetors tell your children/ Not to do as I have done*
> *To come right out of graduate school and coordinate comp-o-si-shee-un.*

Taking It Personally

Redefining the Role and Work of the WPA

Alice M. Gillam

> By the risks of its writing, personal criticism embodies a pact, like the "autobiographical pact" binding writer to reader in the fabulation of self-truth, that what is at stake matters also to others: somewhere in the self-fiction of the personal voice is a belief that the writing is worth the risk.
>
> —Nancy K. Miller

Twice in my life I have had the same nightmare. The first time was in the fall of 1962. I was a freshman at Wittenberg University, a small liberal arts college in Ohio. The evening before, we had gathered in South Hall's lounge to watch President John Kennedy somberly announce that he was sending battleships to the Bay of Pigs. Eighteen, only a month away from living at home, we sat in stunned silence at the prospect of war. That night I dreamed of nuclear holocaust—fire storms, flesh burning off of bodies like charred scraps of paper, unbearable heat, acrid smells, a palpable sense that I was about to die. I awoke in a cold sweat.

Nearly thirty years later, in the spring of 1992, I had the same dream as I was preparing to take over as writing program administrator. The nightmare occurred in the midst of a painful controversy which inaugurated my work as a WPA. In the spring before I was to take over the writing program, a committee of TAs and lecturers recommended *In Search of Gay America,* a nonfiction collection of narratives about gay life in America, as a text for second-semester composition. As the incoming WPA it was up to me to give final approval. Any hope I had of making a grand entrance, of leading off my tenure as WPA with a decision or act that would be applauded by all, that would unequivocally demonstrate my professional talent for this job quickly went out the window. This was a no-win situation. If I approved the text, I risked betraying my professional judgment and obligation to the undergraduate students in this course. If I rejected it, I risked betraying lecturers and TAs whom I respected.

On the one hand, I support the use of books dealing with controversial social and political issues; indeed, one of the texts we had been using, Frances

FitzGerald's *Cities on a Hill*, included a chapter on gay issues. And in recent years, we had adopted a number of texts which dealt with highly charged political issues: Jonathan Kozol's *Savage Inequalities*, Angela Davis' *Women, Race, and Class*, Barbara Ehrenreich's *The Hearts of Men*. Further, I had a deep commitment to this issue for personal reasons I felt I could not and should not discuss publicly. On the other hand, it appeared that the only way I could demonstrate political solidarity with TAs and lecturers was to approve this text and that seemed a professionally irresponsible reason for approving the text. I talked for long hours with a TA representative who was also a personal friend. For both of us, this issue was intensely personal and for both of us, this issue dramatized the tension between professional judgment and personal concerns. I wracked my brain for a solution that would hurt or distress no one. I tried to think of ways to minimize the damage that would result no matter what I decided.

For the two weeks of this ordeal, I felt as if I was reliving the nightmare of my divorce, the loss of my husband and the family life we had built to a gay lifestyle. Although this professional crisis paled emotionally in comparison to the crisis in my personal life, the two experiences evoked related feelings and a similar sense of loss. On some level, I felt as though I was being required to give up my hopes for an idyllically successful professional life just as I had been required to give up my hopes for lifelong marriage and an intact family for my children.

In both cases, I felt trapped by circumstances beyond my control. Again, it seemed as if my support of gay and lesbian rights was being unfairly tested and was, at the same time, effectively beside the point. Yet again, I was being deeply affected by an issue that was not mine, yet somehow mine. Oprah and Geraldo aside, there are deep and legitimate sanctions against "confessing" painful personal experiences in public, professional forums. Even now, it feels somewhat gratuitous and unprofessional to reveal my personal experience as a way of asserting my credentials and my commitments to gay and lesbian rights.

Because I could not share my frustrations publicly, they boiled up privately: How dare people question my support for gay and lesbian rights on the basis of one decision? How dare gay and lesbian instructors assume that they were the only ones deeply affected by homophobia and that they were the only ones who had suffered from it? I, too, have a stake in seeing homophobia eliminated. The permeability between my professional and personal life could not have been more powerfully evident.

Ultimately, I decided against the text for a range of what I felt were sound pedagogical and programmatic reasons. Not only was this a required course for students but also the course involved high-stakes, large-scale portfolio assessment, the outcome of which decided whether or not students attained junior standing. Prior experience suggested that students had more difficulty writing analytical essays about narrative texts. I worried that students' discomfort with the subject might interfere with their ability to demonstrate their writing competence. Students might feel that they were being asked either to argue for or against homosexuality. Moreover, while I support the inclusion of politically charged issues into the curriculum, I believe that inclusion must be done carefully and with due consideration of the curriculum's overall aims.

Not unexpectedly, some interpreted my decision as censorious and homophobic. There was a petition circulated urging me to reconsider my decision. At the suggestion of the TA I mentioned earlier, TAs, lecturers, other faculty, and I met and proceeded in Quaker meeting fashion to discuss the decision, the issues involved, and the feelings engendered by this experience. Teachers spoke of the success they had had in teaching the Castro chapter of FitzGerald's book. Gay and lesbian instructors spoke eloquently about what it meant to them to have this issue included in the first-year curriculum. Others spoke of the message this sent to our gay and lesbian students. And some, of course, echoed my concerns about adopting this particular book for this particular class. I tried to explain as clearly as I could my reasons for rejecting this text on gay and lesbian issues. The meeting went some distance in healing the hurt on both sides but it did not leave everyone happy with the decision.

The lessons from this initial WPA experience were many. Ironically, my decision to set aside personal bias in favor of professional judgment was interpreted as evidence of personal bias. People who knew nothing about me as a person made judgments about me based on this decision. It was interpreted and evaluated out of the context of my life experience. I came to realize one of the realities of administrative work: one cannot control public perception of public decisions. And I learned paradoxically the inevitability of taking things personally and the necessity, at some level, of not taking things personally.

I tell this story because I think that most of the discourse about writing program administration separates the personal from the professional, denies the tensions between the personal and the professional, and denigrates the personal in relation to the professional. I think there are two related reasons for this: (1) efforts to legitimize the WPAs' professional status and identity have resulted in coding the ideal WPA as male; and (2) these same efforts have required that personal concerns be separated from and subordinated to professional ones.

Challenging the Professional/Personal Binary

Laments about the WPA's lack of professional recognition and status often describe this dystopic state in female terms and represent the utopian ideal in male terms. Olson and Moxley in their oft-cited "Directing Freshman Composition: The Limits of Authority" bemoan the fact that department chairs value WPAs most for their distaff role and for such "insubstantial" duties as being accessible, training and supervising teachers, and communicating effectively (53). In "I Want a Writing Director," Lynn Bloom invokes Judy Syfers' "I Want a Wife" to satirize the perception of WPA work as "housework"—nurturing new instructors, cleaning up students' writing, protecting the time of more important department colleagues by taking care of administrivia.

The predictable counter move has been to define the WPA role and professional success in this role in male terms. The most dramatic example of this is Ed White's "Use It or Lose It: Power and the WPA." Not only does White associate power with male sexual prowess in this title, but also he employs military metaphors in describing the behavior of the strong and successful WPA. WPAs must "size up enemies" and "assess [their] weapons"; they must "marshal [their] own forces," garner their own "weapons," and develop shrewd tactics to use in "fighting" for their program's interests (6–9). Acknowledging his militaristic tropes, White asserts bluntly that if you don't agree with this figuration, you are either naive or self-deluded (6). He concludes by insisting on his particular construction of WPA work and his definition of WPA success: "The only way to do the job of a WPA is to be aware of the power relationships we necessarily conduct, and to use the considerable power we have for the good of our program" (12).

This discourse sets up an economy of values in which the most "public" professional acts are deemed most important and the more "private" trivialized. Work that resembles the stereotypical private labor of women is dismissed as unimportant and as evidence of unprofessional status while the stereotypical public labor of men—winning battles and running things—is associated with professional achievement and recognition. More specifically, in-house work with students and teachers is "insubstantial" while negotiating budgets with deans is "substantial."

The personal enters White's discourse only as an illustration of professional success and failure. White's essay begins with a heroic personal anecdote about his use of power to out maneuver a traitorous Dean of Humanities. White's essay concludes with the clear implication that failure to use power aggressively, decisively, single-handedly, makes one's personal fitness for the job questionable: "If we really don't want to deal in power, we had better step aside, or we will be doing more harm than good" (12).

Recent articles by feminists critique this gendered coding of the WPA, proposing alternative administrative models and analyzing its negative consequences for women. Directly addressing White's portrait of the "heroic" and "individualistic" program administrator, Rebecca Howard acknowledges the importance of gaining "institutionally sanctioned power," but advocates an approach that refuses a "militaristic spirit of antagonism" in favor of "collective methods for effecting change . . . that will [themselves] transgress the discourse of hierarchical competition" (40). Alternatively, Marcia Dickson, in "Directing Without Power: Adventures in Constructing a Model of Feminist Writing Program Administration," proposes a feminist administrative structure which eschews traditional power games and "privileges the personal" (148). She writes not of swashbuckling victories over deans but of seeking "a simple, feminist conversation about the problems at hand" (147). She credits her successes, the best things she has done, not to her prowess as a power broker but to her collaboration with others (148).

In "Decentering the WPA," Jeanne Gunner discusses the negative consequences of the powerful WPA-centric model of administration which elevates the professional WPA at the expense of the writing instructors who are treated as perpetual "novices" or apprentices (12). And Mary Ann Cain in a forthcoming article, "The Feminization of Writing Program Administration: Naming Conflicts, Resisting Resolutions," examines the complicated ways in which these gendered constructions of the WPA work against women: penalizing those who do not behave as men, denigrating those who do, and dividing female WPAs from the mostly female writing teachers they supervise.

Offering yet another alternative to masculinist models of administration, Hildy Miller argues for a "postmasculinist" approach which blends masculinist and feminist administrative models in light of the practical reality that "masculinist assumptions about power, leadership, and administrative structure permeate the academic, affecting feminist approaches at every turn" (58). "[I]f feminist teaching is at odds with the larger masculinist academic structure," writes Miller, "feminist administration is doubly so. . . . At every turn, established authoritarian forms of leadership threaten to destroy nascent programmatic structures that would cooperatively guide such concerns as teacher training, mentoring, and curriculum development" (49). For Miller, this reality calls for a strategic hybrid approach which entails working collaboratively or according to feminist principles with those who are technically under one's supervision and assertively or according to masculinist principles with those who are one's peers and "superiors."

While not all of these reformulations of writing program administration directly invoke the personal, I would argue that they all do so indirectly in their insistence on equitable interpersonal relationships and collaborative ways of working. Other challenges to the "heroic" conceptualization of the WPA and the separation of the professional from the personal emerge in recent narratives by feminist WPAs.

Accounts such as Mary Ann Cain's previously mentioned essay and Wendy Bishop and Gay Lynn Crossley's "How to Tell a Story of Stopping" narrate not heroic administrative deeds but rather complex experiences which lend themselves to multiple interpretations. Cain, for example, tells the story of her difficult tenure as a WPA and particularly of her unsuccessful effort to share power with adjunct faculty through the formation of a teacher-research team. As Cain makes clear, the talk which occurred during these teacher-research meetings was a blend of the personal and the professional: it was "wide-ranging, free-flowing, almost decadent in its richness"; it was "informal, anecdotal, even gossipy, definitely outside 'official' institutional discourse." Ultimately, however, these consciousness-raising/professional development sessions went awry due to conflicting agendas and a variety of misunderstandings. Rather than casting herself as the victim, Cain turns this troubling experience into an occasion for self-reflection and critical inquiry.

Bishop and Crossley offer a dialogic account of Bishop's decision to resign from her WPA post. Interspersed throughout this narrative are "confessional" journal entries—"I decided the more I teach the less open I am to talking to others about teaching"—references to the personal dimensions of program administration—Bishop's "personal connection" with GTAs and interactions with office staff—and even mention of at-home experiences with kids and cats (70–71). Although the ending of this story, Bishop's resignation over arbitrary decisions made by higher administration without her consultation can be interpreted (and was by an early reviewer) as an all-too-familiar victim narrative, Bishop and Crossley resist the defensive response and go on to explore why "victim narratives" are such "a characteristic way of telling our professional stories" (75).

These essays illustrate that full, richly textured accounts of our professional lives not only include the personal but also break down distinctions between the personal and the professional. Further, these accounts demonstrate how candid, self-reflective narratives enrich and complicate our understanding of WPA work. Arguing for the value of reflective narratives generally, Kathleen Blake Yancey writes: "Without it [reflection] we live the stories others have scripted for us: in a most unreflective, unhealthy way. The stories we make construct us, one by one by one, cumulatively. So I think it's important to tell lots of stories where we get to construct many selves" (60).

Reclaiming the Personal Beyond the Professional

To date, most feminist critiques focus on the professional consequences of these gendered constructions for women WPAs. In conclusion, I would like to focus on the personal consequences of this figuration. Although we hear personal "horror" stories of exploitation and failure to get tenure, these stories emphasize the professional costs rather than the personal ones. A recent case in point is Sally Barr-Ebest's "Gender Differences in Writing Program Administration." Based on her survey of WPAs, Barr-Ebest reports that "the men fare far better than the women. They publish more, they are paid more, and they are more likely to be tenured" (53). While some of these differences can be accounted for by the fact that the male WPAs are more senior than female WPAs, the finding that women's careers, particularly their ability to "move on," is more severely jeopardized is disturbing. However, what disturbed me more were Barr-Ebest's recitation of the effects of writing program administration on the personal lives of women WPAs:

> "I might be able to have a healthier life if I weren't always in service of the institution."
>
> "I think I'm an angrier person!"
>
> "No time to breathe, much less to publish."

"The overwhelming struggle for respect and acceptance makes it difficult to continue believing in oneself."

"I work from 10 PM–3 AM on weeknights to get my writing done—and arise at 6 AM to get kids to school."

"Essentially I gave up my personal life in order to sustain my scholarship and teaching while doing administration."

"Hard to tell, but a divorce happened after 7 years."

"I am a mess" (59–60).

This litany of personal costs is but a sampling of responses by women WPAs reported by Barr-Ebest. Male respondents, I hasten to add, also report paying a heavy personal price for their work as WPAs—damaged or lost relationships, reduced quality of "personal" life, lost time with family, stress-related health problems. However, since the focus of Barr-Ebest's article is on the gender-difference in the professional costs of writing program administration, the similarity in personal costs is noted only in passing. One might conclude that while both men and women suffer terrible personal stress as a result of this triple expectation to research, teach, and administer, at least the men are able to gain tenure more readily, to publish more, and to be more mobile. However, I want to decry a professional ideal that ignores or minimizes the personal costs of attaining that ideal.

When I began my tenure as WPA, a former WPA advised me to keep in mind that decisions and actions related to the job should be "professional, not personal." As one who has never been able to divide her life neatly between professional and personal commitments and identities, I worried about my suitability for this job. After four years, however, I am convinced of the impossibility and artificiality of this distinction. Although the intersections of the personal and professional have not always been as conflicted and obvious as in that initial WPA experience, I have found that personal and professional considerations mutually inform and often vex each decision and action.

I think it is crucial that we talk about the convergence of our personal and professional lives and that we redefine our work in a way that does not exclude or denigrate the personal. For our own sakes and for the sake of those who follow us, we must insist not only on professionally acceptable terms of employment but also on a concept of professional work that does not require us to sacrifice our personal lives, our personal relationships, and our health.

Postscript

A few days ago, amidst work on the final revisions of this essay, I received a flyer in the mail inviting faculty to designate their offices as "safe places" for gay and lesbian students to come for academic counseling or simply conversation and support. I readily filled out the form and sent it in, grateful, at last, for a angst-free opportunity to integrate my personal and professional commitments.

Works Cited

Barr-Ebest, Sally. 1995. "Gender Differences in Writing Program Administration." *WPA: Writing Program Administration* 18 (3): 53–73.

Bishop, Wendy, and Gay Lynn Crossley. 1996. "How to Tell a Story of Stopping: The Complexities of Narrating a WPA's Experience." *WPA: Writing Program Administration* 19 (3): 70–79.

Bloom, Lynn Z. 1992. "I Want a Writing Director." *College Composition and Communication* 43 (2): 176–78.

Cain, Mary Ann. In press. "The Feminization of Writing Program Administration: Naming Conflicts, Resisting Resolutions." *Dialogue.*

Dickson, Marcia. 1993. "Directing Without Power: Adventures in Constructing a Model of Feminist Writing Programs Administration." *Writing Ourselves into the Story,* edited by Sheryl I. Fontaine and Susan Hunter, 140–53. Carbondale, IL: Southern Illinois University Press.

Gunner, Jeanne. 1994. "Decentering the WPA." *WPA: Writing Program Administration* 18 (1/2): 8–15.

Howard, Rebecca Moore. 1993. "Power Revisited: Or, How We Became a Department." *WPA: Writing Program Administration* 16 (3): 37–49.

Miller, Hildy. 1996. "Postmasculinist Directions in Writing Program Administration." *WPA: Writing Program Administration* 20 (1/2): 49–61.

Miller, Nancy K. 1991. *Getting Personal: Feminist Occasions and Other Autobiographical Acts.* New York: Routledge.

Olson, Gary, and Joseph M. Moxley. 1989. "Directing Freshman Composition: The Limits of Authority." *College Composition and Communication* 40 (1): 51–60.

White, Edward M. 1991. "Use It or Lose It: Power and the WPA." *Writing Program Administration* 15 (1/2): 3–12.

Yancey, Kathleen Blake. 1996. "Portfolio as Genre, Rhetoric as Reflection: Situating Selves, Literacies, and Knowledge." *WPA: Writing Program Administration* 19 (3): 55–69.

Orient Express

Marguerite H. Helmers

Prelude

The present

subject. the conscious or thinking subject, the self or ego.[1]
> **literature unceasingly 'produces' *subjects,* on display
> for everyone. So paradoxically using the same
> schema we can say: literature endlessly transforms
> (concrete) individuals into subjects and
> endows them with a quasi-real hallucinatory individuality.**
> —Etienne Balibar and
> Pierre Macherey[2]

> *the subject is site rather than centre or presence.*
> —Jeremy Hawthorne[3]

"In the shadows of the tractor wheel I crouched, looking out toward the tree line that encircled the fields of my father's farm. I imagined them to be the tall buildings of some distant city, Boston or New York, some city in the east. Someday, I thought, I would go to college in one of those cities." So wrote a young woman in one of my classes about the meaning of place. Her college was a place where imagination met reality. Her dreams were of Harvard; her reality is Oshkosh, Wisconsin.

As a college student, I too had dreams, images of teaching nurtured by films. Professors wore tweed coats and smoked pipes and discussed literature by stone fireplaces. In that world, I was one of many young women who joined the academy. We settled into overstuffed floral chairs in our carpeted offices, poured cups of fragrant tea for our colleagues and our students, and studied literature in a circle of golden lamplight at long tables in the library. When I was twenty one, I met such a professor in England. Her Jack Russell terrier curled in a corner during her tutorials; her tea was made from water boiled in an electric kettle. She was a frail Victorian figure in the robust world of men in tweed jackets who coached the field hockey teams and who gathered to drink a pint of bitter in the late afternoons.

73

My life is quite different from these images. Yet these dreams do not make me think I have become what I don't want to be. I spend three hours a day in my car, where I plan the composition program by jotting notes on a yellow legal tablet by my side. My car is littered with McDonald's coffee cups, pencils, books, and empty Ritz cracker boxes. At work, I seldom sit still. I walk quickly to the library, or to the administrative building, or to my class, or to the student union. My office is a site of motion and meaning; two doors ceaselessly admit people carrying papers or bearing questions. The phone rings as I am in the middle of an important theoretical point:

Interpellation means . . .

I am comfortable with these surroundings. My office is purple. My walls are covered by art prints. Postcards of Elvis are taped to the back of one door. My daughter's dragons adorn another. At the end of the day, I drive ninety miles to my home in Milwaukee, to Yellow House, where my husband, two daughters, and two cats greet me in the kitchen.

I. Orient

1995

A landscape that is incomparable[4]

orient. *refl.* to put oneself in the right position or relations; to ascertain one's "bearings," find out "where one is."

> New Student Orientation is the process and program by which the university welcomes and celebrates the arrival of new students into the university. As an integral part of the process, new students begin to learn to take responsibility for themselves and understand the values and expectations which are a part of the foundation of this new community.
> —Statement of Purpose[5]

> Incorporate the entire university, its sense of place and its people.
> —Statement of Purpose

Oshkosh, Wisconsin, can trace history visually in the rings of its urban growth. At the center, a two-story brick Main Street, modernized by aluminum awnings and plate glass windows. Then, in waves, bungalows, ranch homes, the K-Mart, the airport, the outlet mall, and the condominiums that stretch Oshkosh southward and northward into a continuous city with the other towns that rest along this central Wisconsin plain: Fond du Lac, Neenah, Appleton, and Menasha. Beyond them, farms, paper mills, canning factories. To the east, Lake Winnebago. Farther east, the icy implacable Lake Michigan. In summer, the Fox River ripples with silver slivers in its waves. Pewter-headed fishermen dot the bridges and banks. On winter evenings, the brick smokestack at the edge of the university campus becomes prominent, revealed by the blackened, bare branches of snow-dampened trees, lit by an eerie apricot light from the halogen street lamps along Algoma Boulevard and High Avenue. Clouds of steam billow from its base and drift across parked and snow-crazed cars.

The chimney is an ironic, but powerfully associative, icon on the campus. Its height distinguishes it as the most noticeable campus landmark, constantly churning, forbidding, yet indicative of a place where industry and industriousness are combined. Even more than the picturesque brick and stone offices that marked the old teachers' college, the smoke stack is the symbol of democratic education in the modern age, faintly redolent of Progressive and Victorian idealism, of Carlyle, Ruskin, and Matthew Arnold. The university is at the center of the outward development of the town. Less than one mile to the east, the same High Avenue that extends along the campus intersects Main Street.

Others have marked the absence of a spire or a campanile as a metonym: the campus has been frequently referred to as "U W Zero," a place where the climate effects chill temperatures and where the center of the campus seems an empty center, physically and—by association—mentally. The center should be life, blood, the heart. It should be a womb, a site of intellectual and social life, a place of shelter when, venturing far afield, one needs to retreat. And thus the irony is infectious: How can one orient oneself in a zero, a not-place?

Practically speaking, to ascertain one's bearings as a student on the campus, one must be inducted through an orientation for new students. This is where I enter the story. I am the writing program administrator and a few years ago I was asked to attend meetings in order to develop a program for a common intellectual experience among entering students. The plot of my story is fairly simple, yet it is replete with inspired moments, clashes of ideals, and misreadings.

Since 1994, the University of Wisconsin–Oshkosh planned to involve new students in a reading program. As the WPA, I was assigned the job of integrating the chosen reading into sections of College English I to ensure reading participation, accountability, and a stimulating learning environment—and to move the allotted time for discussions between faculty, staff, and students beyond the hour given to it on the first day.

My own progressive rings of outward growth and responsibility were broadening: With a daughter nearly two years old, I had just become a mother for a second time; I was a teacher; I was responsible for the faculty, staff, and students in first year and advanced composition; and I was entrusted with selecting and developing the reading selection for all faculty and new students. I was overwritten by voices: official documents, fragments of poems, half-remembered lines from novels, Foucault's translated prose, student essays, and the lovely echoes of Margaret Wise Brown's *Goodnight Moon*. My own life and preoccupations began to echo the statement of purpose that would come, in time, to govern the New Student Orientation activities: "Incorporate the entire university." While it is a cliché of sorts to compare mothering with teaching, it is significant to me that I took on the roles at the same time, beginning new academic ventures at the onset of my own parenting adventures. While the twin roles of academic and parent have often led to sentimentality on my part about the inevitable separation from my own daughters, I have also discerned that the ability of faculty to envision New Student Orientation as parents seems crucial. To that end, New Student Orientation is less a process of intellectual challenge, immediately permeated by rigorous critical thinking, than a moral process of creating a new family for the students to join. The object is to settle the students within a *topos* that—through myth, legend, and immediate experience, "a set of references, a congeries of characteristics," as Edward Said writes—assumes responsibility for structuring the students' lives. It is a figurative aerie. The campus itself must become that which is the Orient, a place where "There" resides, to paraphrase Gertrude Stein. Consequently, for three years my university has been determined to orient new students to the *topos* of the university: the initiation of a universe of ideas, a polyvocal space of inquiry unified by common respect for intellectual pursuit.

In the first and second years of the formal New Student Orientation Program each new student received from the Provost a slender book and an invitation to meet with faculty on the first day of school in September to discuss their reading. First, in 1994, there was *Siddhartha* and one thousand students on their first day of college grouped into circles of ten in the sports arena. The next year, with *The Way to Rainy Mountain*, a thousand new students collected loosely into groups of wire chairs in the arena. In 1995, the third year of the program, the theater program launched a performance of *Death of a Salesman*. There were no wire chairs, no arena, rather, a snapshot: five hundred students in two long lines at dusk face the opening doors of the Fredric March Theater. Each year has represented another ring of outward growth, a step in the quest to re-create in a day or a week the process and vitality of collaborative, interactive inquiry.

While some reading program and some expression of intellectual idealism is better than nothing, the university would admit that the *Siddhartha* and *Rainy Mountain* years left little to celebrate, other than the inspiring visit to campus by *Rainy Mountain* author N. Scott Momaday. For one, the environment of the sports arena was more conducive to cacophony than polyphony. Over one thousand voices racing over names and plots, scraping wire chairs against each other and scuffing the tarpaulin floor is more like an impromptu game of musical chairs than an environment that encourages "the habit of taking thought," as our university mission statement phrases the ideal. The ventilation system roared. Power boats rumbled along the Fox River, just beyond the opened doors of the gym. A chorus of anxious dogs barked from the animal shelter. The microphone, set before the keynote speaker, hissed, hummed, crackled, and turned off,

leaving only the hollow sound of scraping metal and the dusty hum of
quizzical voices.
Thirty minutes to inculcate a lifetime of shared inquiry simply wasn't
enough.
And yet, there were flickers of magic, sparks of common interest
and a
fraternal dialogue between professor and student outside
the classroom.
We later discovered that just over forty percent
of the students   read the books.
In March 1996, amidst the planning
sessions for the coming, third year, the
Dean of Students
announced to us all:
Disaster.

II. Ludus

1996

13-MAR 09:14:57[6]
Subj: Disaster
I have just left a meeting with the Deans Group and the Vice Chancellor.

They have asked us not to proceed with the "common intellectual
experience."

They believe that faculty will be reluctant, at best, to take part in this or
any other event that conflicts with departmental meetings and faculty bond-
ing that takes place during the meal period. The conversation was much more
extensive than this capsule version. The Deans Group was very laudatory of
the committee's efforts.

The agenda for Friday's meeting is to discuss next steps. Have a nice day!

The German word is *bildung*, an academic quest. The quest must begin as the
hero sets out on a journey to rectify a wrong or to solve a problem. On the journey, the hero meets those who will guide and those who mislead. Thus, the
committee, acting through a mission of benevolent guidance, sought to welcome students to college with a party on the mall, hot dogs and potato chips and
cookies and music, the "Three Bs: brats, beans, band." UW Oshkosh doesn't
have the natural beauty of oak trees or beds of dahlias. Its broad intersections
of cement are lined by low, utilitarian postwar architecture. A striped big top
encircled by puffs of white smoke from a charcoal fire and the heady, spiced
aroma of Wisconsin bratwurst was rich food for the imagination. Although the
haze of smoking bratwurst drifted across the campus mall and the campus
clubs held their recruitment fair, there was little formal talk of books on the first
day of university life, September 1996.

Yet, it was important for the university to remain committed to its intellectual mission and to stress that mission immediately. The New Student Orientation committee had hoped to counteract the negative effects of what was nationally publicized as a "riot" in the spring of 1995. Following arrests at a house
party and a fire drill at a nearby dorm, several hundred students took to the
streets, pulling down street signs and kicking in windows along Main Street.
Establishing a common intellectual experience at the center of the New Student
Orientation would stress that the university life was more than the Three Bs
of beer, bong, and bawdiness. To forestall the abandonment of the common intellectual experience, the English Department assumed responsibility for administering the entire program. We stepped in to the Vice Chancellor with a
petition and a departmental resolution because we believed in the program's
potential for unifying the students and faculty.

Thus, in 1996 celebration became its inverse: *carnival.* Two forces, one
official culture and the other transient, vied for control over the first day of
"celebration and frivolity." From carnival, however, arises free play. Russian
writer Mikhail Bakhtin theorizes that the carnival exists in the present, freely
inventing and reinventing the reality of the moment.

III. Orientation, *spec. in Zool.*

1996

A time that is gone forever

orient. *spec. in Zool.* the faculty by which birds and other animals
find their way back to a place after going or being taken to a place
distant from it. . . .

**Throughout all programs and processes is the need
to assist new students in feeling comfortable
with their new surroundings, both physically
and emotionally.
—Statement of Purpose**

The journey herein recalled
continues to be made anew each
time the miracle comes to mind, for
that is peculiarly the right and
responsibility of the imagination. It
is a whole journey, intricate with
motion and meaning; and it is
made with the whole memory, that
experience of the mind which is
legendary as well as historical,
personal as well as cultural. And

> the journey is an evocation of three
> things in particular: a landscape
> that is incomparable, a time that is
> gone forever, and the human spirit,
> which endures.
> —N. Scott Momaday,
> *The Way to Rainy Mountain*

> *"Why am I trying to become what I don't*
> *want to be? What am I doing in an office,*
> *making a contemptuous, begging fool of*
> *myself, when all I want is out there,*
> *waiting for me the minute I say I know*
> *who I am!"*
> —*Biff Loman*[7]

Encircling the disaster site were the clouds of dissent. Faculty and nonteaching staff had not been happy with the direction that the 1995 *Rainy Mountain* New Student Orientation work had taken, finding the book obscure. They were angered, too, that the students showed so little interest in exploring the book. By the time the planning sessions resumed again for the 1996 New Student Orientation, resentment brewed. Such an atmosphere needed dispersing, lightening, and a festival of academic adventure needed to take place rather than an enforced penury of reading well. Thus, the idea of theater was born, with the classic play *Death of a Salesman* selected by the theater program as an immediate textual experience, something the students could not escape through inattention.

And then it was the turn of the New Student Orientation committee to be angry; they were disturbed by the intimations of mortality in the title of Miller's play, death being incompatible with celebration and an inappropriate subject for the celebration of the students' entry into college. At the manifest level, the play's rigorous critique of capitalism and the American Dream through the tragic, disillusioned Willy Loman seems to condemn all that the university values: growth, self-development, refinement of the intellect. Willy Loman believed in capitalism—sold it even—and it let him down. This bold affront by the New Student Orientation planning committee towards *Death of a Salesman* led to some levity: English department members committed to integrating the play into their sections of College English I made a pact to never refer to the play publicly as *Death of a Salesman*, or a shortened version *Death*. Instead, we found it more convenient to think of it as *Salesman*, even some nonsexist carnival versions surfaced to occlude the negative assumptions: *Demise of the Sales Profession as a Viable Means of Income in America, Curtains for the Seller, Dissolution of the Transient Trader*, or even *The Loman Play*.

Some critics feel that Willy Loman is not the hero of the play, but Biff Loman, who achieves a self-revelation and breaks with his parents and with self-deception in the play. As Miller himself noted in the introduction to *A View from the Bridge*, drama should draw attention to the plight of human beings to realize their potential as thinking, acting, and ethical individuals rather than focus on beings reified into dehumanized social occupations, "positions" such as salesman, teacher, or student (Hagopian, 35). The poignancy of *Salesman* is that Willy Loman is not able to achieve transcendence from his position as salesman. Yet Biff, "the one who struggles most for understanding, who faces the most crucial question, who achieves the most transforming insight, and whose motives, decisions, and actions most influence the total situation" of his and his family's existence, is a more appropriate main figure (Hagopian, 35). Certainly it was the young actor portraying Biff in the UW Oshkosh production who impressed the students. He invested the character with every ounce of disorientation and intense emotion that a college student could have, underscoring that underneath the gayety surrounding the entrance into a new life is real pain for many of the students. Pain arises at the moment that students leave their parents, friends, and home. Later, a recognition surfaces that life means saying good-bye to many things: to friends when you promise to write, to family, to brothers and sisters who move to the coasts to pursue their careers or who become involved with their children's soccer teams and music lessons. It is this threshold that the students who enter college from the surrounding plains are on: a borderland between self and academic other, between daughter or son and individual.

Educators operate *in loco parentis*. As a work of art that can help to articulate life experiences, *Death of a Salesman* speaks to the pain of misunderstanding, clashing goals, differing self images, and the pain of separation, causing us to reconsider what we value about family, work, and education. After a few weeks of working with *Death of a Salesman* in College English I, I discovered how proud my students were of their parents who had completed college, worked hard, and attempted to create a good family life for their children. I could see that New Student Orientation, thus, extends into the *future* lives of students, enabling them to find a place in academics, something their own children can take pride in later.

IV. Pastorale

1995

> *In order to see much one must*
> *learn to look away from oneself—*
> *every mountain-climber needs this*
> *hardness . . . you must climb above*
> *yourself—up and beyond, until*

> *you have even your stars under*
> *you! Yes! To look down upon*
> *myself and even upon my stars:*
> *that alone would I call my* summit,
> *that has remained for me as my*
> ultimate *summit!*
> —*Friedrich Nietzsche,*
> Thus Spoke Zarathustra

The idea took shape on the patio in Santa Fe, New Mexico, where my family and I were spending the summer in 1995. I was preparing a packet of teaching materials for College English I instructors who would be incorporating *The Way to Rainy Mountain* into their courses in the fall to help further the goals of New Student Orientation. I took out my road atlas to locate Rainy Mountain in Oklahoma, but I couldn't find it, so I searched for textual clues: west of Anadarko, near Lawson, near the river and it was then, following the traces of the map that an idea began to grow: on the way home to Wisconsin, why not go to Rainy Mountain? I thought about climbing the hill ("a single knoll" in the Wichita Range, writes Momaday) and I noted the directions from his book: between "the fork of the Arkansas and Cimarron" (6) and Fort Sill, near "the great bend of the Washita" (10). That put me in a likely spot, Mountain View. I carefully circled it in pencil in the atlas.

And then, one day, turning the pages of the *Santa Fe Reporter*, I saw that Momaday would be reading from his fiction and poetry at the meeting of the Santa Fe Writer's Conference at Plaza Resolana. After the reading, lingering under the pines and clear sky, I stood at the tail end of a long line of people waiting to meet Momaday and, introducing myself, asked him a single, key question, "How do I get to Rainy Mountain?" His directions were a story themselves: Drive to Mountain View and ask anyone there.

A few weeks later, we left Santa Fe early on a Sunday morning. We stopped in Clines Corners, New Mexico, turning onto Interstate 40 and trying to ignore the story at the gas station: a woman, her mother, and two children killed in a car crash, worn down from the road, leaving home in California or Nevada or somewhere west and on their way to a new life in Florida.

At Amarillo, we stopped at the legendary Big Texan restaurant, home of the 72 ounce steak. Now the real part of our journey began. We were alone, no guides to help us with our route. It was one thirty in the afternoon and we had to find Rainy Mountain in Oklahoma and a hotel before dark. The children hummed and giggled in the back seat of the car. We talked about the summer in New Mexico and the coming months at home. We talked about winter, and snow, and the cold drafts that whistle through our kitchen windows and extend like invisible icicles from the crevasses in the pocket doors. After many hours, we turned our car onto US 183. In the distance were three ghostly gray hills. There were mountains in Oklahoma; there was Rainy Mountain. There were deep river gullies, and red earth, and cottonwood trees.

My hopes of climbing the hillock were dashed by the setting sun, but there was still time for the photographs—if only we could find the road! Suddenly we noticed a small white sign, almost obscured by the waving long grasses: Rainy Mountain Baptist Church. The car ground loose gravel under the wheels as we spun onto the narrow paved road.

I wandered through the cemetery near the Baptist Church. Prehistoric-looking grasshoppers of tremendous size buzzed and snapped at my legs. Momaday writes that "green and yellow grasshoppers are everywhere in the tall grass, popping up like corn to sting the flesh" (5).

Into the dying light of day, I snapped my photographs. Later, I assembled them with pictures of storms on the New Mexico grassland, Chief Dohasan's tipi ornamented with battle pictures, George Catlin's portrait of the Kiowa Kotsatoah, an encampment in the Wichita Range, and an unassuming picture of the Kiowa sacred Tai-me. While I had lived the adventure of the quest, the students in Oshkosh would at least have my pictures.

V. Orienteering

1997

The human spirit, which endures

orienteering. the competitive sport of finding one's way on foot across rough country with the aid of map and compass.

> **In modern Western society maps quickly
> became crucial to the maintenance of state
> power—to its boundaries, to its commerce,
> to its internal administration, to control of
> populations . . .**
> **—J. B. Harley,**
> **"Deconstructing the Map"**

> Ah, but a man's reach should exceed
> his grasp,
> Or what's a heaven for?
> —Robert Browning,
> *Andrea del Sarto*

Of all the ways to think about planning New Student Orientation, my preferred metaphor is to think of it as orienteering, a quest. Orienteering represents travel, learning to read maps, assimilating the differences between home and away. An orienteering project occasions writing, charting, planning, constructing—and deconstructing, the kind of decentering that unfolds from shifting histories that underlie every word, every concept, every text, every place. Thus New Student Orientation is more than just a choice of texts and a passing on of information. The program requires commitment to a philosophy and a *destination*. The university administration and teaching community must lay out an environment from a metaphor that enables students to journey toward a conceptual destination: education, *bildung*, growth, achievement. There is no escaping the reality that faculty, students, administrators all exist within an integrated environment, a space both physical and ideological. No single person and no single office can assume responsibility for all conditions in this environment, for they are intricately linked by ideology, history, idealism, promises, memories, and physical circumstance. The metaphor is absolutely central to a conception of the project and the individual's place within it. French historian and philosopher Michel Foucault records that his metamorphosis into an intellectual took place "between the book and the lamp" (trans. Miller 109). His prolonged tenure in the library forged an academic identity described as ascetic and renunciative. While the myth persists of the solitary genius—taking shape amidst the long shadows cast by Einstein, Picasso, Bill Gates, and Robert Bly—a university that arises from the central plain clearly requires a richer, more communal concept to guide it. The myth of individual achievement constructed America's acquisition of the Western territories of the continent; ultimately questioned, finally disproved, it is today a less fruitful metaphor than orienteering. New Student Orientation is enterprising and communal, even radical in its efforts to suggest the blurring of boundaries between disciplines and to offer a shared responsibility for the welfare and intellectual life of students new to the college campus.

If education represents for students a threshold and a frontier, New Student Orientation is a frontier for faculty and administration. Like writing, it requires planning, several attempts to map the terrain, and thoughtful revision. There is adventure, excitement, and uncertainty in learning; in planning the New Student Orientation, there is a similar degree of adventure and uncertainty. The story I have told is intended less to represent the facts of the process or my own administrative role than it is meant to suggest ways of interpreting the site and the process. I entered a complex situation in 1995, without a blueprint for my own position as director of the writing program, without an outline for maneuvering the isolating wilderness of a junior faculty member's responsibilities, without tactics or strategy for developing a safety net for incoming students. Yet, with the assistance of a committee committed to the academic, social, and spiritual well-being of the students arriving on the campus and to the same uncharted emotional territory as I, I was able to sketch a program into which those students could excel—and put my stamp upon it.

Most recently, the World Wide Web has enabled New Student Orientation to create a virtual space that unifies the campus. The *Einstein Web* pages are based upon the two common texts for the 1997 orientation program: Alan Lightman's speculative novel *Einstein's Dreams* and Steve Martin's comedy *Picasso at the Lapin Agile*. The web site is designed to open up communication between faculty and students, providing the illusion of an intellectual environment that transcends time and space. For in 1997, New Student Orientation has transmogrified into Odyssey, an archetypal reconceptualization of the academic, administrative, residential, and social aspects of the students' lives that invokes the mythic Greek quest of the hero Ulysses. Yes, Odyssey charms us with the grand narrative and the essential truth of being; it is ripe for deconstruction, central to controlling the campus population during the summer months and the first days of the school year, and inspirational enough to inspire students to reach beyond their grasp.

> *For in this world the passage of time brings increasing order.*
> —*Alan Lightman,*
> *Einstein's Dreams*

Paths may diverge in a yellow wood, as Robert Frost once speculated, just as the paths of those crafting the odyssey once diverged from a flue cast in pale orange at the fringe of the campus. For all my love of poststructuralism, I have discovered that it is the intellectual center that is vital. It is that which allows us to remain and to return.

Notes

1. All definitions are taken from the *Oxford English Dictionary*, unless otherwise noted.

2. Quoted from Etienne Balibar and Pierre Macherey, "Literature as an Ideological Form," translated by Ian McLeod, John Whitehead, and Anne Wordsworth, and published in the *Oxford Literary Review*, volume 3, 1978, pages 4–12.

3. Hawthorne writes this in his discussion of *subject and subjectivity* in *A Concise Glossary of Contemporary Literary Theory,* page 205.

4. This heading, and the headings which subsequently underscore sections three and five of my essay are part of a longer quotation by N. Scott Momaday in *The Way to Rainy Mountain*, the full text of which appears under section three of this essay. The excerpt from Momaday's work appears in his prologue to *Rainy Mountain,* on page 4.

5. The "Statement of Purpose" was a document forwarded to the Provost and Vice Chancellor of the University of Wisconsin–Oshkosh on December 1, 1995 by the New Student Orientation committee.

6. The message that begins the section "Ludus" is the complete text of an electronic mail message received by the author on March 13, 1996. The name of the writer has been omitted, however, to preserve the writer's privacy.

7. Biff makes this comment in Act II of the play *Death of a Salesman*. In the Dramatists Play service edition of the play, his lines may be found on page 96.

Works Cited

Browning, Robert. 1949. "Andrea del Sarto." *Selected Poems of Robert Browning.* Edited by William C. DeVane. Arlington Heights, IL: AHM.

Foucault, Michel. 1993. "Un 'Fantastique de bibliothèque." Translated by James Miller, *The Passion of Michel Foucault.* New York: Doubleday. Miller notes that this idea is expressed in "Distance, aspect, origine." *Critique* 198 (November 1963): 938.

Hagopian, John V. 1972. "Arthur Miller: The *Salesman's* Two Cases." *The Merrill Studies in* Death of a Salesman. Edited by Walter J. Meserve. Columbus, OH: Merrill.

Harley, J. B. 1989. "Deconstructing the Map." *Cartographica* 26 (2): 1–20.

Lightman, Alan. 1996. *Einstein's Dreams.* New York: Time Warner.

Miller, Arthur. 1980. *Death of a Salesman.* New York: Dramatists Play Service.

Momaday, N. Scott. 1969. *The Way to Rainy Mountain.* Albuquerque: University of New Mexico Press.

Nietzsche, Freidrich. 1961. *Thus Spoke Zarathustra.* Translated by R. J. Hollingdale. New York: Penguin.

Mothers, Tell Your Children Not to Do What I Have Done

The Sin and Misery of Entering the Profession as a Composition Coordinator

Keith Rhodes

Introduction—The Song

I often play my guitar for attitude adjustment. One night in February of my first year as a composition coordinator, with things in my new job at their bottom, I sang this song late one night in the middle of reading papers:

Coordinating Composition
(sung to the tune of *House of the Rising Sun*—creatively scanned)

There is a job in academe / coordinating composition
It's been the ruin of many a young prof / And Lord, I know 'cause I'm one.
Now my mentor was a rhetor / She showed me the world of 4Cs
But my department chair does not venture there / And suspects it's a social disease.
The only thing a comp teacher needs / Are students, pens, and paper
And the only time she or he is satisfied / Is . . . well, frankly, never.
Now I've one foot on dismissal / And the other foot on too much work
But I'm going back to my colleagues / Even though they think I'm a jerk.
Oh rhetors, tell your students / Not to do as I have done
To come right out of graduate school / And coordinate composition.

The Trend

Shortly after, at last year's 4Cs, I discovered that I was part of a trend. At session after session, I found new Ph.D.s who had been hired at regional state colleges and universities to "coordinate" composition. I'm rarely fashionable, so I should have been happy; but I wasn't. Two things bothered me. The first I'll let pass, for a moment—that few of the new peers I was discovering had written dissertations in rhetoric and composition. The second, though, hit harder because it raised pangs of guilt.

A bit of background before the revelation. I had heard, vaguely, of the "Portland Resolution," an administrative follow-up to the mythic Wyoming Resolution on conditions for writing teaching. My understanding had been that there was a call to avoid hiring non-tenured rookies to run composition pro-

86

grams. I recalled, too, Elizabeth Wallace's article in a *College Composition and Communication* forum pointing out that the Wyoming Resolution had no chance unless teachers started refusing to accept bad conditions for writing teaching. Turning that logic to the Portland Resolution, I should have refused my job; but I hadn't. Apparently, I was far from alone.

For myself, for my own sin, I had excuses. I wrote a dissertation in rhetoric and composition; my Master's was with a "focus" in composition; even my undergraduate work was mainly in writing and in Latin; and my first career as a commercial litigator had given me knowledge, experience, and insights that—or so I thought—could lend me some of the authority needed to guide a writing program, even without tenure. Experienced warriors in academic politics may begin laughing now; I won't be insulted.

Finding that I was part of a trend changed my perspective—aided, of course, by my fresh understanding of the importance of hierarchy in academic politics. An entire cadre of us was being recruited—tempted—to enter the profession as nominal authorities over composition programs. In other words, it was becoming normal to ask people with no job protection and usually no genuine, unsheltered experience in academic politics to take on one of the most critical, exposed, and troubled tasks in academe. I was helping to create that trend, no matter how many glosses I wanted to put on things. So, ashamed, I started reflecting and inquiring, trying to figure out what this trend indicated, and it shortly became fairly clear to me: within a heavily status-driven system, the actual status of composition programs themselves still fell beneath the power of even the most lowly new assistant prof. I could "coordinate" composition because composition was beneath even me. Even the possible silver lining to this dark cloud was getting tarnished as I continued my investigations; after all, if bringing fresh expertise about rhetoric and composition was the point, then how come so many of my new peers had dissertations in literature? I suspected the worst: the answer might be that they were expected, eventually, to grow out of their larval stage in composition and flourish in their tenured years as gloriously winged literary scholars.

Regional Overseers?

I'd had fair warning. I knew that James Sledd's paper at 4Cs in Nashville the year before had been a masterpiece. Entitled "Where's the Emperor? or, The Revolution That Wasn't," it argued with scathing wit that composition had developed a facade of professional status, privileging a small elite without improving conditions for the overwhelming majority of writing teachers. Adding almost one metaphor too many (though good metaphors are like good bourbon in my favorite eggnog recipe [Rombauer and Becker, 51]—too much is just enough), Sledd pointed out that composition's elite has become an overseer class, altogether too ready to rationalize continuing composition "slavery" for others as the price for their own gains. From the sound of things, that seems like what many a composition coordinator has been hired to facilitate now at the more far-flung margins of regional colleges and universities. The word does seem to be getting out that writing teaching takes some specialized knowledge; and among my new peers—all former composition teaching assistants in good programs—I found only one who seemed noticeably ignorant of the important issues (and he knew it and admitted it and was working on it). There still seems to be an impression, though, that the problems of composition are more a housekeeping matter than one of profound change; and I found very little concern that the *status* of writing teachers and writing programs might be the most important issue in the field. My sense is that many "coordinators" have been brought in on a naive faith that if we add some better textbooks, a few new assignments, some fresh grammar drills, then composition will be as it should—spiffy, tidy, forgotten and forgettable, a place to which to assign the residue of real academic resources.

To some extent, in fact, even this may be optimistic. Just as once there could not be a proper English department without a Chaucerian (even if the Chaucerian mainly taught comp), perhaps now there is a growing impression that a proper English department must have a composition coordinator. In which case, merely having one may be the point—heaven forbid the upstart should actually try to do anything about composition. I've even had reason to suspect that some places use the coordinator of composition as a corn king—a ritual sacrifice, offered up to the rest of the faculty periodically to atone for passing on "students who can't write a proper English sentence (Harumph!)."

Sin and Misery

Still, let's indulge in the assumption that it might be good in theory to hire a new Ph.D. to coordinate composition. After all, knowledge in this field has expanded and become specialized, leaving many small, outlying departments out of the loop. New graduates from large research universities, especially when they are former teaching assistants, often come with not only theoretical but practical knowledge about the emerging field of Greater Composition. Why not bring in some of that kind of new knowledge? Why not turn the light of this new knowledge to immediate practical use in benighted composition programs? And, while we're at it, why not look for someone who can also help out with new movements in critical theory and literature pedagogy? (By the way, can she also teach Chaucer every fourth year? It is our Chaucerian, after all, who is retiring). It is like shining a light into the cold night, right? Well, growing up in North Dakota, I learned that when the sun shines through the bitter cold, it generates the epiphenomenon called sun dogs, extra points of light marking atmospheric crossing points; and sometimes it's hard to tell which is the real sun. My sense here is that these good intentions generate the sun dogs of Sin and Misery, to the extent that it's hard to tell what is the point anymore.

The sun dog of Sin forms around the *public* nexus of power and virtue. It seems virtuous to bring in the fresh knowledge no matter what the power issues; but to bring a fresh assistant professor in to run a program that is already subordinated to the "real" mission of the English department is in effect to bear false witness, to tell a lie on which employer and employee collaborate. Institutionally, the hiring declares that writing is a sub-issue, a lower world over which the lowest angel in heaven can be given charge. Any pleas by that angel for any higher recognition of composition are clearly, then, purely self-aggrandizement, and hence further sin. That was exactly my predicament when I asked my higher colleagues to enter into any sort of dialogue with me (on any terms) about what makes up the best writing pedagogy. Few could find any reason at all to respond—and those who did were mostly affronted. Now, the issue was not really that I had no authority to compel response (though that had some role); the issue was largely that examining the writing program was not worth their time—after all, a mere rookie could run the thing. Thus, my lack of tenure itself was really only a minor contributor to the more ringing message sent by the linkage between my status and the writing program. Writing could not be the more serious discipline I was trying to make it if I were in charge of it; hadn't I implicitly agreed to that? Sin, though a cultural construct, has a nasty way of clinging to the designated sinner; and I was a sinner, and I knew it. I could begin to see how corn kings were created, even led to leap in the fire themselves.

The sun dog of Misery collects around the *personal* power/virtue nexus. I came to this job hoping to do things both powerful and wonderful, hoping to improve my own teaching by interaction with experienced hands and to encourage them to re-engage the world of composition theory from which they have felt so long alienated. Writing classes ought to be student favorites, if you get down to what they really are for, what they really could be; I wanted to be part of generating that result. Instead, I found myself largely following in the footsteps of my departed predecessors, working mostly with a small group of already committed writing teachers (who tend—though not universally—to be of the most vulnerable rank), alienating older faculty, and increasing the sense of risk felt by untenured and untenurable faculty who associate themselves too closely with any "radical" composition program changes. Perhaps what hurts worst, though, is that some of my own better students, aware how differently their own classes progress compared to those of many of their peers, suspect me of experimenting on them—even when they know how far they have come.

I apologize for not getting into the details more, but whining is the opposite of good bourbon—too little is too much, already. Perhaps one incident can stand for the entire problem. Toward the end of my first year, I sent out a very cheery request for positive stories about what is good about writing teaching—enjoyable aspects, big successes, lessons from experience. I called it my "summer reading," inviting any old thing any time. I did get one real—and very

valuable—response, after some delay. The first answer, though, was my own
note, crumpled then restored to reasonable flatness, with one margin note next
to the first sentence: "C.S." And the worst part is, it was not really a comma
splice at all!

"Good in Theory"

So I come down to the point that what sounds good in theory about the recent
Diaspora of new composition coordinators has its bad aspects in practice. But
"good in theory" is still worth something. My own unique problems come in
part from unique advantages, incremental advances in the field that have paid
dividends in my department. The school demands a common assessment at the
end of any general education core course, a potential nightmare. My predecessors, before being run off, left behind an excellent final assessment rubric and
a method for using timed writings in a relatively humane fashion—two drafting sessions, multiple tries, a portfolio back-up option. One of our excellent
group of full-time instructors has taken over the coordination of this effort
quite capably. We normally have no part-time or adjunct teachers, and our non-
tenurable instructors have full benefits, full departmental privileges, and full
votes. Every member of the English faculty, right up to our lone distinguished
professor, teaches composition. That was instituted by an old hand in the department—the same one who sent the *real* response to my reading request—
who has learned composition theory interestingly well by keeping his eyes
open while teaching. Meanwhile, every member of the English faculty (except
me, by choice) gets at least one course that is not composition each semester—
and this is based on relieving the time pressure of writing teaching almost as
much as on giving people the work they "really want to do." Finally, I work as
part of a trio of co-coordinators, each with released time, so that I do not have
to run writing assessment or the Writing Center. While in part this was explicitly designed to limit the influence of my position (paying for the sins of the former generations), it has really been a godsend. That's another article.

Still, it comes down to this: many of our teachers still focus on grammar-
based instruction, and some tend to use composition courses as mainly another
place to teach New Critical literary study; and there's really nothing I can
do about it, which means that most of our Writing Center tutors, upper-level
students largely the product of the department's literature program, think developmental writing teaching means grammar exercises—and there's little
anyone can do about that, either. Like their esteemed—and genuinely humani-
tarian—mentors, they can at times get in a regular dudgeon over the notion that
student writing needs anything other than a good, thorough editing. Here we
come to the poignant flavor of my particular misery. Ultimately, I like these
new colleagues; I find them to be fine teachers in general, and immensely concerned with their students' welfare. There is, in fact, a rather large sub-group
that works actively on writing teaching, and my fellow co-coordinators, despite

being non-tenurable instructors, are devoted and knowledgeable composition professionals. My notion is that we could be a stellar writing department; but no composition coordinator or director yet has been able to combine expertise with enough staying power to test the notion.

Real Needs

I'll get real. Despite the Portland Resolution, these jobs will not go begging; and despite my song and my early despair, I do not really want new Ph.D.s—especially rhetoric and composition Ph.D.s—to refuse jobs like mine. Eventually, the sun rises higher and higher, the earth warms, the sun dogs disappear, and—even in North Dakota—spring comes and flowers blossom. The question becomes what we should do about this rookie coordinator of composition trend. Forgive me, but I'm thinking fairly nakedly about what would have made my life easier.

Mentoring

First comes mentoring—not just in the sense of how graduate students are educated, but how they enter departments and professions. I latched onto that old curmudgeon who wrote to me. He doesn't know James Berlin from Irving Berlin, but he knows departmental history, campus governance, and academic life in general; and his students know how to write. But I found him basically by instinct, and I had to suffer through some fairly stern and personal rebuffs before we could get to this point. He's exactly the sort of person we newbies ought to be taught to find, though; and exactly the sort of person every hip English department ought to know their newbies need. Indeed, from that beginning I've found multiple paths toward better collaboration and learning from my elders; but with only slightly different luck, I could have been gone myself before any of us ever realized these possibilities. Mentoring, to be successful, has to come from those in authority; and to some extent it takes a conceptual change to realize that composition coordinators have any call on those with real authority.

For that reason, I suspect that organizations like WPA should be encouraging mentoring both within and across institutional lines, and actually institutionalizing it to an extent. Relationships with former professors and dissertation advisors tend to mature into something less "mentor-like" by the time we actually get done with our degrees. It's natural to try to find ways to be fellow adults after all that, even despite the usual disparity in savvy. Besides, not all of our best learning relationships are with people who are experienced administrators—something that will grow more likely if composition and rhetoric expands into full disciplinarity. Yes, you who are eligible administrative mentors all already have too much to do, and there are too many of us for you; but the need is stark.

Public Relations

So, even more demands. We need to foster informed administrative support for rhetoricized composition programs, both through a process of moving WPAs up into University administration and a concerted public relations effort. Unfortunately, rhetoric and composition scholars as a whole are curiously indifferent to these needs or bad at meeting them—as the almost annual George Will or John Leo flaps on WPA-l expose for those of us online. WPAs as a group have more at stake and more to offer in such an effort than the field as a whole, though; so, again, more work for the weary.

Skills

Finally, though, I have to admit it: I could be doing my job better. There was another memorable article in that *College Composition and Communication* forum on the Wyoming Resolution: William Robinson's rather parental retort that before composition asks for respect it should be sure to deserve it. Here is looking a gift horse in the mouth: I was let out of my doctoral program with an excellent background in composition theory, scholarship, and practice, but no direct experience in composition administration—even though my dissertation advisor was herself a sterling administrator. And yet most of the jobs for which I applied with any hope of success included an administrative component. Fortunately, in my own case, this is my second career, following one in law. My litigation background—and, frankly, my age—both help. Still, the reputation of academic politics is well-deserved, I find, and a challenge even to a former commercial litigator. Like most students, I did what was required as well as I could, even did a bit extra; but administrative posts are rare, and they are difficult to fit into a class schedule. I am beginning to suspect that, for just that reason, composition may need to go beyond laudable efforts to get the top students involved in moderately sheltered administrative posts. The field may need to *require* such work, make it riskier, and send a clear message that the student without such a post on the resume is a less than desirable candidate. The school from which I graduated was beginning to make that switch even as I was leaving. Heaven help us, I know what sort of grad student politics such policies can ignite; but better to lose good people there than to burn them up after they think they have made it through. They can always switch to law school before it's too late.

Conclusion

Our professional organizations cannot do all of that, of course; but they can make much of it more likely. Perhaps we could envision The Council of Writing Program Administrators in particular as a grass-roots guild—a guild devoted to developing people who know how to implement writing instruction, not just teach writing themselves. The WPA summer workshops look wonderful, but offered at just one location, sometimes in a corner of the country, they become rather exclusive. Workshops and conferences are different animals, and can do different things. The workshop effort does not have to be linked to the annual conference. Local workshops could draw larger numbers and help collect people at disparate but nearby institutions into collectives for further action. A guild could spread its influence right into the apprenticeship process, becoming a second strain of education, supplementing graduate school— perhaps with more extended summer programs, perhaps even with local working apprenticeships at schools other than those doctoral students normally attend (or just schools other than those they are attending). A guild dedicated to the practice of implementing writing instruction would also be in a superb position to take on the public relations challenges facing the field, even to the point of becoming a nationally recognized "one-stop" source for public information about rhetoric, composition, writing, and related literacy issues. I'm thinking of something along the lines of a national writing *administration* project.

With such an organization behind them, new coordinators of composition would know more. They would also be in a position to have more of the courage of their convictions: courage to question, even to refuse; courage to demand better and know that qualified peers will stand with them in rejecting unreasonable positions and demands, even in the face of an "English glut." Ultimately, that glut itself might be eased. It seems likely that there is much more balance than currently appears between the demand for literacy professionals and the supply of them. What is missing is the will to apply the resources to the needs. This, of course, is the larger problem—the one we're all really trying to solve. Maybe I am just whining, after all, in trying to encourage moves that would support new composition coordinators in regional schools. It could also be, though, that this is a genuine point of leverage, one of the many things that all need doing at once that ought to come first. The trendy vanguard of which I am a part could be affecting a huge number of students—many of whom, by the way, are going to be teachers. Meanwhile, behind the sometimes misguided immediate intentions of some of our colleagues at these schools there lies a precious storehouse: a genuine desire that our students should all be writers of the first order, coupled with a love of language and a great deal of classroom experience. In other words, this trend is a site where enormous resources are already present, and just need the right guidance.

How sweet it would be to sing, someday, of redemption.

Works Cited

Robinson, William S. 1991. "The CCCC Statement of Principles and Standards: A (Partly) Dissenting View." *College Composition and Communication* 42: 345–49.

Rombauer, Irma S., and Marion Rombauer Becker. 1962, 1973. "Eggnog in Quantity." *The Joy of Cooking.* New York: Plume-Penguin.

Sledd, James. 1994. "Where's the Emperor? or, The Revolution That Wasn't." Paper given at Conference on College Composition and Communication, Nashville, Tennessee, 18 March.

Wallace, M. Elizabeth. 1991. "A One-Time Part-Timer's Response to the CCCC Statement of Professional Standards." *College Composition and Communication* 42: 350–55.

Catching Our Tail

A Writing Center in Transition

Ralph Wahlstrom

In the pages that follow, I chronicle an uncomfortable, ambiguous period in my professional life, the time I was given the responsibility of directing our campus writing center. I was at once pleased and distraught, fortunate and unfortunate. I had designed and directed remedial education, ESL, disability, and other service programs for twelve years, but this was a chance to become more involved with the upper level faculty and curriculum and to pull back, even if slightly, from the barrage of tedious administrative tasks that took up much of my day. It was also a welcome opportunity to work with bright student tutors and to put my own stamp on the writing center concept at the university. As a longtime writing instructor and a scholar profoundly interested in advanced literacies and access for the disenfranchised, I was eager to have a more direct impact on the writing competency at our small university, and I felt confident that I would.

I admit, my approach to my role of Writing Center Coordinator is often based more on good intentions than practicality. I am much the stereotypical middle manager, buried in reports, statistics, committees, and all the assorted redundancies of bureaucracy. Nevertheless, I am committed to creating a writing center environment that promotes equity and accessibility while providing a substantive scholarly learning experience. My ideal center is managed largely by well-trained tutors who display that balance of nonconformity, intellectual prowess, and responsibility that we "Baby-Boomer" parents long for in our children. It is a place in which theory meets practice in smooth linen folds, where informality meets professionalism, where topics for publishable articles leap out at me at regular intervals, and where espresso and Earl Grey tea sit side by side always fresh and pungent, always hot. My writing center is equipped with computer carrels, islands of creative people and the software and machines that give them the power to create wonderful text. Finally, it is a center of learning where faculty and students bend over projects learning and teaching together. This story is not about my ideal writing center.

This is not a theoretical work on the place of the writing center in higher education or, for that matter, in the clashes of culture and attendant battles for equity that rage in our institutions. It is not a thesis about the superiority of my

95

approach to the writing center over the style of my predecessor or of English departments in general. It is, by its very nature, illustrative of the writing center's questionable role and its low position on the hierarchical ladder at universities across the country and of the second-class status of its staff. This is a story of frustration, anger, disappointment, joy, and, of dubious, momentary victory. It is, obviously, my view of events, and I acknowledge in advance that other perspectives certainly exist. Let others tell their stories. This is mine.

I had the university writing center thrust upon me two years ago in one of those administrative initiatives that demonstrates all too well the haphazard and short-sighted ways we often make institutional decisions, and which put into perspective what Nancy Grimm has called "the conflicted nature of writing center institutional positioning" (527). In the middle of a fairly typical financial squeeze, the powers had decided to save money by putting the then director of the Writing Center, an English faculty member, back in the classroom instead of continuing to provide the one-quarter time release she had been given to direct the center. My supervisor called me in one morning and asked, "Could you handle the writing center coordinator's job?" I said that I could, as I had directed the campus center in my previous position, and I was currently director of remedial learning and tutoring at the university. Writing, and research into advanced literacies and instruction was also a focal point in my doctoral studies, so the prospect of becoming the coordinator was appealing. "Great," said my boss, "because the Chancellor just assigned the center to you."

Coincidentally, the current (former) coordinator was, at the same time, talking to another university administrator who would give her the news. Neither of us had been involved in this decision, nor had the English department and writing faculty. As a result, I was being offered a role that appealed greatly to me, but which, in view of the circumstances, I felt did not rightly belong to me.

The consequences of this administrative fiasco were both immediate and enduring. First, the former director, surprised, angry, and more than a little insulted, refused to talk to me for several weeks and, in the absence of anyone else to blame, aimed much of her frustration at me and the center. This was particularly unfortunate because she and I had much in common philosophically and pedagogically, and I had always counted her as a kindred spirit on campus. Her hurt and, subsequently, her anger transferred to other members of the English faculty, and relations were, for some time, frosty, even for northern Wisconsin. The problems were not simply attitudinal. When I walked into the center a week or so after the coup, I found it empty. Student files were nonexistent, materials for recording sessions, scheduling, evaluation, and information on the day-to-day operation of the center had all disappeared. As I stood in the empty suite of four tiny rooms, I knew this was not going to be easy.

I set to work putting together the basic materials I'd need to put the writing center back on its feet and developed a tutor manual based on bits and pieces I had gathered from other institutions, my own teaching, and the record keeping forms we use in Student Support Services. And, I began to try and re-connect with my bruised colleagues in the English department. This new be-ginning was going to be rocky.

First, the graduate assistant the university had hired to direct the daily goings-on of the center was a non-English person who confessed to me that she was not comfortable with writing. One week into the start of a chaotic fall semester, she resigned, saying that she needed more specific direction. Frankly, I was grateful. I was trying to write a doctoral dissertation and already had a full-time staff position, which did not include the writing center, so I felt that I needed someone who could work independently and who had experience with writing tutoring and with writing centers. Fortune smiled in the form of Susan Simpson, a returning adult who had applied to be a writing tutor, and who, it turned out, was one semester from officially becoming a graduate student in the Master of Communicating Arts program. She had eight years of experience teaching high school English, was fluent in several languages, and had done a good deal of administrative work. After a bit of reconfiguring of the job de-scription and a temporary shift in the way we budgeted for the position, the writing center had a remarkable, new graduate assistant. Nevertheless, our difficulties continued.

Most tutors had been hired in previous semesters, and many had developed a strong loyalty to the former director. They were angry. The Student Senate and other university faculty were also up in arms over her shoddy treatment at the hands of the administration. In our first meeting the tutors and I talked openly about the issues. They were concerned about the former director's feel-ings, of course, and many shared her anger and disappointment, but they were, I discovered, primarily apprehensive about the fate of the writing center itself. Good writing tutors, as we know, share a commitment to the discipline of teaching writing and of helping students. That day, as a group, these tutors took it upon themselves to see that the writing center would survive and would con-tinue to offer the kind of writing assistance that so many of our students need.

So two weeks into the new semester the Writing Center was open, tutors were scheduled, new tutors were hired, students were coming in for assistance, and I was beginning to make changes. I had mailed newly printed manuals to English faculty and university administration, and Susan, the tutors, and I were getting notices, posters, and notes out to the campus community to let every-one know that the Writing Center was alive and well. Within weeks, the new and veteran tutors had settled in, and business was brisk. On two occasions, one of our documents appeared in the mail cluttered with red editing marks, marks more indicative of their anonymous creator's background in obscure Latin grammar and desire to find mistakes, where typically none existed, than of a real interest in improving the writing. I am a firm believer in the power of publicity. Thus, many of the flyers that floated across the campus featured ir-reverent, humorous, and off-beat approaches and graphics that, as it turned out, appealed greatly to our students and not so much to faculty.

During the first three months of the semester, the number of students coming in for assistance matched previous years and, in spite of my lack of time and the mad pace of the change, we were settling into something of a routine. In view of the difficulties the transition had created, I was pleased.

Early in the second semester of that first year I received my next major surprise. A colleague called and told me that a representative of the English department had gone before the Academic Senate and had complained bitterly about the mismanagement of the writing center and the apparent incompetence of the new director. The presentation was, it turned out, based on outdated and false information. An angry segment of the English faculty, it seemed, was going after the only agent who was perceived to be vulnerable in this unfortunate affair. When I confronted him, the English professor apologized sheepishly and admitted that perhaps he should have talked to me before making his presentation to the Faculty Senate.

That would have been the end of this misunderstanding. English departments, in spite of the ambiguous relationship they tend to have with writing centers, are ultimately concerned with the successful development of student writing proficiency and pedagogy. The writing center is designed to support these faculty and instructional efforts. I soon learned, however, that English departments also harbor specific bureaucratic and political objectives that can override the interests of students. The struggle for budgetary control and faculty release time took precedence, in some minds, over the objectives and operation of the writing center. Some time after the first incident, I found a transcription of a Budget Committee meeting in which this same individual again decried my management of the writing center and stated, "This is a blow to the literacy efforts at this university." I sighed, put the document in a file folder, and tried to move ahead.

Shortly thereafter, English turned its attention to other matters, and the writing center focused on helping students negotiate their college writing assignments. The center operated smoothly, although without much distinction, in spite of its usually absent director. At the time, I was working feverishly to complete my dissertation and direct the Office of Student Support Services, my full-time job at the university. So, the writing center was, by necessity, nearly as much the poor cousin to me as it often is to the university. I give enormous credit to Susan, the graduate assistant, and the tutors for its success. And there were other bright spots. In December, the Minority Services Coordinator had come to me with a request. The state had some unspent grant money for initiatives that could enhance educational opportunities and services for disadvantaged and minority students. He asked if any of my service areas might fit into this niche and asked if I knew a local woman of Nigerian descent who had graduated from the university with a Master of Communicating Arts degree, and who had been a professional journalist for a number of years. I did. Could I fit her into some part of Student Support Services? My colleague and I drafted a proposal to place this remarkable woman into the writing center as a professional staff, tutor, and public relations employee. Within a few weeks, she was working with students, establishing outreach initiatives, and opening the writing center to some of our students who, otherwise, might not have been comfortable in that very northern Wisconsin, very white, very middle-class environment.

During this period, the relationship between the faculty and the writing center warmed. One professor who told me he had never sent students to the center simply because he did not trust student tutors began to suggest to his students that the writing center could help them, and they began dropping in. He did this in response to our conversations and because, when students approved, the center established a policy of sending summary reports on the tutoring sessions to faculty. This growing sense of confidence in the writing center's work was common among faculty, particularly non-English faculty.

The end of that first year found a writing center that was relatively healthy, vibrant, and well-accepted in spite of poor funding and a rather rocky transition. Unfortunately, as is more typical than not, the center's place in the hierarchy of the university had not changed a great deal. If anything, the shift from its place in a legitimate academic department under the direction of tenured faculty to an add-on segment of a service department under the unofficial direction of an academic staff middle manager suggested that it had diminished in stature. Even so, one good year behind us promised a smooth beginning for the fall. My dissertation was complete, but by the summer, I was already deeply involved in writing the major Department of Education proposal that would fund the Office of Student Support Services for the next four to five years, so my attention would continue to be, by necessity, on other matters. Still, the staff would remain constant, and the system that we had developed was established, so I expected few surprises. The series of events that followed would further demonstrate the institutional lack of commitment to the writing center and its mission.

The interim Chancellor embarked on a plan that was benignly called restructuring.

In August, the Vice Chancellor called me in to tell me that the center's location was to be included in a shift of administrative offices that would displace the writing center and a number of other student service offices. The plan was, ostensibly, to concentrate a number of administrative offices in one location of the main campus building. The university leadership may well have had good intentions with this move, but with four weeks left before the start of the fall semester, I was handed an enormous problem. While a number of offices were being displaced, it seemed that only the writing center was being displaced to nowhere. The Vice Chancellor explained that there was no place to put the Center—unless, of course, I had a suggestion.

I did. A suite of offices that had housed a recent, short-lived crop of deans was vacant and was, I was told, to remain empty for the next year or so while the planning process progressed. I suggested that the Vice Chancellor put the writing center in the empty space. After all, we were small, had few possessions, and could move fast. He said he would consider my suggestion.

Three weeks later, no decision had been made. At this point my supervisor, a man of rare integrity and effectiveness, suggested that I simply move the writing center into the empty offices. Within several days, I had requisitioned keys and made a request to have the threadbare, salvage quality furniture moved into the expansive, carpeted, well-lighted, brightly painted rooms. We even had a kitchen with running water. A friend likened our ragtag collection of tutors dressed in various grunge, alternative, hippie, camouflage, and polyester styles to an alien occupying force. We simply did not fit into the polished, suit-and-tie image that typically lived here. Nevertheless, that was it. The writing center, ensconced in luxury, opened on time and, within a week or so, clients knew where to go for writing assistance.

At that time, this maneuver seemed almost amusing—the takeover demonstrated in some appealing way the resistant nature of many writing center directors and their creative, energetic staff of tutors. In fact, this was a vivid illustration of the "otherness" of the writing center and its role in the university. In the institutional hierarchy, in the midst of budgetary and planning shifts, there was no place to put the writing center. The illustration would become even more vivid in the weeks to come.

During this period of restructuring a new Chancellor had been hired, and those of us who had been restructured were settling into our new homes. By October, somebody noticed that the unconventional writing center was taking up some of the most desirable space on campus. At the same time, most of the other departmental moves were proving to be unworkable, and the administration decided to rethink the plan, essentially to restructure the restructured structure. By the end of the month, the material of the writing center was stacked in an unused corner of the university's generally unused Administrative Library. The tutors, graduate assistant, and I immediately set about locating room dividers, moving furniture, and posting signs across campus, and we were in business again. The Administrative Library is a beautiful old room reminiscent of an English study—tall vaulted ceilings, oak woodwork and shelves, painted glass windows—a makeshift plywood financial aid counter stood on one end of the room, a particle board storage closet was tucked in another corner, and steel foldout chairs were scattered about for the occasional standardized test. Some years before, perhaps during a restructuring, the university had installed motion-sensing electric eyes that clicked on the room lights whenever people entered the library. These timed lights then clicked off several minutes later, so throughout the day the flashing on and off of lights accompanied the tutors and clients in cadence with their movements. Again, temporarily, we were home.

Shortly, we were working with clients again. By now, the numbers for the year were well down. We had moved twice and had lost more than a week in transition. In November I was notified that the center would be moved again, this time back to its original location. We will have finally caught our tail. The move would be easy. We could all leave for the holiday break, and when we returned in January, the Writing Center would be back in the small offices it had occupied for the past thirteen years. We were asked to box up the files, books, and such and told to have a nice vacation. Unfortunately, Susan, the tireless graduate assistant, also chose this moment to announce that she had discovered that she had earned enough classroom credits to graduate and would not be returning after the break. Of course, students are supposed to graduate, so as much as I hated to lose Susan, I wished her well, wrote her a glowing, well-deserved letter of recommendation, and began the search for a new Susan.

As I was neither faculty nor student, I did not immediately skip off on Christmas vacation. I was still working a few days later when I received an e-mail message: the move had been postponed.

- It is early February, three weeks into the semester. Curtis, the new graduate assistant, promises to be another exceptional find, and the writing center is operating under full sail. It remains in its temporary, albeit palatial, location. I'm told we'll be moving soon.

- It is early March. Tutors have been working closely with me to create publicity for the center. One, a journalism major, has seen that the writing center plays prominently in the campus newspaper. Another is producing a tutor training film, while a third has joined me to lobby English faculty and university administration. Two more have been visiting campus organizations and setting up campus e-mail notices, and all are involved in developing a proposal for the upcoming National Writing Centers Association conference. For the first time in two years, tutors are being welcomed into English classrooms to talk about the center.

- Finally, we're home again. It seems that we've caught our tail.

First (Happy) Ending

This saga is not meant to suggest that our faculty, staff, and administration do not value the writing center for the experience that it provides both student clients and tutors and for the service it provides instructors. The center has consistently received high marks for the quality of writing help students receive and few would question the value of this experience for tutors. In the months of being pushed and pulled about the campus, I was able to get two proposals funded, due largely to the strong support of my supervisor and the Vice Chancellor. The first allowed me to add several tutors and a significant amount of tutoring time to the schedule at a time when we were terribly understaffed and underfunded. The second was a proposal I wrote jointly with a member of the economics faculty. This "Writing to Learn" proposal entailed extensive tutor training in economics-based technical writing. Tutors were prepared to work with students in two writing-heavy economics courses. Their training included role playing, multimedia presentation, discussion, and hands-on work with sample papers. They then were to keep detailed records of their sessions with this group of students, and at the end of the semester faculty would evaluate the quality of student writing in comparison to other semesters. This second proposal included funds for several tutors to attend a regional writing centers conference and to join me in a presentation about the project. In addition to these encouraging and exciting proposals, we were getting writing center publicity out to the university community, a new composition specialist hired by the English department was turning out to be a great friend and ally to the center, and we were helping students become more effective writers.

The place of the writing center in higher education is dubious in the best of times, but under the strain of academic/institutional politics and mismanagement, it can become an afterthought, if not an inconvenience. In spite of institutional and departmental biases, our writing center, like moss growing on stone, has continued to flourish as a center of writing and learning. This momentum has little to do with me, the English department, or the administration. Tutors know that they are doing important work here, and student writers will seek out the writing center in spite of all efforts to hide it.

- It's getting towards the end of the semester. Great things have happened in the writing center. The tutors are becoming better teachers and learners as they connect with different writers and kinds of writing. They are beginning to see themselves as more a part of an academic community and learning that this is not merely a student job. It is a meaningful, often demanding, collaborative experience that will help mold them intellectually, professionally, and personally. Some will be attending a conference in the fall to make a presentation on their experiences with the "Writing to Learn" project, while others will present the program to campus audiences at home. All will continue to tutor and participate in an ongoing dialogue about student writing and writing centers. Chances are, we won't be restructured again in the foreseeable future, a future that looks relatively stable and uncomplicated. We should be so lucky.

- It's the end of May, and I've been offered a position with Buffalo State College in New York. I'll have the opportunity to teach and direct a writing center under departmental and institutional auspices. I accept.

Second Ending

In my enthusiasm, I was leaving the institution with the conviction that the writing center had reestablished its place in the institutional hierarchy, and that its viability was not dependent on my political and fiscal savvy. Questions arose as I was walking out the door, however: Who will direct the writing center? English would like to have it back but only if the director is given release time. The administration is unwilling to take salaried, tenure-track faculty out of the classroom. This is an economic decision. The Writing Specialist in Student Support Services is qualified, committed, and could be assigned the task without incurring additional costs. Perhaps she would be interested in developing the center further.

As I left for Buffalo, these questions remained unresolved, but as I began to put down roots in my new home, I was confident in the administration's enthusiasm for the writing center.

Curtis, the returning graduate assistant, telephoned this weekend. He is distraught. In the month since I left my previous position, much has happened.

- The writing center's budget has been cut. The funds can be used more directly in other student service areas. What was once inadequate has become half.

- There is no director. Instead a number of administrators have proposed to fold the center into their student service departments where they can more directly serve minorities, students with disabilities, and high-risk students.

- The Writing to Learn project is in disarray. Peer-tutor participants may not be permitted to attend the upcoming conference because the funds might be used elsewhere. As two of the tutors are my copresenters, this is a problem.

The writing center will endure in some form; of that I am fairly confident. Yet its place in the institutional hierarchy, the institutional mindset, has not changed. Stephen North has written that the progressive writing center defines itself "in terms of the writers it serves" (27). He says that such writing centers and their staffs "have about them an air of shrewdness, or desperation, the trace of a survival instinct at work" (35). Writing centers are, by their nature, marginal sites, and in the very best instances, this marginality—North's instinct for survival—opens possibilities for resistance, critical scholarship, and growth. It is something of a badge of honor to hold the place of the "other" in the too often hidebound academy. Indeed only the resistant tutor and writing center can engage student writers in the critical conversations that, as Grimm says, "invite undergraduates into the intellectual work that makes a difference" (546). Yet this marginal status can force writing centers into the role of beggars, of service units at the beck and call of those who hold the purse strings and the academic capital. Until institutions recognize the legitimacy, the intellectual power of what we do, we will continue to expend far too much energy on simply surviving, and in many cases, as my old Vice Chancellor said, there will be "no place for the writing center."

Works Cited

Grimm, Nancy Maloney. 1996. "Rearticulating the Work of the Writing Center." *College Composition and Communication* 47 (4): 523–47.

North, Stephen M. 1995. "The Idea of a Writing Center." *The St. Martin's Sourcebook for Writing Tutors,* edited by Christina Murphy and Steve Sherwood. New York: St. Martin's Press.

How to Be a Wishy-Washy Graduate Student WPA, or Undefined but Overdetermined

The Positioning of Graduate Student WPAs

Stephen Davenport Jukuri and W. J. Williamson

Bill and Lance

I followed Lance into the classroom where he taught two sections of HU101 (the first in our three-course, first-year English sequence). It was early in the term, and I was there to observe him, just to see how everything was going. Because Lance was concerned that something wasn't right in his classes, he had asked me to meet with him to discuss his lesson plans and then to go observe his class. He had also asked Don, a fellow GTA and newfound friend. I try to keep a low profile in other people's classrooms in such situations, so Don and I started to move quietly toward a back corner, intent on slipping unobtrusively into the last empty chairs.

"We have some guests today," Lance began. "This is Don," he said, indicating my companion, "and this is Bill, the God of Teaching."

They all turned to look at us.

Stephen and Kris

When I got back to my office that afternoon, Kris was there, again, sitting in my chair waiting for me.

"I need help. I don't know what to do in class tomorrow . . . what am I going to teach these people?"

I couldn't respond any more. It was late in his second term of teaching and it felt like nothing had changed. I was beginning to think that he just couldn't develop basic classroom activities on his own. Yet I knew he wasn't just an idiot; in fact, quite the opposite. My respect for his intellect had grown proportionately with our close friendship in the past six months. I sat down on my footstool and thought for a second: as a young kid, I would ask my grandpa the same questions over and over just because I liked to hear him explain things. Our relationship was defined by all that mutual attention: I always wanted more, and Grandpa liked to talk.

Is that what's going on here?, I asked myself. And if so, what's it going to take to make this kid more independent?

- Since Spring 1994, we have required first-year GTAs to participate in a portfolio-based response and evaluation system.
- All GTAs are required to provide copies of their syllabi and assignments to the Director of GTA Education and to the Writing Center.
- All GTAs can expect at least one classroom visit per year and an opportunity to talk about their pedagogy before and after that visit.
- All GTAs conduct annual self-evaluations of their teaching practices and theory, and discuss these evaluations with the Director.

Balanced against this relatively open support structure, however, is a general commitment to provide support as it is needed for all GTAs. Although this short list of requirements for GTAs begins to provide structure for their roles in the program, it is structure at an operational level, rather than at a conceptual level. We do not clearly define the roles that GTAs have to or ought to adopt in relation to their students or to the administration. We are mostly comfortable with this partial structure, and recognize how valuable it is although we recognize at the same time that it creates a number of dangers for us, particularly as graduate students working with new GTAs. Where there is a structure vacuum, structure gets built in any number of ways.

In fact, it might seem unusual—even unprofessional to some—that our roles as graduate students, administrators, friends, and colleagues merge so much in the interactions of the stories we will tell. Yet this blurring of boundaries makes sense in the working context. Michigan Tech's Writing Program is not large—six to twelve new GTAs enter the teaching program each year, joining twenty to thirty GTAs who continue to teach until they complete their MS or Ph.D. work. The humanities community in general is insular, often somewhat separate from the rest of a predominantly engineering and sciences campus and the surrounding community. Students and faculty alike are thus likely to socialize mostly within that community.

From the moment of their first invitation to the program, we encourage GTAs to seek a comfortable way of joining our teaching community. However, given the programmatic commitment to this kind of open administrative structure, it is incumbent upon us (and other administrative personnel) to impress upon GTAs that this moderate degree of autonomy actually requires greater personal responsibility than programs that are highly formal or informal: GTAs cannot be a mere extension of a hierarchical program, nor can they simply "do their own thing." And yet, the exact nature of this responsibility is difficult to pinpoint, though its general elements are easily determined: it is part university mission, part program policy, part community lore, part professionalism, wholly contextual, and continually subject to renegotiation. In this regard, everyone—GTAs, GTA administrators, and faculty—is complicit in the construction of this community. The challenge is to become and remain aware of that negotiation. It is an ongoing struggle.

To move another step closer to capturing this struggle for positioning, we need to move toward a more specific understanding of where that positioning begins in the job description of the Assistant Director of GTA Education, and where it goes from there.

The Position

There are few specific duties required of the Assistant Director. We help arrange and administer the GTA orientation. We assist with the first-year teaching seminar. We meet with GTAs and visit their classrooms, respond to drafts of syllabi and assignments, participate in reading and responding to student writing, and provide general assistance upon request. We participate on the Writing Program Committee and serve as liaisons to the Writing Center. Beyond these basic expectations, our responsibilities are subject to our own expertise and initiative, and are therefore variable. Other than assisting the director in these ways, there is little official (and less conceptual) definition of just what function and purpose a graduate student in our position is expected to serve.

In that "structure vacuum," expectations of us—from other graduate students, from administrators, and even from other faculty—can range anywhere from file clerk to spy to substitute teacher to pedagogical theorist. And so perhaps one of the greatest difficulties of the position is understanding what any particular individual expects of you, and how they will react when you conduct yourself and define your work somewhat differently from those expectations. The true nature of the position is that of constant negotiation. Ultimately, however, what we have worked toward is to be positioned as a colleague in relation to other graduate students, someone who is there to help guide new colleagues into a system that, despite similarities to the systems those colleagues may have come from, is nonetheless unique and requires some form of orientation to work productively within. And for those who have never taught before, we are there to help them make that shift from student to teacher, something that often looks easier than it is.

At the same time, given the openness of the position, each assistant director has his or her own individual agendas and concerns. For me (Bill), one of the most important elements of the position was "being there." During my tenure as Assistant Director, I instituted "roving office hours," times when I wandered from office to office and through public places where GTAs could typically be found. I wanted to be as visible as possible so I could engage in as many conversations with GTAs as possible as frequently as possible. Although many of those conversations turned to teaching, many turned to other topics as well. "Open door" policies are invitation enough for some people, but for others there is a need to seek them when their own doors are open, when they are comfortable in their own domains and confident of their own security (or insecurity). Conversation, engagement, presence—these were keys to some of my success in the position. In addition, and of much more significance to the program, my presence served as a reminder that the work of GTAs was significant enough to the program that they invested in a full-time GTA position for the expressed purpose of serving the teaching needs of individual GTAs.

For me (Stephen), I realized early on that the main focus of my work would be the new GTAs, in part because of the relatively large size of the new group (ten) and the fact that half of them had had no previous teaching experience at all. Having come into the program three years earlier with no teaching experience (and having been away from the university entirely for almost three years before that), I had struggled to remember anything at all about school, much less what it means to gradually learn how to pull together a classroom. Thus, my main goal was to help new GTAs gain some perspective on what they were experiencing. I could share with them what I had learned by working through those challenges, and I could help them analyze and reflect on their own experience. More than anything, I wanted to reassure them that even though those first experiences were often difficult, learning from them was the best way to build something better as time when on—especially if they were willing to talk about them, rethink, try different things, and pay close attention to how their students were responding to their teaching.

As we tell the stories of Lance and Kris, it should be evident just how much our particular "take" on the position fed into the development of the roles we defined for one another.

A Look at Two First-Year GTAs

We'll return now to the stories of our interactions with Lance and Kris that opened this chapter. Both GTAs were master's students. Neither had any prior teaching experience, but both were very willing to discuss the struggles they were experiencing in their classrooms.

Bill and Lance (Continued)

I didn't know what to say after my introduction as "the God of Teaching," so I just looked back at Lance's students, making eye contact with as many as possible and trying to gauge their reactions. They were pretty stony. I figured the best thing to do then was to slip into the role the *program* had appointed for me—that of observer. It was an easy choice considering my inexperience as the God of Teaching.

Lance's introduction to the day's work didn't make me any more comfortable, unfortunately: "Bill and I worked up something to do with today's readings," he began as he shed his black leather jacket, "but as I was walking over here, I started to think about it and decided we would try something else. And I think this is gonna be a lot cooler."

From my discussions with Lance in preparation for this class period, I knew that he was struggling to rein in his energy and enthusiasm for the classroom. He indicated to me that, although he had many ideas about what might happen in his classes, he could rarely decide on one thing to do—possibilities seemed endless to him. But the results were pretty chaotic.

Lance's practice of revising his lesson plans as he entered the classroom became his teaching signature. For the most part, this only made him look unorganized in front of his students. Because he didn't take the time to think through the goals and ends of these revisions, however, he faced greater difficulties later on. This pattern extended beyond classroom work, however. What was worse for his students in both the short and long run was Lance's unwillingness to see an assignment through to its original conclusion. His initial ideas were sound enough though he struggled (as do most first-year GTAs) to articulate exactly what he expected of his students. However, as his students questioned his motives and the specific logistics of each assignment, he revised them as well, "on the fly." What I was observing in his class that day were the beginnings of this pattern. Some of Lance's students were quick enough to follow his lead, and they tried mightily to help their peers navigate the leaps and bounds that characterized classroom discussion. Most seemed unable or unwilling to follow, however, and contented themselves with watching the rest.

Lance was frustrated that quarter because his students continued to write safe, uninteresting essays that skirted around the tough issues he attempted to engage them with (e.g., the role of religion in everyday life, occultism as social resistance). He questioned on several occasions my claims that Michigan Tech students are intelligent, savvy, and hardworking. He didn't sense that kind of ability in his students. At the end of the first quarter of his teaching, several of Lance's students protested their final grades. They complained that they had little idea from one day to the next what they were supposed to do in class, and that they rarely knew how to complete his writing assignments.

My observation that day sparked a long series of discussions and observations focused on moving Lance toward a more secure position in his own classrooms. It was a project that was never entirely successful though in the end I became more aware of some of the motives behind Lance's teaching strategies and the values he connected with university life.

Lance came to Michigan Tech from a BA program in philosophy and comparative literature at the University of British Columbia–Vancouver. He entered the rhetoric and technical communication program to pursue interests in business communication. He had notions of entering the global corporate environment prepared to deal with issues of management and intercultural communication, expecting to work on making his business communication more effective and more efficient.

His previous personal experience with writing included dozens of term papers—assignments given early in the term and expected in full, grammatically correct versions at the end of the semester. His instructors were mostly male, people who had been raised in the academy as career philosophers and literature professors. They cultivated eccentricity and calm.

Although I assumed from the outset that Lance needed guidance in his teaching—and at the time I struggled to figure out what that guidance might mean—I realized later that what he probably wanted from me was simple validation for the way he approached teaching. Teaching was as much a matter of personal style as it was a matter of academic excellence for Lance. He wanted respect from his students, but hadn't figured out the kinds of things he might have to do to earn that respect. Certainly, walking into class as their teacher on the first day earned him a certain measure of respect, but that wasn't the kind of respect or validation that Lance was seeking. He wanted to cultivate a friendly distance from his students, the kind of distance that would allow him to remain slightly aloof, but still leave room for casual joking before and after class, and that would encourage long head-to-head exchanges during office hours with students who wanted to explore increasingly philosophical dimensions of the discussion topics raised during class.

What Lance discovered when he attempted to achieve that degree of scholarly nonchalance with his students was that he didn't know how to do it. I changed my approach when I realized how he imagined himself leading a successful class period. I tried to convince him that professors who could walk in and lecture like that, without notes but with eloquence and style could only do so because they had *lived* in the material they were teaching, that they had so completely immersed themselves in the work that it had become part of their everyday vocabulary. They seemed so casual because they came to class so well prepared. They had taken the time to develop lectures and assignments and see them through to fruition or failure. The changes they made in their pedagogical strategies were changes that resulted from focused reflection on what worked, what didn't, and why. Lance later confided to Stephen that he had come to recognize that much of what he "naturally" did in the classroom was ultimately unproductive . . . but that he simply could not change himself. To him, making changes threatened his individuality and creativity. He would rather appear unprepared than become what he perceived as a "cookie cutter" GTA.

Like the story Stephen presents regarding his relationship with Kris, Lance and I created complications for ourselves by forging a friendship. Although friendship among colleagues isn't beyond the realm of possibility, it wasn't something that either of us expected. When Lance arrived with the other four members of his teaching orientation group, he did not expect to find a graduate student in a position as a writing program administrator, especially one that, at twenty-five, was only three years older than he. Two chains of events happened during that first week of our acquaintance that blurred the boundaries between our official, programmatic roles. First, Lance sought opportunities to talk to me but not only about teaching. We connected in many ways and as a result became close friends very quickly. Second, Lance was a bit intimidated by my casual confidence regarding classroom practice. When he asked "how" and "why" questions, I often gave him several possibilities to consider, rather than just one. I saw this as good administration—show him a range of possibilities and encourage him to gather together a repertoire of practices that feel comfortable to him. Unfortunately, this strategy backfired and created a gulf between us professionally; once Lance began to struggle in his own classroom, he assumed that I was far more accomplished than he was likely to become and decided he could never attain a similar level of expertise.

I became a teaching mentor for Lance through my position as the Assistant Director of GTA Education, but we were also enrolled in a postmodern philosophy course together during that first quarter. In that setting, I became one of Lance's guides to succeeding in the program on an academic level. In that class, we collaborated on writing assignments, spent long hours engaged in discussions of the readings, wrestling with the work of François Lyotard and Emmanuel Levinas. We developed a friendship that extended beyond the parameters of school as well. He entered the same circle of friends, giving us more and more opportunities to connect socially. In all of this, Lance tapped into my need to offer assistance. I like it when people come to me to talk about things they need to talk about, for whatever reason. With Lance, those conversations began with my advice on teaching and graduate studies, but evolved into conversations that were less connected to school—life experience, goals, relationships. And of the four first-year GTAs in the first "class" I administered, only Lance and one other GTA seemed willing to acknowledge that I had anything to offer. (The others had significantly more teaching experience than I did and remained more distant until well into that academic year.) Initially, Lance and I came together on a much more personal than professional level. Although I entered Lance's classroom as one of his supervisors, I worked with him more as a friend than anything else.

That mix created tension later on. As I worked with Lance, often spending an hour or more with him to develop strategies for drawing out his educational goals in the classroom through everyday teaching practice, I invested more and more time and energy in support of a friend, and became increasingly frustrated over time with the reluctance of a colleague to take his teaching seriously. At least, I assumed for much of that time that Lance just didn't take his teaching seriously. Although I know better now, at the time the attempt to maintain both a friendship and a professional relationship wore me down.

Stephen and Kris (Continued)

. . . *What's it going to take to make this kid more independent? It's not like he can't think through this stuff himself. I've seen him analyze and work through ideas a lot more complex.*

"Okay," I said to him, "rather than me just giving you ideas, why don't I just ask you what your students need right now? What are you asking them to learn at this point in the term, and what do they need from you tomorrow in order to do that successfully?"

Kris immediately began to answer the questions, skillfully. I had to do little more than provide follow-up question, keep track of what he was saying, and validate his plans. It worked . . . or so I thought for a while, until I realized that it simply became the pattern for our ongoing discussions, and he still seemed so dependent upon me, even if it was only to ask him questions that I thought he should be able to ask himself. We were stuck.

Or so I thought. I can see now that even though it felt as though Kris was not progressing, he was progressing in very individual ways. His strengths were clear: he responded in very meaningful and productive ways to students' writing, he was able to assess very accurately what they needed, and he was able to talk very clearly about how his students were responding to his class. When he told me, early in the year, that they were not responding well at all, my first visit to his class confirmed that assessment. He was struggling to get through the hour, every single day and every class. Despite his desire to have open-ended discussions and his careful preparation, the unpredictability of such openness made him so nervous that he frequently could not finish his own sentences. When students provided answers to his questions, it was clear that he was not sure what to do with those answers: at best he would repeat the answer and nod his head, and then ask the question again in hopes of an answer he could work with. At times he misunderstood what a student was saying, as we all do from time to time, but instead of taking a little time to negotiate an understanding, he would panic, give up, and move on. And when students asked for clarification on something, he could only repeat the exact words he had used earlier rather than explain it in another way.

He wanted, desperately, to do what he was least equipped to do: to make the classroom a shared space, to open it up to discussion and dialogue, to learn along with his students. Rather than militantly follow his syllabus, he wanted to build a classroom that would shift and adjust over time to the needs of his students. Yet his background education and certain individual characteristics made that a constant struggle. The contradictions between desire and skill were painful to watch, and it was natural that I would give him all the time I could spare.

And it was complicated. He quickly learned to evoke his engineering education to establish some ethos with his students, who were predominantly engineering and sciences majors. But that authority was limited, I believe, because some students intolerantly interpreted his classroom struggles, in conjunction with his Indian identity and British accent, as a lack of facility with the English language. They could not see just how proficient he was, and over time I learned the irony in that misunderstanding. Having grown up with a serious stutter, Kris had learned that he could control his stutter best by avoiding certain word combinations: his ability to speak "normally" meant, first, developing a vast vocabulary to choose from and, second, an extremely quick and sophisticated ability to revise syntax and meaning. Yet the additional stress of talking to an entire classroom, and responding to a wide variety of comments from students, would short-circuit his coping methods and his stutter would return.

Thus it was only my classroom visit that convinced me that he was telling me the truth: this person who was highly capable and articulate in both writing and in person was, in front of a group of students, frequently at a loss for dealing with anything unpredictable. It was no surprise that he came to me continually to provide some kind of security and structure for his classroom. And, given my sympathies with his struggles, it is not surprising that I would readily provide it—over and over again—along with a lot of reassurance of how well he was performing in every other aspect of his teaching. Having to work with all of the GTAs, I could not visit Kris' class as much as he (or I) would have liked, but he was skilled at making use of every other available moment in my day. And I reassured myself, and him, that so long as he was continuing to try, and was open to the strategies I and others would offer, he would gradually pull together the classroom discussion as well.

When I look back on Kris's experience, I realize that he came into the program with a background that would necessarily cause struggle with our program: an undergraduate degree in electrical and electronics engineering from India and a master's degree in engineering management from Australia. His educational experience was highly formal, one in which students did not approach the teachers for any but the most formal and official reason. Yet he had wanted, for years, to be an English major, to work with language rather than electronics, and he was highly motivated to succeed. He was also willing to do just about anything, including teaching, to be in our Rhetoric and Technical Communication program. And our program is willing to place almost anyone into a classroom for their first year and see how they will do.

His determination was, more than anything, what I admired in Kris and the reason why I wanted so badly for him to succeed. And in all honesty, it was a refreshing difference from the attitude of some GTAs who were not sure they wanted to be in our program, some of whom had been attracted by funding offers or were still uncertain about their goals and direction for graduate school in general. I was still very enthusiastic about my decision to come back to the university, and had found that the GTA "attitude" could be draining. Thus it was entirely natural that I would gravitate to somebody like Kris who was adding energy to our shared goals. In our ability to meet our mutual needs, we developed an intensely close friendship rather quickly—actlly, faster than we could control.

And of course, he was also meeting my professional needs as well: I found, early in my new responsibilities, that many graduate students were unwilling to share with me what they were doing in their classrooms, reluctant to talk about their experience, highly protective of their teaching strategies. Kris, on the other hand, welcomed my presence in every aspect of his work, allowing me to feel as though, at least with one graduate student, I was doing my job. I was giving him the kind of attention that I had needed, myself, during my first year of teaching—thus fulfilling my own goals for the position.

Although I was confused, amazed, excited, and at times frightened by the intensity of our relationship, it is easier to see, now, how snugly our particular needs and individual personalities fit together and how quickly the relationship developed and settled into a structure of its own. Ironically, it was the very settling down that left me feeling unfulfilled, for I somehow expected, in that first year, for Kris to become entirely independent of me (and me of him), and that just didn't happen. By the end of the year, my patience had worn dangerously thin. I began to doubt my methods, wondered if close friendship had stunted his professional growth, and realized that at some point the connection had begun to drain my energy rather than sustain it. I was struck by the feeling that, somehow, I actually had not been doing my job. And the friendship—which in the midst of all of our shared work, school, and pedagogical concerns had grown so close—seemed imperiled as well.

Some Conclusions

We have chosen to tell stories that feel, at least to us, thoroughly ambiguous. In one sense, we maintain a certain level of uncertainty and personal dissatisfaction with our work with these individuals, though at the same time we value their efforts and recognize the progress that each made. Lance worked hard to understand what was going wrong, but ultimately didn't want to change the personal habits that were interfering with his goals. He positioned Bill not just as a mutual friend and helper, but also as an administrator who would benevolently and continually bear witness to the fact that his students just couldn't adapt to him. Kris wanted desperately to change so many things, and worked hard at it, but never quite overcame the fears that prevented his goals from fully developing. He positioned Stephen not just as a mutual friend and confidant, but also as his administrative security blanket, a "reachable" supervisor who would drop everything else to talk him through every step of the way.

We don't find fault with the fact that our close friendships and working relationships became inextricably intertwined, and we continue to value these friendships even as those GTAs are now working in industry. But it is also true that the comfort and security of those mutual positionings began to feel, over time, unproductive and constraining to us as administrators and to Lance and Kris' development as GTAs. It may simply be that the foundational strength of our position—the fact that it is undefined and can develop as individual needs direct it—may have become our greatest weakness. We were unprepared to find suddenly that we had settled into comfortable but inert relationships. And although it seems so very productive to be able to understand GTAs as individuals, particularly in how it might help us to direct their development, the real complexity of that "individuality" also clarifies why that development was not easy, quick, or particularly satisfying. Thus we worried constantly about the classrooms they were providing for their students.

At the same time, we readily ask: would the teaching of Lance or Kris have *developed* (not *been*) better if they were merely handed a book and told to teach, as would have happened in some programs? Or would it have been any better if they were given a syllabus and lesson plans developed by somebody else, and told to implement them as their own? We know that some GTA Education Programs, for a variety of good administrative reasons, maintain a strictly defined teaching curriculum for GTAs, providing standardized syllabi, textbooks, and assignments for all classrooms. Other programs have few resources for GTA support and can only employ the "here's your class; come ask if you have any questions" method of training that we have heard about or experienced directly ourselves. In both extremes—one a carefully structured context, the other lacking structure entirely—there is a certain security that comes from knowing exactly where one stands in relation to others. Many GTAs react negatively to too much structure, feeling smothered and untrusted, yearning for absolute freedom and, at times, subverting administration in order to gain it. Meanwhile, those who have "absolute freedom" often resent their lack of support and guidance and create their own security by privatizing their classrooms and abhorring any "administrative interference" with a project for which they have had to be entirely responsible.

Yet we know that many other programs, like ours, are shooting for something in between: we wanted Lance and Kris to take their teaching seriously and develop and evaluate their own pedagogy somewhat independently, but we wanted them to do so in the context of a coherent writing program and a responsible community of colleagues with whom they provide mutual help, guidance, critique, and in which they would participate in the construction of its negotiated goals and values. Becoming such a colleague means taking a serious interest in teaching and students, talking about the issues that are raised in the daily activities of teaching, talking about what we value in our teaching, in others' teaching, in the work our students do in our classes. It means learning to think like a teacher and wanting to accept the responsibilities of being a teacher (both in practice and in position) in a university. Our experiences with Lance and Kris show us that these qualities are, by their very nature, relatively indefinable prior to their specific reality, and thus may not be easily fostered by the extremes of highly traditional hierarchies or laissez-faire administrations.

Ultimately, the ambiguity we feel comes from the very strength of a program and administrative position that operates with and within a partial structure: the ability, in that relatively open space, to see the complexity of what is happening to particular individuals as they attempt an act as complex and personal as teaching. It is true, perhaps, that Kris might have felt more comfortable at first with a highly structured program where he would have had little need to be flexible and accommodating to students. And Lance would have perhaps welcomed a complete lack of such structure, enjoying the freedom to make up his class anew every day. Yet undoubtedly, Kris would have grown to resent the structure as he gained confidence in his own ability. And Lance would have grown into the realization of his own failings, though he would likely have faulted whatever forces "permitted" him to go at it alone in the first place. Instead, what seems significant here is that the same program was able to provide two very different GTAs with something that they both could value and work with: a very realistic sense of the complexities of developing an effective classroom, of negotiating their particular personal abilities with what does or does not constitute effective teaching, and a taste of what it means to be a colleague.

Context does greatly determine the positions we take up and work within. In the context of our program, relationships like ours with Lance and Kris emerge from our daily interactions with GTAs—without our even realizing it at the time. What might be most important in these stories is our recognition that when we attempt to work within the kind of partial structure that might provide continual growth toward collegial interdependence, structure of some sort will develop anyway. A position such as ours that seems so open to possibilities and personal direction can easily turn into a role, serving the past experiences and needs of those who construct it. If there is one thing that we have learned, it is that although it is often difficult to change or work productively with the mutual positionings we suddenly recognize between ourselves and other GTAs, it is relatively easy to fall into them.

And yet, to end on a more hopeful note, our stories tell us also that so much more is possible, even when that "danger" is realized. The real antidote to discovering these positionings "too late," as we sometimes fear we have done with Lance and Kris, is to be aware of the openness of the structure and the tendencies of the individuals involved, including our own. And from within that awareness, to work at understanding what it really means for individuals to attempt to teach others, how valuable it is to see the reality of our teaching through the eyes of another colleague, and how important it is to consciously shape and nurture the relationships that we develop with one another. Those endeavors are perhaps what is most important to GTAs' long term development, as well as to their present participation in GTA programs that are also communities of colleagues.

Note

1. These first glimpses of the ways we are positioned are often unsettling, particularly when they reach a certain exigence. How do you respond, for example, to a fellow graduate student who declares to you (when the Director is away) that he now works exactly 20 hours per week, and suggests that "the Program" must accept responsibility for the things that are not accomplished in any one particular week. What do you say to

the GTA who takes the Director's memo (to GTAs, about their work with students) and projects it on an overhead while you are observing her class? And why is it that the GTA leaves messages all night long on your answering machine, seeking approval for his expressed inability to give his students anything but As for final grades? We see what seems obvious, and we see the more subtle positionings as well: we notice which GTAs duck down the hallway when they see the Director coming, and which ones feed us compliments and classroom stories that they hope will filter up to the Director in favorable ways.

The Peer Who Isn't a Peer

Authority and the Graduate Student Administrator

Johanna Atwood Brown

During my first year as a TA, I remember watching an administrator—who happened to be a graduate student—facilitate a tense teaching assistant training session. At the time, I thought to myself, "Great experience . . . but bad karma. Isn't the life of a graduate teaching assistant complicated enough without supervising recalcitrant peers?"

A few years later, the lure of "great experience" won over "bad karma." I applied for and obtained a position as an assistant administrator toward the end of my Ph.D. work at the University of Wisconsin–Milwaukee. I was a little uneasy about the potential problems, but the benefits of leadership training, hands-on experience, and professional development outweighed the fears. Indeed, I did gain new perspectives on the "big picture" of university decisions and policy making. I also learned more about teacher training, committee and liaison work, politicking, supervising, memo writing, and all the detail work that administrators face. So I continue to believe that Ph.D. candidates in composition studies can learn much from a taste of administrative work.

What I didn't expect was a lesson about the pitfalls of a supervisory position. I discovered, for example, that fellow TAs often had odd reactions to my position of authority. At first, I thought the reactions were the result of my easygoing personality. But now the reactions strike me as endemic to the position of graduate student administrator: that is, being a peer who isn't a peer. In fact, this role may be familiar to any WPA who supervises—or even works with—faculty peers, and I believe it's likely to remain a struggle in my professional life. Naturally, I wanted it both ways: I wanted to be a peer—a friend or just another TA—on social occasions and an "authority figure" at school. I learned that it is very difficult to be both at the same time.

My official job title was Assistant Coordinator of English 101, but I was called the 101 Coordinator, a title more suggestive of the authority I held. English 101 was an important course: it was first in the composition sequence and most incoming students took it. It was also the course that new TAs (and some new lecturers) taught for the first year. Its instructors participated in mandatory portfolio assessment each semester to determine student competency. My job, therefore, was to organize and facilitate the evaluation process

120

from beginning to end. During a given semester, I supervised TAs and lecturers, visited classes, talked to students, and held mandatory staff meetings. At these "norming sessions," instructors read model essays and worked toward consensus in scoring. I was also responsible for implementing the final week-long assessment process. In this position, then, I was in charge of the day-to-day administration of 101. I more or less told other graduate students (and lecturers) what to do.

But I was not a WPA, and I felt as though I had no real power or authority. One day I was another TA who went about my business, taught my classes, griped about meetings, and resisted institutional policies—just like everybody else. And the next day I was someone who had to uphold the rules, run the meetings, and tell people what to do. I was suddenly making real decisions that affected people's lives. I often careened back and forth between being a graduate student and an administrator, inhabiting one role or the other, depending on the situation. Of course, I thought I was never in the right role at the right time. When I wanted to be "friend," I was "coordinator," and, of course, when I wanted to be "coordinator," I was "peer" if not "friend."

The first year was the hardest, for many reasons, but particularly in terms of role-switching. When I began to work as coordinator, the first group of TAs I worked with included six friends of mine. Five were in composition studies working toward Ph.D.s, one or two years behind me, and one was a candidate in literary studies. In our program, graduate students often have to wait a year or two before becoming TAs, so we had been taking classes and hanging out together for awhile. We had attended parties, drunk coffee late at night, and discussed the finer points of Berlin, Shor, and Emig after classes. I felt very insecure, therefore, in my new position as coordinator—and, more specifically, in my sense of authority over TAs, especially TAs who were also friends. So, part of the difficulty was located in my discomfort.

But part of the position switching I experienced—from peer to supervisor—developed out of the TAs' attitudes or reactions toward me. 101 "baggage" tended to intrude sometimes when I was trying to relate to my friends as friends. I would become mired in the role of coordinator and would not be able to disengage, even if I wanted to. For example, one day I was talking on the phone to one of the new TAs, who was also a friend. We were planning to meet for coffee or something. I was laughing and enjoying myself when my friend suddenly switched conversational gears. She began listing complaints about 101, TA orientation, the calendar, and meetings. She said, "So now that you're coordinator, you can make these changes. Most of us feel the same way, you know. But of course you know; we've talked about what needs doing." My friend began to demand—literally—that I make changes in all the procedures she disagreed with. "You've got to make changes; you have the power now," she stated vehemently. "You have to do it for the students."

I was not shocked by her attitude: I knew all the usual complaints. But I was stunned by the suddenness of the "attack" in the middle of a friendly conversation. I told her that I could not take most of the suggestions, which included revamping the entire system that all the composition courses followed. I explained that just because I had this new position as 101 Coordinator didn't mean that I was in charge of the composition program.

She paused briefly, then said, "Well, you can change the books we use for 101, can't you?" I hesitated and replied, "If a new book were warranted, I suppose I could." "We should be asking students to read a novel or at least some short stories," she said, expectantly. In 101, students read articles and essays but no fiction. I said, "No. Students use the essays as models in 101, and they learn through imitation. Let's leave the fiction for the lit courses."

To make a long story short, we argued for the next half hour about 101. I was annoyed first because I was not at work nor was I expecting such a discussion. My friend had shifted into TA-who-resists-101-mode, and somehow I ended up playing "coordinator" when I thought I was playing "friend." But, more importantly, this person caught me off guard—and it might have been a purposeful manipulation. She wanted very badly to have a friend on the inside who could make changes, and I didn't turn out to be the coordinator she expected.

Similar situations, though not as upsetting, began to happen with increasing frequency in the next three years. I found that when I met 101 TAs or lecturers at graduate student gatherings—parties, cookouts, or movies—I would remain "coordinator" in everyone's mind. Fine, I thought to myself, after all, it is my current job. But, to tell the truth, I didn't want that position to eat up my entire life—and I felt as though I had no other social gatherings to attend except those hosted by other graduate students. I wasn't a faculty member and I knew no one outside the university in Milwaukee.

Unfortunately, some of the 101 TAs and lecturers looked surprised to see me at social functions—as if I stayed locked up in my office at night. It was like when kids see their teacher at the grocery store—what an unreal experience that must be. Some TAs kidded me that I was spying on them, implying that I was not a graduate student and therefore didn't belong at the party. Others asked me 101 questions or discussed their problems with classes. That would have been fine, except I didn't always want to answer 101 questions or be coordinator at social events. I remember once avoiding a holiday party because I couldn't face playing 101 Coordinator all evening. I felt trapped: I either had to answer the questions or ask people to see me later about their concerns. *Then* what do we talk about? Because I was finished with course work, I wasn't in anyone's classes, so the common ground topic was 101. The upshot is that I did not know how to function within this situation.

In contrast, at school, in meetings, and in other professional situations, I desperately wanted to be seen as coordinator. Of course, in those situations TAs coded me as "peer," "friend," or "graduate student" and could easily dismiss what I was asking—or telling—them to do. Again, the first year was the most difficult, partly because I had shifted from friend/peer to coordinator over the summer.

Some of my friends had trouble making the transition from Johanna-as-friend to Johanna-as-coordinator. These were the folks who started sentences with words like: Do I really have to? Or, can I get away with? My crossover to administrative work made relationships very tense. One of my friends, for example, turned out to be what I considered, quite simply, a horrible teacher. Of course, because he was a new TA, I had no idea what kind of teacher he was. I guess I knew he wasn't "into" teaching, like those of us in Rhetoric and Composition, but that fact didn't register until he was working with me. Almost immediately, he showed his lack of commitment to teaching writing and to 101 in particular. For example, he wrote inappropriate comments on student essays: "turn this so-called essay back in when it's worth reading." Often he made no comments at all, and, according to students, he rarely talked about how to write, preferring to discuss controversial ideas. "Today this one student," he complained to me over coffee, "jumped up in the middle of class, called me a communist, and walked out. I just shouted 'good riddance' after him and I hope he doesn't ever come back. What am I supposed to do with that attitude?" Many of his students, including that one, ended up in my office, complaining—and rightly so. They couldn't stand him, and he seemed to despise them as well. I tried, in my official capacity as coordinator, to help him work on teaching, but he wouldn't respond to my suggestions. They were too much work, he claimed, for a stupid course: "no offense, of course." As I increased my demands that he back off on his attitude and do his job, he became more hostile and quit talking to me. Because I truly had become coordinator in his eyes, I was his enemy.

Friends, I learned, could easily ignore what I told them to do. Obviously, I'm describing worst-case scenarios, but some peers put enormous pressure on me to make concessions and do them favors, big and small. I certainly felt a conflicted sense of loyalty between friend and job—as well as a desire to give in for the sake of friendship.

Even those TAs who didn't know me well also tended to test the limits of my authority. Alice Gillam, the writing program administrator at UWM, used to refer to some TAs or lecturers as "free spirits." Hers is a perfect description of these people, and I subsequently incorporated the term into my personal lexicon. Free spirits—and I saw a few in three years—ignore authority altogether, preferring to do things their own way. Often, they disagreed with the program's philosophy, either believing we are too easy or too tough on our students. Their attitudes consisted of "Hey, it's nothing personal against you, Johanna. The program sucks." But this was an insidious position because students got caught in the crossfire of utter rejection. They suffered the consequences of teacher disagreement. 101 instructors had to do their jobs, whether they personally disagreed with the program's philosophy or not. Because instructors did not evaluate their own students' work, all teachers had to adhere to 101 standards both in terms of teaching and participating in portfolio assessment as readers. One cannot be a free spirit, in part, because students may fail the course.

For example, one goal of 101 was work on analytical writing skills to prepare students for the next course in the sequence; therefore, summary papers, informational reports, and strictly narrative papers were not acceptable demonstrations of competency. One free spirit decided that this was a horrible and demeaning requirement to force upon students. She wanted to allow students to express themselves freely, which seemed to mean through narrative and descriptive writing only. While I appreciate narrative and descriptive writing, I know they will not help students become fully prepared for the tasks of the next writing course. This teacher, in fact, was doing her students no favors by rejecting analytical writing. We had so many meetings that I lost track. I reasoned with her, and it didn't work. I harassed, bullied, and plagued her, and that didn't work very well either. She found ways to make her dissatisfaction heard. More than once she told me I was wrong and said she would not do what I asked her to do. She took little I said very seriously.

The last straw for me was when I found her passing every portfolio she read during the final assessment process. I told her she could not do this. She told me she disagreed with portfolio assessment and with the 101 philosophy—which I already knew—and that she would not stop. She stalked off. I let her go so both of us could cool off, but after a while, she began to read more reliably, so I said nothing. I also said nothing because I thought I lacked power to speak.

I have never felt so weird about my position among friends and other peers as when I was coordinator. I never fully understood what my power consisted of in this position and felt profoundly uncomfortable exercising it. I was unwilling to test its limits because I felt keenly aware of my other position as graduate student. I wanted to be a graduate student, too—at parties and other social events. Furthermore, any power I had came from the WPA, and I was unsure of how to use that second-hand power. I never knew exactly how much pressure I could put on other graduate students and lecturers to do their jobs. What could I do? What could I say to these people? "I'll tell Alice if you don't shape up"? If direct or indirect confrontation, such as reminding people of obligations to the program, to their students, to the job, doesn't work, what other choice do I have? I didn't really know. I often felt very divided about what I was doing and what my identity should be, especially when I saw a picture of myself reflected in someone else's eyes. It was frequently a portrait I didn't recognize.

As I was finishing up my tenure as coordinator, I wrote a job description and coordinator manual—and I thought a lot about my experience. Alice and I talked about how to modify the coordinator experience to enhance it for the next candidate, but we didn't talk as much about the emotional impact of being a peer who isn't a peer. I have done so in this article. What would I do differently myself? I don't know. But perhaps there are some general recommendations I can make to WPAs who work with graduate student administrators. My first recommendation would be for WPAs to write down what the limits and boundaries of authority include. What kind of troubleshooting action is appropriate? What would be over the limit and what's not doing enough about a problem? I also recommend formal discussion of this issue before the student administrator begins working. While learning to deal with authority issues are part of the professional development process, some guidelines concerning authority are warranted. TAs get to know the limits of their power in the classroom, why not graduate student administrators?

Second, I recommend that, if possible, WPAs devise more than one administrative position and create a support network for all graduate student administrators. When almost all of my friends became 101 instructors, I might have had no one to talk to about my problems. Fortunately, my office mate was also a new coordinator (of the basic writing courses) and a graduate student. We spent a lot of time the first year talking over problems informally and he became a good friend. Similarly, there were meetings with all composition coordinators throughout the year with social luncheons at the end of each semester. These meetings made me feel part of a distinct group and less of an anomaly in the graduate student world. In addition, I was able to ask for help from a different peer group; in other words, I didn't have to talk about my difficulties with TAs who were not administrators. I even invited other coordinators to sit in on my staff meetings to help me with discussions and give me feedback. WPAs should encourage graduate student administrators to make contact with others in their position perhaps through e-mail or on the phone to build another type of support network. I believe that this kind of support is absolutely essential.

Third, formal training for the graduate student administrator is vital. It not only offers the candidate graduate credit for professional development but can help new administrators learn to work more effectively with people. Graduate student administrators need to read material on management techniques, such as task delegation, confrontation strategies, and conflict management, and tactics for working with superiors as well as subordinates. WPAs could initiate reading groups to discuss these issues and might think about including others in administration from the university or even from the community. In addition, reasonably-priced training seminars for managers are offered in many areas and can serve as crash courses in management techniques.

I believe that there are many options for helping a graduate student adjust to a different kind of work environment. Fortunately for me, many of them were already in place when I became 101 Coordinator. The key is to be prepared for some difficulties, discuss them ahead of time in detail, and make sure support networks are in place.

Finally, in thinking more about my experience, I think it mirrors—albeit in a small way—the challenges many WPAs face when they must supervise tenured faculty. It seems to surface most vividly when untenured WPAs work with administrators or faculty who "outrank" them. It's a challenge that I certainly feel more equipped to face now that I've been there and done that.

Part III
WPAs in Collaboration

One of the best things about being a WPA is that when faculty across campus start thinking of collaborating with someone in the English department, they often check out the WPA first. In their home departments WPAs may struggle to explain what they do and how they might be evaluated, but outside our home departments we are likely to be the most visible resource on campus. Of course, that visibility is not always a blessing, especially if it's campus-wide assessment that is the issue at hand. And, it isn't that faculty outside our departments necessarily have a clear picture themselves of how we would talk of our own work. Far from it. Still, I doubt that anyone would have called me three years ago to ask if I would help design a new Faculty Orientation Program—one without all-day talking heads on the benefits of the Benefits Package—if I had not been a WPA at the time. Like most WPAs, I didn't need the extra work, but the opportunity to collaborate with an interdisciplinary group developing a year-long workshop series focused on teaching was just too good for the WPA in me to let pass.

When we think of working in collaboration, most WPAs are likely to think of programs like Writing Across the Curriculum where many of us discovered that writing instruction was welcomed in a very different way and sometimes much more enthusiastically than it was in our home departments. Of course, that response hasn't been universal. I do recall one faculty member's skepticism after he had listened to a presentation on WAC at Michigan Tech: "Writing across the curriculum," he mused. "It just sounds like another the-sun-never-sets-on-the-English-department scam to me." End of conversation. Yet, WAC has provided some of our richest cross-curricular experiences, and it has been the place where we had to work in collaboration, in dialogue with others; no WAC program can exist long as a soliloquy.

Collaboration is, I would argue, how any writing program functions both in and outside its department. We work in collaboration to build departmental programs, as Toby Fulwiler and his colleagues at the University of Vermont demonstrate in the way they have chosen to tell their story. And, we work in collaboration with staff and faculty both in and outside our departments to create useful writing experiences for our students. Beth Daniell's morality play on the lessons of e-mail is a wonderful example of this kind of project. Through it all, what we might be looking for is the Baklava Experience that Kathleen Yancey writes of—not just the good food, though we wouldn't turn it down, but the too rare opportunity to create an ongoing Teaching Circle made up of faculty from many disciplines who simply want to talk about teaching.

I know few WPAs who really work alone. They might sometimes feel isolated by departmental politics or by the workday patterns any administrative position can impose, but most will admit that a program run by one person making unilateral decisions isn't much of a program at all. Worse than that, it's a program that's tough to pass on to the next person or to talk about with colleagues because it has little existence outside the head of one person. The selections that follow all tell stories of working with others, sometimes easily and sometimes not.

The Teaching Circle, the WPA, and the Work of Writing in the University

Kathleen Yancey

The last Monday in August 1994, and I'm sitting at my computer revising a syllabus for my advanced writing course when the ring of the phone pulls me back to the present. Reluctantly, I take the call. It's from a colleague of mine, a biologist I don't know well, but (given what I do know) I like. She hates to bother me at home, she explains, but she's got a favor to ask. Would I attend a two-day, systemwide University of North Carolina conference that will focus on teaching, in particular on enhancement and evaluation of teaching? Sure, I reply. You'll be working with others from our campus, she says, then names five faculty I've never heard of, and yes, one whose name I have heard of. "You won't be going?" I reluctantly inquire. No, she can't make it. How can I get out of this, I think.

But it was too late; I'd said yes. Besides, I'd already planned to do something to let my campus know that I appreciated their support of me; this seemed to work. And really, as I thought about what my colleague had outlined, this was both easy and clean: two days at the conference, a report to write up, and we were done. I could see the end of the project before it began.

You can see what's coming, I'm sure: the five strangers and the one not-quite-a-stranger and I have become friends and colleagues and partners, a collaborative team that we have come to understand as a teaching circle. The story of how we became a teaching circle, what that means, and how teaching circles can support and enrich the work of writing in the university is the story I want to tell here.

It's a story that adds texture and depth to the picture of Writing Program Administration.

The faculty going to Western Carolina University for the conference met once before we departed for Western Carolina's Center for Teaching Excellence. I wasn't the only stranger: no one really seemed to know anyone else. And we were diverse: a sociologist who specializes in race relations; an engineer from Lebanon who directs the graduate program in his department; a business professor whose specialty is social science communication; a faculty member from the College of Education who'd been a dean as well as department chair; a professor of dance and theatre of Greek descent whose recent work includes adapting African performance into American arts curricula; and the biologist,

129

whose primary work, partly in conjunction with the American Association of Higher Education, has focused on ways to engage both disciplinary and cross-curricular faculty in teaching. We agreed on a time and place for the conference departure, on what we wanted to learn at the conference, and on the kind of report we would file with the provost's office.

Another meeting concluded, I think as I walk back to my own department.

The thing was that this conference didn't turn out as (I'd) planned, the end wasn't in sight at all (still isn't), and what I've learned, if explicated, would take more than the number of pages I'm allotted here.

What did happen, and how does it connect to writing?

The conference happened, and it did its job. In North Carolina in 1994, we had a new legislature-mandated ordinance to put into place: what is, in a kind of shorthand, known as Memorandum 338. It specifies that faculty must be observed teaching, its intent to assure that teaching remains—or in some cases, becomes—the focus of academic attention.[1] At the conference, representatives from all the campuses worked—alternately, in small groups and large groups—to consider how 338 might best be implemented—how to structure a three-part process of pre-observation, observation, and post-observation; how to conduct the post-observation conference; how observation (with student evaluations and faculty self-reports) contributes to a "triangulated" way of understanding and evaluating teaching.

Inside this conference, two other events took place. First, at the initial small group I was assigned to, we learned about a model of faculty enhancement that UNC Asheville was using, something they called a teaching circle: a group of faculty, usually inter-disciplinary faculty, who come together for a specified period of time to take up one or more questions. As it was explained, the teaching circle sounded like an interesting vehicle for faculty development—voluntary, self-defined, inquiry-oriented, diverse, (to my mind) academic in the best sense. I liked it.

Second, the members of the UNC Charlotte group, working together at the conference, began to like each other. Of course, partly, this kind of phenomenon is encouraged by a conference structure: for a couple of days, we eat, work, and play together. But as we rejoined our campus group after participating in multicampus sessions, we found ourselves reacting similarly to suggestions, thinking with each other about how we could enact some of what we were learning, laughing at some of the same observations. Sometimes we didn't laugh. At the last meal of the conference, a breakfast, we found ourselves in the midst of a serious discussion about illness and death: my father was dying of cancer, one member of the group is a survivor of a serious illness, another the survivor of a massive heart attack. We had sadnesses to share as well.

We trusted each other.

When we returned to campus, we scheduled a meeting whose purpose was to frame the report to the provost. My end was in sight. But not: In addition to outlining the report, we made two decisions that took us beyond that report, that conference, the technicalities of that memorandum. First, we decided that, within the university grant-funding structure, we would try to offer a three-day UNC Charlotte Summer Institute on peer observation and evaluation. Second, borrowing what we had learned from our colleagues at UNC Asheville, we began to define ourselves as a specific kind of group, a teaching circle. In retrospect, both of these moves—and they are fundamentally rhetorical in nature—were crucial.

The decision to commit to offering a Summer Institute gave us a purpose beyond simply fulfilling our earlier obligation, and it was our purpose, not the state legislatures or the university administration's. Particularly because we are located in different disciplines, even within different colleges (and as is fairly typical, our range of collegiate cultures is considerable), the unified focus was important: it was concrete, the larger tasks could be broken down and parceled out, there was much to learn in completing them, and it was a focus that was university-wide. It brought us together, and from the beginning, it meant that we would write together, first, of course, on the grant.

In order to write the grant to offer the Summer Institute, however, we needed to decide what kind of group we were. In other words, from the university's perspective, we were an ad hoc group appointed to complete a task. Could we write the grant as this ad hoc group, or did we need to become official? If so, official how? As a committee? As part of an already existing committee? Several of us frowned on the idea of joining a preexisting committee, and some of us believed that if we were made official—as making us a committee would do—we'd lose a part of what it was that we liked, the autonomy that comes from not being official. And as we reflected on what we had learned at the conference, we saw that the model of the teaching circle gave us an alternate way of thinking about who we might be: a group of faculty who work on our own projects, explore our own questions.

It's only fair, however, to point out that we weren't then, and aren't now, the typical faculty circle. As we learned about faculty circles, we encountered two models.

- One is university-supported, thus public in nature, highly focused—typically, on a specific like "methods of collaborative learning in class," for instance, or "use of the Internet in teaching"—and short-lived. The faculty meet regularly for a term or a year: say, once a month during this time. The support is, from the university perspective, small-scale: typically used to buy lunch for the members when they meet and to allow copying of materials. Sometimes a concluding report is presented to an academic office, sometimes not.

- A second teaching circle is informal and self-generating. It plays no official role in the academy, except that interested faculty are interested in the same topic and thus agree to pursue collaboratively.[2] This model of teaching circle has no set start-up nor concluding date.

Our circle seemed, from its inception, to be a hybrid model. Like the first, we wanted some university support, and the Institute wasn't going to be financially small-scale either. On the other hand, we weren't part of the university or faculty governance structure, and we were self-generating. As interesting, even by trying to sponsor the Summer Institute, we were assigning ourselves a public role, since the proposals are read by faculty and administrators across campus. Given that several members of the group are faculty leaders—for example, three of the seven have served as President of Faculty Council—playing a public leadership role seemed appropriate.

Still: what to call us? The "Ad Hoc UNC Charlotte Team on Faculty Enhancement and Evaluation" was accurate but not very handy. One member suggested the name "Baklava"; to my surprise, it stuck. For its somewhat opaque quality, it did make a kind of sense. The group likes to break bread (or in this case, Baklava) together, and given the ethnicities of the group members, we've had a kind of running contest between Middle Eastern Baklava and Greek Baklava. As important, and what I didn't fully appreciate then, was that assigning ourselves a name provided us with a kind of identity—both for ourselves and to others.[3]

In the intervening three years, Baklava has taken on various tasks.

- We were awarded the grant and presented our Summer Institute on Peer Observation in two sessions, one in May, one in September 1995.

- We have peer-observed many faculty in many colleges.

- We have hosted many "Faculty Dialogues"—short sessions on pedagogical and professional issues for faculty across campus—on topics as various as the evaluation write-up based on peer observation and the controversy about post-tenure review.

- We began to explore teaching circles as a vehicle for faculty development, and we presented a session on them at the American Association of Higher Education conference on Faculty Roles and Rewards in Atlanta in 1996.

- We started teaching circles for faculty new to UNC Charlotte in 1996–97, and we continued that effort for 1997–98.

- We presented several sessions on peer observation for a UNC system conference, the Carolina Colloquy, in the summer of 1997.

- We proposed, in conjunction with AAHE, a campus workshop for faculty in selected disciplines on teaching portfolios in 1997.

- We have written one article on peer observation and are considering writing a monograph on the topic.

- We just been asked to host a Teaching Dialogue on teaching circles.

What we have contributed through this teaching circle has been considerable. For one thing, we've demonstrated a new model of cross-curricular faculty leadership. Not unlike a research group, we consider what questions we want to take up, how we will go about seeking answers to them, if and when and where and how we will share them. Our particular focus has been on enhancing teaching—through peer observation, primarily—and on clarifying and maintaining the distinction between the enhancement of teaching and its evaluation. In forwarding that agenda, we have, I think, enhanced teaching itself.

My argument, then, in part: teaching circles contribute to better teaching, and better teaching is at the heart of WPA work. But (you may well be thinking) what's the connection here to writing? Is there a connection? There is, but it's not always direct; it's more subtle, every bit as lasting.

When I was asked to attend the conference with Baklava, I was not asked as a Writing Program Administrator, nor was I asked as a writing person. I was asked because I knew something about faculty development and about portfolios. My sense of faculty development, however, is that it necessarily involves writing—always indirectly, often directly. This has been true in the case of Baklava as well.

Our first task, for instance, was to write the report to the provost, then to write the grant for the Summer Institute. So writing together became the norm for the group. Then, through faculty development efforts, we found that a case study methodology provided a way into many of the issues we wanted to discuss. We reviewed the case studies that others had used, then began to develop our own—to illustrate some of the philosophy behind peer observation as well as some of the pragmatic issues that such observation entails. And we were developing our own experience, partly as a function of the many observations we had participated in, partly as a function of workshopping the ones we had developed. Through both kinds of work, we saw complications we'd been unaware of, we revised the case studies, we re-theorized our own understanding. In sum, we wrote, we learned, we wrote some more. Like the experiential model of faculty development practiced in the National Writing Project and in many WAC programs, we engaged in the same learning and writing practices we hope to see in classrooms. As important, the writing tasks were real; they were required in order for us to do what we had set out to accomplish. This, then, is one kind of writing work in the academy that teaching circles can assist.

A second kind of writing work takes a more direct form, though it's merely a function of knowing more people and working with them. Several Baklava colleagues and I have worked together in a sidebar way, at their request, on classroom questions and issues that are quite specifically writing-related. For instance, Debbie Langsam, the biologist, and I have taken up the role that e-mail can play in large lecture classes and have written about it together as well (Langsam and Yancey). The sociologist was interested in using portfolios in an honors class he was teaching; he asked me to assist him with that. The move in the class away from a comprehensive exam toward a portfolio that included reflection motivated several writing assignments in addition to the final reflective essay; different learning styles were valued in the new model. So Baklava is making writing work in the academy a part of classroom practice as well.

I claimed earlier that Baklava is a hybrid kind of teaching circle; that's true. It's also true that through thinking about Baklava as teaching circle and about what we were gaining from it, we conceptualized its value in yet another way— what we called a collaborative mentorship. When you bring together faculty with diverse interests and backgrounds who choose to work together, they can mentor each other. It's a relational, horizontal model of collaborative work— rather than a vertical, hierarchical model. In this model, then, what matters isn't academic rank, but the experience and expertise related to the topic at hand. I'm the most junior member of the group, for instance, but when it comes to assessment issues, given my research, I'm considered one of the seniors. When it comes to case study methodology, I'm back to junior again, not because of rank, but because several of my colleagues have both a breadth and a depth of knowledge and experience here that I don't. We assume expertise on everyone's part; we both share from and benefit from distributed expertise.[4]

And as I thought about teaching circles as collaborative mentorship, I realized that I'd been in another teaching circle. During my second year at UNC Charlotte, I'd been intrigued by if and how our first-year writing program connected to the kinds of writing going on within other departments. So very informally and on my own, I asked some faculty I knew were interested in teaching—my biologist colleague from Baklava, two faculty in English, and two more from geology and earth science—to form what I'm was coming to call a teaching circle, this one quite specifically focused on writing and teaching and learning. For two years, we met monthly. Other than my general inquiry, we had no set agenda, but this wasn't a problem; each one us seemed to have questions and issues that we wanted to think about with others. One colleague, for instance, was very frustrated with the ways some of his assignments were (not) working, so we looked at texts some students had produced, reading and comparing readings and interpreting together. In these discussions, we also talked assignments, methods of invention, ways of reading and responding to student texts. Another colleague shared with us her survey of the writing practices typical for biology majors on our campus: the frequency with which students wrote, the kinds of writing asked of them, the patterns we saw across years and courses. Was this sufficient writing, we considered. Did it include a sufficient range of writing, we asked.

As I say, we worked together for two years, and then we slowly found our schedules full, our selves occupied with other questions. Put in terms of the language of teaching circles, this one had run its life cycle. As it did, we learned a lot. We became better teachers.

One of Baklava's initiatives last year focused on providing a teaching circle for all interested faculty who were new to UNC Charlotte. Our purposes were few but crucial, we thought:

- to welcome UNC Charlotte faculty and provide them with a small sampling of our campus culture
- to associate new faculty with a cross-disciplinary group to help them gain another extra-departmental perspective on the campus
- to bring together new and experienced faculty to address faculty issues (e.g., insurance, our students, tenure, and promotion)
- to provide an additional faculty resource

With a colleague from the math department, who has also been involved in the AAHE Teaching Initiative and who is as well a Nations Bank Teacher of the Year nominee, I led our group. Again, my role was not to act as a WPA or to put writing in the classroom on anyone's agenda. But again, I assumed that if we talked good teaching, as I hoped we would, writing would be part of that discourse.

As it turned out, that belief was (again) correct. One of our first discussions—including faculty from business, information systems, and biology—addressed collaborative learning: why to use it, how to use it, how to be sure it worked well. Writing was identified as a vehicle for monitoring such learning, for demonstrating and documenting it. In other words, writing thus became a topic in a contextualized way related to a real rhetorical situation: as an item in a larger pedagogical inquiry. Writing as work in the university also appeared with reference to specific faculty member's needs. At a later session, for example, a new colleague asked that we focus on her teaching: she provided us with a living case study.

Like many who arrive on our campus, this faculty member had assumed that our students would behave as she had when a student: they would study hard and often, they would exercise diligence about their work, they would be devoted to (her) academic agenda. Our students don't quite satisfy these expectations. Fully 27 percent are nontraditional: they have families and jobs and churches and (surprisingly often) crises. Even the traditionally aged students typically have jobs, often have crises, and (even without those) are frequently not dedicated to studies in the way this colleague had assumed. She discovered this in two quick steps: (1) when the students failed the first written assignment of the term, the midterm; and (2) when the students reacted to this failure. In my view, there is a real misfit here, one that is all too common: the faculty member wants to be a good teacher, but doesn't understand the students, relies on a graduate seminar model of teaching (that doesn't lend itself to our undergraduates), and has no idea of what to do next. Nor should she, given that her graduate education provided no work in pedagogy. So now: she is ready to learn, the teaching circle a safe place for her to do so—about teaching and writing and bringing them together, among other things.

My colleague in math and I knew that we were doing something right the last time we met with our teaching circle. It was late April, we were moving relentlessly toward exams, and we were all tired. At the same time, the circle had been helpful, he and I had learned, too, so there was a feeling that we could bring it to a satisfactory conclusion.

They didn't want to conclude; rather, they wanted to adjourn temporarily; they requested that we continue meeting again the next year, even though they wouldn't be new faculty any longer.

I've described here three kinds of teaching circles: one explicitly focused on writing in the classroom; one providing acclimation for new faculty members; one faculty leadership model. They all "worked," if what we mean by work is that they allowed faculty to choose and pursue questions related to good teaching. What common practices assisted in this working?

In each case, we have had a nominal leader or leaders for logistics: someone who assumed responsibility for finding places to meet, food to eat, duplication of materials, and so on. Depending on the group, this person also may facilitate as well, helping raise issues, set priorities, play back what group members are saying. In providing this assistance, the leader helps shape the group.

In each case, we did break bread together. It's a truism that WAC programs have been built through the stomachs of faculty, and we used that understanding to good effect.

In each case, we set an agenda for the meeting, though we felt free to alter it as the need arose.

In each case, we established a routine for starting a meeting and closing it. In Baklava, since we are friends, there is a lot of social chat that precedes the work of the meeting; for the new teaching circle, we began by telling a funny story about something that had happened since we'd last met. Overall, then, there is a real mix between the social and the academic, which accounts in part for why these have worked, I think. Faculty in some ways are not unlike their students, and students tend to stay longer in college and do better when they form study groups that have both a social and an academic function. It may be that this is precisely what successful teaching circles do as well.

My story here is intended, of course, to make several arguments: that teaching circles contribute to good teaching in new ways; that to the extent that writing is a part of good teaching, writing is a part of teaching circles—in ways more multiple than I've outlined here, I expect. But this gives us a start. And I want to echo Barbara Cambridge and Ben McClelland in their argument that the work of the WPA involves collaboration of the official and unofficial variety.

On our campus, we have two official WPAs: one who directs the first-year composition program, one who directs the writing across the curriculum program. The faculty/administrators who serve in these positions have enormous opportunities: in general, to accept the invitation to work with faculty and graduate students to enhance teaching; to make connections across campus that only they can make; to provide vision for our university community. This kind of change-making is direct, systematic, coherent. There is another kind that works hand-in-glove with the first: the faculty-initiated, indirect. That is where the teaching circle fits in.

Good teaching involves writing: I believe this. Because I take this as a given, I simply wait for its appearance as a topic, and precisely because I'm included as something other than the writing person—the non-WPA—I have a kind of credibility I might not command otherwise. My colleagues know that I am a writing person, certainly, but that's not the role I play here. So I bring a kind of disinterestedness to the topic, and that, I think, enables me to exert more rather than less influence.

It is through bringing the programmatic change together with the indirect change that academic cultures are formed. To the extent that they work together, we create change that is meaningful. The work of writing in the university gets done in multiple ways. We have official programs, and we have quieter agents of change.

Teaching circles are one of those quieter agents of change.

Notes

1. In practice, what has happened on many campuses is that only junior faculty are observed, senior faculty are asked to observe without being provided with any assistance in doing so, and the exercise becomes merely that. Our efforts were intended to resist its becoming merely this exercise.

2. Because this variety of teaching circle is ubiquitous but not documented, less is known about it.

3. Lunsford and Ede report on research teams that take their own names, but in general the taking of a group name is uncommon. It seems to have benefited Baklava: for instance, it allows us a common identity apart from our individual identities; it permits some members of the team to participate when others cannot.

4. And we have developed our own expertise, as well, as I indicate. Also, there is research elsewhere to suggest that even when senior faculty are asked to mentor junior faculty, the senior faculty find themselves learning as much as the colleagues they are mentoring.

The Writing Committee at Work

Toby Fulwiler, Committee Chair
Susan Dinitz
Christina Doykos Breen
Paul Eschholz
Jean Kiedaisch
Tony Magistrale

To tell the story of the writing program at The University of Vermont is to describe the everyday work of the English Department's Writing Committee, which is exactly what I told my editor, former colleague, and friend Diana George when she invited me to write a chapter for this collection. Vermont's current writing program has evolved over the past three decades through the visions and actions of a number of committed individuals, most of whom continue to make sure it works.

In the late 1960s Paul Eschholz established the current first-year writing program and in the mid-1970s started The Vermont Writing Project to train state teachers in the writing process. In the 1980s Sue Dinitz and Jean Kiedaisch developed our writing center into a thriving campus institution while Mary Jane Dickerson, Tony Magistrale, and I took turns developing the several dimensions of our ongoing writing-across-the-curriculum program. On and off, most of us have also taken turns training the graduate teaching fellows who teach most of the first-year writing courses and take turns serving on the writing committee. In other words, no single person speaks for the whole writing program.

Accordingly, my colleagues and I who serve on the Writing Committee have composed the following set of verbal snapshots to explain where our writing program came from, to describe how it operates, and to suggest where next it is going.

Toby Fulwiler
Chair, Writing Committee

1969

Paul—There is no writing program. When I arrive ABD in American Studies from the University of Minnesota, the College of Arts and Sciences has voted no single course important enough to be required, and the Department of English has just abolished first-year composition. However, it doesn't take long for colleagues around the University to start murmuring about weak student writing. More importantly, students begin asking for opportunities to work more deliberately on their writing skills, but few writing courses are now offered. In reading the work of Don Murray, Ken Macrorie, and Peter Elbow, I start to think that just maybe it's time to consider a process-oriented first-year writing course.

Toby—Paul's story is, of course, before my time at Vermont. In 1969 I'm still at Madison, finishing my doctorate in American literature, still believing that Ph.D. English professors, after paying their dues, teach only literature. None of my grad school professors still taught writing courses—why should I think any differently? The only book so far to influence my own teaching of writing is Strunk and White's *The Elements of Style*. It is not until 1976, when I take my first tenure-track job at Michigan Tech and meet Art Young, that I, too, learn from Murray, Macrorie, Elbow, and James Britton who teach me about "writing to learn" which becomes the foundation for my ideas about writing across the curriculum.

1973

Paul—"Eschholz, can I see you in my office," an obviously upset department chair intones. "You've got a problem!" It's late June, I have a softball game tonight and cannot imagine what's wrong.

"What's the matter?" I inquire.

"Just got the enrollment figures back, and there's a crisis. Your new writing course didn't go. I don't know what we're going to do with all these teachers and the schedule."

"What do you mean 'didn't go'? I don't follow."

"According to the registrar's figures, only twenty-three students are enrolled and you talked me into offering all those sections of 'Written Expression.' You were sure they'd all fill up," he says, looking me square in the eye.

Talk about feeling alone. I haven't really started my new post as Director of First-Year English, don't have tenure, and now am already attending the funeral of our new writing course. Has my gamble on the students' interest in writing backfired?

No. It turns out my chair has misread the enrollment figures, and instead of twenty-three students enrolled in thirty sections with twenty-two spaces in each, only twenty-three openings remain. When he realizes this, he breaks into a smile and says, "WE have a winner!"

1976

Paul—We start the Vermont Writing Program. Building on the success of our new first-year writing program, we apply to the National Endowment for the Humanities for $200,000 for two years to introduce writing process ideas to Vermont public school teachers. With NEH funds, Al Rosa and I host eighty-nine Vermont public school teachers in a four-week summer institute on the teaching of writing. Guest faculty include Don Murray, Don Graves, Janet Emig, Mary Ellen Giacobbe, and Walker Gibson—the best in the business to support our early work in Vermont.

1983

Toby—I become the Director of Writing at The University of Vermont. Teaching seven years at Michigan Tech has taught me that teaching writing is serious academic work. UVM hires me because its College of Arts and Sciences is on the verge of passing a four-course writing requirement. I teach first-year and advanced writing, introductory American literature, and a two-credit graduate-training seminar. I also join the College task force whose agenda is selling a four-course composition requirement to the faculty and begin a writing-across-the-curriculum program called the Faculty Writing Project to introduce instructors from all disciplines to using more writing in their teaching.

Sue—The new Writing Center begins to take root. In 1982 Kathy Skubikowski, an adjunct instructor, created a writing center by locating it in and funding it through our Living/Learning Center, a dorm complex combining residential and academic programs. When Kathy is offered a position at Middlebury, I write the grant to fund the center for another year. Ten tutors, several of whom live together in a suite, set up appointments, keep records, do publicity—in short, run the whole show. Training the tutors and running the Writing Center is considered a 3/8th time position; as director, I am invited to join the Writing Committee.

1984

Tony—In conducting faculty writing workshops I learn that some issues translate more easily than others: the messy nature of the writing process, the importance of audience, purpose, and voice, the usefulness of multiple-draft assignments. Other ideas prove harder to sell: the concept of writing to learn, the use of journals in science courses, and the value in early drafts of ignoring spelling. Now a second-year assistant professor, I rely on my graduate school training at Pittsburgh, under William Coles, for my knowledge of composition theory and pedagogy. But nobody has taught me how to explain these concepts to colleagues across the curriculum who are as vague in their knowledge of writing as I am of the specifics of their disciplines. Some already sense the connection between writing and learning while others seem forever fixated on grammar and spelling. Some trust that something interesting will happen; others are worried this will be another one of those English classes they hated in high school—Did I really give up my last day of vacation to attend a writing workshop?

1985

Sue—The Writing Center joins forces with other academic support programs to create The Learning Cooperative. We establish a budget and administrative support (no more making our own appointments or maintaining the database) by having ties to the Student Affairs side of the university. The other program directors hold full-time staff rather than part-time faculty positions—but I value my faculty status and resist the pressure to keep regular hours or let a secretary schedule appointments for me.

Paul—School districts around the state now advertise for teachers trained to teach the writing process. Two years after federal funding ceases for the Vermont Writing Program, which trained some six hundred teachers between the years 1977–1982, we institutionalize process writing as the cornerstone of our pre-service course for prospective teachers of English—now a regular offering in the English Department. We also offer in-service courses evenings and during the summer to continue training Vermont teachers and school administrators.

1986

Toby—The Arts and Sciences faculty vote in a new core curriculum but leave out a writing requirement. Everybody agrees that one required writing course is not enough, but nobody wants four. We'll deal with it, they say, next year. All the other colleges in the university—Agriculture, Engineering, Education, Allied Health, Business—continue to require first-year writing.

1987

Tony—Writing-across-the-curriculum workshop co-leaders now include full professors Mike Strauss in chemistry and Hank Steffens in history who are able to reach faculty Toby and I cannot. Even so, every time we co-direct a workshop, participants start out anxious and a bit suspicious of one another. After all, we represent different disciplines and, more often than not, have different agendas. But as we work together for two long days—sharing stories, posing and solving problems, writing and rewriting, eating and drinking together—a spirit of cooperation emerges. At its very best moments, these workshops remind us why we became teachers in the first place—a love of learning new things, certainly, but also a renewal of the urge to become a little bit better at reaching students, at the art of teaching itself.

1988

Toby—English major enrollments are up—400 and climbing—but faculty positions remain frozen. Everyone is teaching flat out to meet the demand for upper level English courses, so I end up the only tenure-track English instructor who teaches first-year composition. Eleven graduate teaching fellows and nearly the same number of adjunct faculty teach the sixty annual sections of "Written Expression," which require weekly drafts of personal, analytical, and research writing. In these workshop-style classes, students read papers to each other, submit them for assessment in portfolios, and often publish their best efforts in student edited class books. Budgets tight, the College of Arts and Sciences still doesn't get around to proposing a writing requirement for first-year students.

1989

Jean—My turn to direct the Writing Center, now a full-time faculty position. We schedule hour-long appointments with students, enough time to find out how classes are going and to do some writing during the session, showing students techniques or strategies they might use for future assignments. We also establish relationships with faculty across the curriculum by presenting tutorial demonstrations at the twice-a-year faculty workshops, sometimes followed up by developing projects with faculty and their classes: An art history professor has groups of students meet with a tutor, sketches in hand, to discuss the piece for their "looking exercise." A civil engineering teacher has students bring letters to consumers about their water meters.

Toby—*Reading, Writing, and the Study of Literature* is published by Random House. Ten of us in the English Department write, revise, and edit this textbook for junior English majors: Half the chapters focus on literary genres (e.g., poetry, fiction, and drama), while the other half focus on student genres (journals, critical essays, research writing). This project sparks two other books collaboratively written by Vermont faculty, *Angles of Vision* (McGraw Hill, 1992) and *Community of Voices* (Macmillan, 1992). All three books are written more to keep us writing and working together than to make a profit—which is a good thing, because we don't.

1990

Tony—On the first day of the twenty-first Faculty Writing Project workshop, the guy with gray hair in the back hasn't said a thing all morning. He looks like he once played ball—maybe an interior lineman—guard or tackle. He doesn't look very comfortable, always squirming, running his meaty left hand through his hair and back down the side of his head. After the session on using journals in the classroom, he shifts his weight to the left, then to the right and announces, "Look, I teach concrete. The mathematics and physics of concrete. My students go out and build the bridges that you drive over. If they make a mistake, if they get out there and 'speculate about the possibilities' of using concrete, your families could die. Can't see the relevance of 'exploratory writing' to what I do. I teach concrete, and what my students learn from me is as solid as concrete."

1991

Toby—First-year writing is once again on the College agenda: The new Dean's new writing task force is prepared to recommend first-year and senior writing seminars as core college requirements; to implement these will require eight new faculty positions. In April, the university experiences the first of what seem to be an endless series of financial shortfalls, and the proposal is tabled.

Sue—The Writing Committee convinces the English faculty to separate the training of our Graduate Teaching Fellows (GTFs) from the graduate-level course in composition and rhetoric. GTF training becomes a condition of employment, consisting of a week-long workshop before the first semester begins and weekly meetings throughout the first year. I train the GTFs while Toby plans and teaches "Studies in Rhetoric and Composition," the department's first graduate course in the teaching of writing.

1992

Toby—My colleagues refuse, for the ninth consecutive year, to recruit an assistant professor with a Ph.D. in composition. We have thirty-two tenured faculty with degrees in literature and creative writing, none in composition. I walk out of this September faculty meeting before it's over. The next day I resign from the department Executive Committee and refuse, the rest of the year, to attend department meetings. I teach well, enjoy my students, and sulk in my tent.

Sue—What, I wonder, is the best way to "train" first-year MA students to teach writing? Paul stresses one-to-one conferences. Toby focuses on provocative revision. I see the course as introducing students to academic writing. While we all agree that writing should be taught as a process, it's clear there are many processes.

1993

Paul—I teach "Writing Vermont Life," a seminar for senior English majors. Because we don't offer any journalism courses, students pack writing seminars whenever they're scheduled. Word spreads quickly that students who enroll in "Vermont Life" will also work with a "real," live magazine editor, since my friend Tom Slayton, the editor of *Vermont Life*, assists me every other week. In preparation for one of his visits, Tom asks each of the eighteen students to write a query letter to him proposing a feature story on a Vermont topic. I make transparencies of the letters and, in class, Tom responds to each letter as a professional editor. What an eye-opener for students to see what attracts his attention and what doesn't.

Toby—Ten years now, and our writing-across-the-curriculum workshops continue to enroll from fifteen to twenty-five faculty each time they're offered. We now count on a small annual budget from the Provost's office to pay for facilities, supplies, and meals for two days at an off-campus conference center. Faculty spend the first day exploring "writing to learn" strategies (keeping journals, writing letters), the second day, "learning to write" strategies (composing, revising, editing, and sharing). By now workshop co-leaders include Tony, Mary Jane, and Bill Biddle in English as well as Hank Steffens in history and Michael Strauss in chemistry. Even without a curricular mandate, the pedagogical use of writing now occurs in many places throughout the curriculum.

Sue—The ideas that I introduce in our training seminars are interpreted differently by each GTF. I consider how they bring to their teaching their own pasts as writers, students, and teachers, and how these pasts shape the ways in which they see the course and their roles. I try to teach them how to think like teachers—to be reflective practitioners. I'm less concerned with what they are doing in their classrooms than with their willingness to examine how they get there.

Toby—The Writing Committee proposes and the department passes a new set of upper-level writing courses: "Personal Voice," "Reading and Writing Autobiography," and "The Art of the Essay." These join the already established "Advanced Writing" courses (one each in fiction, non-fiction, and poetry) and the senior writing seminars that Paul and I now offer on a regular basis. With the literary canon under attack from leftists, feminists, and theorists alike, writing courses seem safe additions to the otherwise contested curriculum.

1994

Sue—I discover that freedom has its price. Beginning teachers often founder, hoping someone will right them by telling them the secret of how to teach writing. But I have no secrets to tell. One GTF decides that she will have students write the first paper (interpreting an advertisement) collaboratively in a group, the second paper (a research essay) in pairs, and the third paper (a personal narrative) individually. While I understand her logic, it worries me that students will not experience writing as an individual until the final weeks of the semester. When I raise questions about this sequence, she stops trusting me, creating a tension in our relationship we never work through. How do you encourage people to plan their own courses, yet intervene positively when you see mistakes?

Toby—At times I burn out and tire of being a traveling salesman for writing across the curriculum, organizer of collaborative publication projects, director of first-year composition, and minority voice for hiring a colleague with a Ph.D. in composition. But then I teach my classes, meet my students, and read their writing—and discover, much to my relief, that I love my work and have the best job in the world.

1995

Toby—A new department chair. A new mood. An equal treatment of all areas of English study. And a dissolving of factions. I chair a committee that recruits and hires a tenure-track colleague with a Ph.D. in composition. She has, in fact, wonderfully eclectic credentials including rhetorical and literary theory, ethnographic research, National Writing Project experience, and publishes short stories. Yippee.

Sue—On my recommendation, the Writing Committee proposes that all Graduate Teaching Fellows who teach first-year writing be required to take Studies in Composition (English 340) to help them learn the why behind the what in their teaching. However, the Graduate Committee denies our request, and the graduate student representative on the committee, reporting back to us, bursts into tears, overwhelmed, feeling as if she's the only one representing writing to a committee of full-time faculty who don't respect English 1.

Toby—Ruth Fairchild writes a Master's thesis examining "student-generated rubrics for revision"—the first composition thesis in the department. Ruth is hired immediately to help direct the writing program at Willmar Community College in Minnesota, the job of her choice. I've been in the department a dozen years, and it's the first thesis I direct. Already other graduate students are inquiring about similar possibilities.

Toby—I teach "Local Knowledge, Personal Voice," a graduate seminar focused on writing rather than teaching writing. The reading list ignores David Bartholomae, James Berlin, and Lester Faigley and features instead William Least Heat Moon, Annie Dillard, and the students as writers themselves. The writing assignments include weekly letters as well as essays on place and language autobiographies in many drafts each. The GTFs in the group confess to revising seriously for the first time in their lives—laughing, they explain that now when they teach writing to first-year students, they no longer feel like frauds.

1996

Sue—The seven new GTFs ask the four second-year GTFs to share their current ideas for teaching English 1. The veterans are excited about teaching and confident about the way they have shaped their courses, and I am pleased.

> *Heather Marcovitch:* My course is about thinking. I care less about the written products than about the reasoning I witness in the student papers. I begin with the interpreting a text assignment because that allows us to explore the difference between summary and analysis or interpretation. Then for the research essay we explore what makes arguments effective.

> *Kathryn Morris:* I spend all summer clipping articles from newspapers and magazines and put together my own collection of readings with seven different sections that, as a whole, introduce lots of ideas about American culture. Students use this as a base to create their own books, adding in published articles they find or pieces written in the class. Students write a paper for each section responding to something in the readings and then choose two to revise. An editorial board for each section responds to the drafts.

> *Anthony Shiu:* I only teach readings well when I care about them myself, so like Katherine, I spend the summer choosing readings that I like and that will help students think about how identity shapes perspective—readings by Southern, African American, Asian American, women, as well as gay/lesbian writers. Now, students use these readings to see how people "other" from themselves write about the world that surrounds them. For example, we read and discuss Hisaye Yamamoto's short story "Wilshire Bus" examining "whiteness," which leads students into extended writings on how their "identity" affects their writing, thinking, and acting.

Christina Doykos Breen—Students write about an experience that has changed them, about the experience of reading *How the Garcia Girls Lost Their Accent,* and about experiencing their community (they each do a community service project). But my class sometimes resists. So today I ask students to sit on the floor in pairs facing each other. With no place to turn, no notebook to doodle in, and no friends to distract, they read to each other, listen, talk back, discuss, laugh, question-making a symphony of first-year writer voices. Their involvement comes out of their own writing, out of their own interest in each other's writing. In these fleeting fifty minutes, I have them, they have each other, and I begin to feel like a writing teacher.

Toby—The Faculty Writing Project joins forces with the Committee to Promote Teaching Excellence, jointly sponsoring a series of workshops on the theme "Alternatives to Lecturing." Eighty-five faculty members participate in the all-day January workshop to talk teaching. Many of the sessions are led by alumni of the Faculty Writing Project, and I am pleased. At the same time, I worry that participation in the thirteen-year-old WAC program is dwindling— at August workshops, adjuncts now outnumber full-time faculty two to one. When I attend a February WAC conference in Charleston, colleagues from other institutions explain strategies for preserving and maintaining their writing-across-the-curriculum programs. I wonder, however, if such programs shouldn't be so much preserved and maintained, as allowed to evolve naturally into other dimensions?

Paul—The National Writing Project arrives in Vermont, fourteen years after the last summer institute of The Vermont Writing Program. Although our earlier work paved the way for Vermont's statewide portfolio assessment program, many of the teachers we trained have retired, moved to other states, or left teaching. A new generation of teachers needs training and a writing program to call their own. In July, twenty-three Vermont teachers meet for four weeks at the University to teach each other best practices and to become writers themselves. All of us on the Writing Committee participate in one way or another to make the Project work.

Toby—My new composition colleague resigns from the Writing Committee, the two of us unable to work together. So much for the idea that compatible credentials lead to compatible program development. Oops.

Jean—Now in its fourteenth year, the Writing Center sees 1,000 students in 1500 contacts annually. Ties to the English Department remain loose, maintained largely through joint membership on the Writing Committee, especially, through regular conversations with Sue Dinitz, who makes sure the GTFs learn how the center can help their English 1 students.

1997

Sue—The English Department gains priority use of two new computer classrooms designed into our renovated Old Mill building. Toby and I, along with GTFs Megan and Nicole, are the first to use these rooms:

> *Megan Fulwiler:* Our 75-minute computer class is full of writing: I pose questions, we all write. We end weekly student presentations with a free-write.

Students share papers, then turn to the computers to record feedback. I individualize instruction: "Dave, what did that locker room smell like?" "Courtney, what if you describe only the first hour of your Outward Bound Solo trip?" The computers make writing more immediate, more accessible, freeing the students to cut, copy, paste, delete, and revise on the spot.

Nicole Aljoe: I find myself frequently falling victim to the technology trap. Too often, I focus on the malfunctioning computer and forget to focus on the writing lesson. As a Mac user I have trouble helping most of my students who are Windows users. And the room is too small for 25 people and 25 computers, and 25 comfy swivel arm chairs. And the hum of the computers and the heat from the monitors is sometimes oppressive. Have I made a mistake by depending on computers and inadvertently putting technology at the center of my classroom?

Megan: Computers add a whole new dimension to teaching. I still get the old questions: What is our homework? How many pages? Now I also get:

> "How do I eject my disc?"
>
> "How do I save a file?"
>
> "Why doesn't the printer print?"
>
> "How do I save again?"
>
> "I forgot my disc, should I stay in class?"
>
> "Anybody find the disc I left here on Tuesday?"
>
> "Help! My 'm' key is typing commas!"
>
> "My computer just froze!"

And so I bend to technology. Small group work? Tough in narrow aisles. Student discussion? Hearing over the hum of the machines a challenge. Writing workshop? I limit groups to 2–3 and we spread out into the hallway. Teaching? I limit my presentations to short moments of theatre at the beginning and end of class and still find myself hoarse by day's end.

Nicole: Students write more and more often. What were often lazy four-sentence journal entries in conventional classrooms now become faster full-screen entries. In-class writing exercises, revising and editing are easier and faster on computer. Revision moves explored in class—switching perspectives, changing forms, adding detail—now show up on finished drafts. At the same time, class is, by default more student-centered. While it's hard to get whole class attention, group work and writing workshops work consistently well. A whole class prayer to the happy technology goddess also helps.

Sue—The Writing Committee proposes changing the size and number of the GTF writing classes. The current load is one class of 25 students first semester, two classes of 25 the second, two again the third, and one the fourth. We suggest, instead, two classes of 18 each all four semesters, resulting in a similar number of students taught, but a more even teaching load, a better chance at classroom community, and a better introduction to the teaching of writing. Both the Department Chair and the Graduate Committee support us. This is easy harmony, an unfamiliar way to run a writing program.

Jean—An uneasy relationship between the Writing Center and the English Department: The past and present chair have agreed that the director of the Writing Center is a staff, not a faculty position and has no formal relationship with the English Department, leaving up in the air travel funds for CCCC as well as membership on the writing committee. (What am I doing in this article, anyway?)

Chorus—We think we've come a long way. Looking back on more than a quarter century of work in and around the University of Vermont, we see writing-to-learn taking place throughout the curricula and learning-to-write becoming more realistic, spontaneous, practical, and fun. Why, we wonder, hasn't the teaching of writing always been that way? And we both think the old divisions between composition and literature faculty may be gone forever. In addition, the Writing Center is a fact of life, as are smaller sections of English 1, senior and graduate writing courses, Masters' theses in composition, writing across the curriculum, and the Vermont Writing Project. Throughout the university and the state both writing and the teaching of writing have become highly valued enterprises.

However, there are also things we don't see and are still working on: Few tenured English faculty teach first-year writing, no new tenure-track writing faculty are being recruited, no writing course is required anywhere in the Arts and Sciences curriculum. The Faculty Writing Project, as a focus of faculty development, is clearly slowing down, and the computer-equipped classrooms, so far, have proved a mixed blessing—be careful what you ask for. . . .

At the same time, no one has benefited more from being part of Vermont's extended writing community than we who've developed and guided the university's up-and-down writing program these past few years. By teaching writing, developing writing programs, and observing our students become writers, in the end, it's we, as perhaps this chapter suggests, who have grown the most as teachers, scholars, and writers.

Envisioning Literacy

Establishing E-Mail in a First-Year Program

Beth Daniell

This is a conversion story in three acts. The first act involves an e-mail pilot project for English 101. The second act focuses on the technological meltdown that occurred just as the e-mail assignment was being institutionalized in the first-year composition program. The third act, the happy ending, includes the achievement of electronic literacy and, in addition, transformation.

Act One: Beginning E-Mail

Act One begins in July 1994, immediately after I became the writing program administrator (WPA) in the English department at Clemson University in South Carolina. Someone at the university's Division of Computing and Information Technologies (DCIT) called for an appointment to talk about introducing what they called "computer literacy" in first-year English. I set up a meeting for four or five people from DCIT and four or five people from English. At the meeting, the DCIT people asked for two class days of English 101 to tell first-year students about the computer capabilities on campus—computing, word processing, graphics, e-mail, the Internet. The English faculty—including me, former WPA Elisa Sparks, and department computer expert Tharon Howard—suggested, instead, one day for hands-on learning with no overview presentations. All the English professors agreed that lectures by computer enthusiasts listing the wonders of the machine can bore, bewilder, or frighten the uninitiated. Besides, old hands at first-year comp, none of us put much store by lecture.

We wanted something first-year students could learn to do in fifty minutes and something that would be a genuine part of the writing or reading in the curriculum of English 101. And instead of beginning with all 1800 first-year students or the 1000 in classes taught by TAs, we suggested a pilot program of 10 sections, about 220 students. We asked DCIT for a simple hands-on lesson on e-mail to prepare the students for an assignment that I would design.

During the August TA Workshop, I asked for volunteers for the e-mail project and got five, people who for the most part already knew how to use the Clemson mainframe. I had never used e-mail. In order for me to participate,

Tharon "acquired" a modem for me and hooked it up to my little Mac Classic. The e-mail program was slow, and correcting typos was so difficult that I never did catch on. Since I am a terrible typist, my outgoing messages were damn near unreadable, and my own first-year students complained bitterly.

Among the first-year students there was fear and loathing—and resistance. At that time, in 1994, no more than a quarter of a given English class knew anything about computers. And those two to five students were usually real computer jocks, almost invariably white men from privileged backgrounds majoring in engineering. In 1994 most of our students had never used e-mail. Some from the rural (read poor) areas of the state had never touched a computer. Two African American women in my class, both good students by every other measure, finally just refused to take part in the assignment. Participating TAs reported similar experiences. In that first year, we saw the socioeconomic order dramatically recapitulated in our classrooms.

In the e-mail assignments, however, we saw something that made the clunky mainframe and the insecurities of the first-year students lose significance. The assignment we had given them was a simple 250-word reaction to Maxine Hong Kingston's "No Name Woman" followed by a fifty-word response to at least one classmate's post. What developed, as the participating TAs and I watched, was real conversation, genuine argument. The students, certainly not all 220, but most of them, were engaged in interpreting Kingston's narrative:

It was incest; the grandfather was the baby's father . . .

No, it was the neighbor . . .

She was a tramp who betrayed her husband who'd gone off to America to make money for the family . . .

No, she'd fallen in love . . .

No, the neighbor raped her . . .

Is it rape if she doesn't say no?

But what if she doesn't think she really has a choice? If she believes she has go along with what the man wants?

Man, I'm glad we don't live in such a backward culture as China.

What about the double standard on this campus?

It's not the same.

Yeah, right. If guys do it, it's cool; if girls do it, they get called whores and sluts. . . .

It was wrong her for to kill herself . . .

It was wrong to kill the baby . . .

How is killing the baby different from having an abortion?

But what else could she do?

She could get a job . . .

Oh, get real, women couldn't do that in China back then . . .

The mother told the story so the daughter would know the family history . . .

No, the mother told the story so the daughter wouldn't have sex. Like that urban legend "The Hook" . . .

Yeah, American moms do tell stories like this. Before I came to Clemson, my mom told me this story about a girl on her hall her first year at college . . .

From this, we could talk about the function of stories, multiple points of views, changing our minds when we consider what other people have to say, finding new insights when we look back on stories to ask questions. Interestingly, reports from TAs not participating in the e-mail experiment indicated that the Kingston piece did not engender this sort of give-and-take in classroom discussion. We hypothesized that it was easier for first-year students to talk seriously about a sexual issue when they didn't have to look at their classmates' faces. Even this much anonymity (the messages were signed with real names) seemed to give the women students the courage to contradict the men.

Beginning e-mail had taken, it seemed to me, an inordinate amount of time, but the discussion the students had on the list showed the potential. Thus encouraged, I pressed on.

Act Two: Meltdown

Act Two begins in the summer of 1995 with the good news that—in bureaucratese—it has been decided that the mainframe will eventually disappear and servers will be used instead. In anticipation, a new e-mail program, Eudora, is going to be installed in all the labs. What's more, Eudora will be linked to a Novell server so that no matter what lab on campus students use, they can access their e-mail. Further, I am assured, Eudora is incredibly user-friendly, and, yes, making corrections will be as easy as with a word processing program. The DCIT people promised that we'd have none of the problems we'd had with the old system. Cutting and pasting and spell checking will be simple, they say. From what they show me, Eudora looks like the greatest thing since canned beer.

One day in my office there's a new computer, a left-over from the provost's office, to be sure, but a real upgrade for me, a Mac IIsi. With Eudora. Hooked up to the ethernet. No more modem. No more busy signals. I can talk on the phone and e-mail at the same time. I've joined the twentieth century. I actually enjoy e-mail. It's fast, efficient, and easy to learn and to use. I recall the discussion in *Zen and the Art of Motorcycle Maintenance* about the importance of having good tools. And so, even though I'm nervous about starting with a new system whose bugs have not been worked out, I say yes: All the TAs will participate in the e-mail project. With twenty-three TAs, each teaching two classes with 23 students per class, that's about 1100 first-year students who will have at least one required e-mail assignment. I want to start the project at the beginning of the semester so that we have time to build on the success I anticipate.

The DCIT folks ask for a couple of hours during the August Workshop to show the TAs how to use Eudora. But during Workshop week, they postpone twice: The system isn't ready. It will be ready by next Tuesday. So we arrange a special tutorial for the TAs on Tuesday night. But on Tuesday there's more trouble. The DCIT techs on campus and the Novell designers in California had been up all weekend trying to get the interface to work. On Tuesday night the TAs get a lecture telling them how to log on to the system and what Eudora can do. Because the TAs are trying to get ready to teach for the very first time on Thursday and Friday, they are pissed and let me know it: A waste of our time, they say. The TAs who are savvy about the mainframe can use the old e-mail system, but the inexperienced ones are understandably anxious. I am not happy. But DCIT promises everything will be fine before the next week when the first-year students start the e-mail classes.

After the first two days, however, the server crashes. Students go to the labs in McAdams Hall for the e-mail lessons, but nothing works. They get lectures about potential, not hands-on training. They are told how to log on, but they don't get to practice doing it. (*Lecture about a computer's capability ain't worth spit, I fume.*) Things get better. The next few classes work. Then, as if on cue, when the TAs start giving the "No Name Woman" assignment, the entire system goes dead. And remains so for days. I am constantly e-mailing or calling DCIT to reschedule classes. I am more than not happy; I am furious. They keep telling me things will be fine on Wednesday, and then things aren't fine. Then it will be Monday, and on Monday no one in the entire university can even log on.

I rant. I rave. I say all the bad words I know. I have a thousand students who can't do their homework and twenty-three brand new scared TAs who are trying to teach something that won't work. They want to convey an air of confidence to their students, but instead they feel humiliated in front their classes. The braver ones ask if they can just cancel the e-mail assignment altogether. I am reluctant to agree.

But, finally, after the days become weeks, I e-mail Tharon Howard, our department computer person: "When do I call this off?" and copy to DCIT. My DCIT contact is hurt and angered, since she has worked hard to please me, arranging the new computer and all, and besides, she tells me, it's not their fault that the technology failed; they've been killing themselves to make this work. Now *I* feel like the bad guy, and I respond with self-blame: Maybe I was wrong to get into this to start with. Maybe I was wrong to try to begin the semester with the e-mail project. Surely I was wrong to lose to my temper. Maybe I am wrong now to consider canceling. I should have known.

This is worse than I had ever anticipated. This the WPA version of the dark night of the soul. I never want to see another computer as long as I live. I feel totally alone. No one seems to understand why I'm upset—except my grad school buddy Mara Holt, the WPA at Ohio University, who gets me through the worst. She assures me this fiasco is not my fault, reminding me that clairvoyance is not one of my gifts and so I couldn't possibly have known the technology would fail. Then she tells me to take a day off and read a murder mystery.

In a day or two, I regain some composure. I call my DCIT contact to tell her that I do appreciate all that she and her staff have done. But I give the TAs individual choice: go on with the project or drop it altogether or modify it if they can. Almost all drop it. Clearly, this first attempt to institutionalize electronic communication in the first-year English program is a failure. It is, I realize, the most remarkable failure I have ever been associated with. I realize, as well, that pedagogical failure is not something I know much about. Apparently it is not something I deal with well, either.

By the end of October, Eudora is working fine, but it's too late.

In November I go to NCTE in San Diego to participate in a roundtable Tharon had proposed about computers and literacy. My part was supposed to be a discussion of the e-mail project in 101 as an example of the social construction of literacy, what, in other words, we'd seen during the pilot project and what I had assumed would take place large scale in the second year. In San Diego, the men go first. Tharon, Fred Kemp, and Wayne Butler, all recognized for their expertise with computers, envision a utopian future where everyone will have access to information and the means of political empowerment. They sound—in my bitterness—as if they believe that the computer is going to bring the Age of Aquarius, to say nothing of Liberty, Equality, and Fraternity. I want to scream: It's resting on technology we couldn't make work on our campus just to do one tiny little e-mail project with a thousand first-year students; *this* is supposed to save Western Civilization?

Then Linda Brodkey talks about electronic technology as a male narrative, emphasizing the inequitable ways electronic resources are distributed, pointing out that young white men have access in ways that women and people of color do not, exactly what we had seen at Clemson. I want to hug her. Later Tharon and I talk about how interesting it is that this panel demonstrates that our experiences with computers are gendered. How would I have responded to the technological meltdown if I had been a man? How would the TAs would have reacted if the group had been mostly men instead of mostly women?

When the roundtable comes to me, I begin with two premises: the social nature of literacy and Ann Berthoff's definition of literacy as "the realized capacity to construct and construe in graphic form representations of our recognitions" (142). Then I talk about literacy as a function of technology—sharpened sticks, clay, papyrus, ink, quills, parchment, paper, the printing press, the things that make the graphic forms possible. My point was that when the technology fails—when the pens or quills or software breaks, when you cannot write, when I cannot read what you have written—there is no literacy. The audience cheers. Obviously, I am not the only person in the room who has experienced serious technological failure.

During the spring semester I talk with my contact at DCIT about ways to improve the project. We agree that the meltdown had been horrendous for both of us, but agree as well to try to learn from the experience. She and I realize it probably was jumping the gun to try to institutionalize an e-mail project for more than a thousand first-year students and simultaneously build what has turned out to be the third largest Novell network in the world. And I begin to accept that no one except another WPA knows what it means to be responsible for a thousand first-year students and 23 inexperienced graduate student instructors. Anyhow, by this time Eudora is working swimmingly.

So I try again.

Act Three: Virtual and Actual Community

By the summer of 1996, Clemson's new president has mandated state-of-the-art computer technology for the whole campus, including humanities faculty. The English department surprises me with a new Power Mac; the president's initiative gives me a new edition of Eudora as well as Netscape Navigator. During the summer DCIT and I make plans for the TA Workshop. This time things work. Beautifully. The only hitches are a few TA passwords, easily fixed.

During the summer I had tinkered with the e-mail assignment to give it more weight in the final grade and had worked up two different assignments so that TAs could have not only some choice but some ownership. A few TAs came up with their own assignments in addition to or instead of the ones I offered. Two or three of the TAs moved all the reading responses to the class list. One or two had students critique a peer draft on e-mail. A few asked students to share, by means of the list, the initial freewrites they were doing in preparation for a formal essay; these TAs believe that the resulting papers were better overall than those without the electronic sharing. I was astounded at the initiative, energy, creativity, and enthusiasm of these TAs in using the e-mail lists.

There was still some resistance: from TAs who were adept at the mainframe because they couldn't dial up Eudora from home; from others because going to the labs on campus was inconvenient and reading messages from 48 students was time-consuming. But, overall, these TAs seemed to think almost everything about teaching composition, including the e-mail assignment, was interesting or fun. Watching them try new things, take risks, ask for advice, and work together helped me see the TAs from the year before in a new light. I had believed that the e-mail snafu had caused the TAs in my second year to turn off to me or to the writing program, but now I began to see that it had been more complicated than that.

In the third year, the e-mail project worked for the first-year students. This doesn't mean they all liked it or they became equally adept at using e-mail. But it does mean that most of the English 101 students at Clemson were required to participate in an e-mail assignment. Which means that from here on out, this kind of literacy event is assumed as part of doing English in our program.

But the happy ending came with the TAs. During this third year, I finally managed to get the TAs on a list which they were required to check three times a week and post to once a week. On the list, the TAs traded successful assignments and lesson plans; then they started talking about what didn't work. Next the discussion moved to why. Sometimes they seemed to forget I was reading (*I'm pretty sure Beth wouldn't approve of this, but here's what I did then . . .*). They talked how they were handling student problems. The women who were experiencing what Julia Ferganchick-Neufang calls gender-specific incidents began to support one another on the list and to give each other the words to draw appropriate boundaries. The men replied that they had not been aware that students treated men and women teachers differently and gave the women some sound advice about dealing with these adolescent males.

I entered into the conversations on an irregular basis. I gave a lot of "attaboys." Occasionally I asked for more explanation. Sometimes when they dwelt too long in practice, I would ask them to theorize, though I rarely used the word *theory* itself: *What would Elbow say about this? Does the concept of discourse community help here?* I asked for their responses to practica: *What was the most interesting idea Prof. Lunsford presented in her talk?* And I sent messages: *Read the Berger piece in Reading Culture before the practicum on the ad analysis paper; Make sure students know that the film "Uprising of 34" is at 7 and not 7:30.* By October paper memos sent to TA boxes were a rarity. Because of the success of this conversation, I continued it in the second semester but cut the number of entries required in half. When the discussion about argument or research dragged, I asked the TAs to reflect on the program: *Which assignment in 101 seems the best preparation for 102? In 101, should the interview paper go before the literary paper or after?* A long and intense discussion ensued on this last wherein no one changed anyone's mind but where pedagogy was articulated and defended. We had become a community of teachers.

Contexts and Lessons

The dramas we live become the stories we tell, but the significance rarely resides in the plot alone. It can be found as well in the contexts and in the lessons. The first part of the context of my e-mail narrative is the history of liberal arts in a technologically oriented land grant university. Clemson's beginnings lie in engineering, textiles, and "scientific agriculture," which Thomas Green Clemson, the son-in-law of John C. Calhoun, believed would allow the economy of South Carolina to recover from the devastation of the Civil War and Reconstruction. Educated at the University of Pennsylvania and at the Sorbonne and serving for several years at the Smithsonian, Clemson found himself in the upcountry of South Carolina because he had fallen in love with Calhoun's daughter Anna.

Unlike the University of South Carolina, Clemson College was founded to educate the sons of yeoman farmers, one step in democratizing education in a region where education had often been reserved for the wealthy. History, philosophy, rhetoric, literature—those disciplines Clemson himself saw as the "seminary of higher learning" he names in his will endowing the original college—have long been regarded by Clemson men with less insight than the founder as "merely" general education, courses which would add a little polish but were, in the final analysis, unimportant. English was a service oriented department and is still seen this way by many if not most administrators and alumni, including trustees, despite its two masters programs and its two hundred undergraduate majors. The result has been that the university's resources, including computer technology, did not accrue equitably to the English department.

In addition, both the old Liberal Arts College, which ceased to exist in 1995, and the English department have been traditional in outlook; proud of their excellent teaching, the college and the department until recently paid little or no attention to technology as either a research or a pedagogical tool. When I came to Clemson in 1989, most faculty in liberal arts did not have computers. In 1990 I got that same little Mac Classic that plays a role in Act One, but a sizable minority of faculty did not have, and often did not want, computers until 1996. In other words, the college and the department have been slow to realize that computers would play a role in the work of the humanities, and the university at large has been slow to insist that computer technology should become part of the work of the entire campus community.

Needless to say, when I came to Clemson, there was no computer classroom for composition, nor was the writing center equipped with computers. The situation remains so today. Indeed computer resources are still heavily weighted toward engineering and other majors which enroll primarily men: engineering, business, agriculture, and architecture. Women came to Clemson only in the 1960s, and those fields that enroll predominantly women students—humanities, education, art, nursing—continue to operate on the proverbial shoe string. This is not an unusual situation, I hear, on campuses across the country; nor is the old canard about how engineering and the sciences bring in money from outside grants. Despite dealing with the realities of public education in five states, I still believe educational opportunity ought to be equal, and I'm old enough to remember when this was not a radical notion.

The first important step in the technology-humanities connection began with the Master of Arts in Professional Communication in 1991, which had effected the hiring of Tharon Howard, who had gained experience with computers in his graduate work in rhetoric at Purdue. So when DCIT came calling in 1994, I had at least one ally who knew both computers and composition.

The factor that made our e-mail experiment feasible was the restructuring of the university. In early 1994, the Board of Trustees had announced that the university would be reconfigured. There was talk of getting rid of programs that duplicated those at South Carolina or those that did not pay for themselves. Veteran WPAs will not be surprised to learn that there was also much high sounding discussion of the commitment to undergraduate education. Department heads, deans, and vice-presidents were being asked to justify programs, jobs, expenditures. It was about this time that DCIT approached the first-year English program with their outreach initiative, the goal of which was to ensure the computer literacy of every Clemson student. Even though I am myself technologically challenged, I knew that my department was way behind in terms of using computers. So when DCIT showed up with a proposal, I grabbed it. One hand washing the other. Like most WPAs, I learned quickly to take an opportunity that presented itself, since most of the time support for the first-year writing program is difficult to find.

Another part of the context—and the part where the hardest lessons reside—was the relationship between the TAs and me. During the first year, the pilot project year, most of the TAs were graduate students who knew me from the required comp theory class the year before. They knew my philosophy of teaching writing. They trusted me and were willing to try what I put before them. As a group, they were committed to teaching. I expected a similar experience in the second year.

But the second year was a different story altogether. The second group of TAs did not know me. And it took half the year for me to figure out that they were never going to trust me and would never, ever like me. In fact, during the second semester of that year, once every three or four weeks one or another of the teaching assistants would come into my office and say, "You know, Dr. Daniell, a lot of TAs don't like you." At first I thought the e-mail failure had caused this antipathy, and this increased my sense of failure about the e-mail project and my resentment of it as well.

I now realize that while the e-mail fiasco may have exacerbated the TAs' insecurity as well as my own, it was not the cause of the problems between us. They didn't like me, they didn't like the textbooks, they didn't like the theories (as one woman wrote in her final journal, "I despise composition theory"). Amazingly they didn't like my colleagues Art Young and Martin Jacobi whom they had had for comp theory ("None of that stuff Dr. Young says is true"). They didn't even like each other: (Anonymous note in my mailbox: "Prof. Daniell, you need to know that _____ _____ says that she is grading the research papers really hard, so that she can give low grades to the students she doesn't like.") Almost all of them came to me with an extremely traditional view of English, a view that did not include rhetoric, or novels not already canonized, or film, or process pedagogy, or e-mail—all parts of the English 101 course I had designed. Their view of English did not include, especially, folks like me, who think that teaching writing is an intellectual enterprise. They dismissed me, but also Young and Jacobi, with the term "politically correct."

Yet I kept thinking I'd turn this group around. After all, I've spent my life successfully converting students, convincing them to see the value of something they had thought was awful—Latin, Shakespeare, grammar, Aristotle, even Freud. But nothing worked with this group of young people, who seemed to see new ideas as threats. I realize only now as I write this that these TAs would not have liked the e-mail project even if it had worked. What seems apparent now is that these graduate students were more insecure and afraid than TAs usually are. If I had been consciously aware of this when we were working together, I would have gone more slowly, would have been gentler, would have drawn the boundaries more clearly about what was acceptable behavior in a professional setting and what was not. What I also realize is that I am not accustomed to failure. And there were two failures, not one, in my second year as WPA: the e-mail project and the TAs.

But I also see, though it has taken me two years to do so, that neither of those failures resulted from things *I* did wrong. Sure, if I'd known then what I know now, I'd do e-mail differently. I wouldn't start until I saw the technology work. And I'd treat these unhappy TAs somewhat differently. But there are some things you don't get to control, even if you are the WPA—even if you are organized, knowledgeable, energetic, smart, and hard-working. I cannot, for instance, control the technology. I could not will Eudora to work. And while I certainly have some power over the TAs, my control over other human beings is always proscribed. I could not make the graduate students approve of me or of what I believe about teaching writing. And the very real possibility exists that even if I had said "Show me the technology" or had been more understanding of this group of TAs, the technology may still have failed and the TAs may still have resisted what I had to offer. Reality, I now understand, includes machines that break and people who don't like you. What I learned as WPA is the same lesson the TAs have to learn: You can't make everything and everybody do it right; you only get to work with the conditions and the students you are given.

The Vision

At the beginning I said this essay was a conversion narrative. Who got converted was me. I had known that the writing program at Clemson needed to integrate computers into its pedagogy. But because I am not a "computer person" and in fact have trouble generally with machines, my vision of the computer was limited. What I saw in the first year of the e-mail project was students' ideas written and read, genuine conversation in written form, the constructing and construing of *meaning* in graphic form, something that students all too seldom experience in school-sponsored writing. I had needed to be convinced that this technology had pedagogical functions that would be consistent with my agenda for the first-year composition program, and *I saw* that. In the second year the interface failure helped me see once again that technology is absolutely essential to literacy, a relationship which had become, over the years of thinking about the theory and the politics of literacy, transparent. In the third year when the technology worked, I saw that the computer could provide both an emotionally supportive conversation and an intellectually enriching resource that the realities of schedules may preclude. Now in my fourth year as WPA, I am experiencing that same kind of community on the WPA listserv, where participating WPAs help one another through various crises by means of the graphic symbols we send, in an instant, across hundreds and thousands of miles of geography.

Having spent the last fifteen years studying, reading, writing, and teaching about literacy, I know about literacy. I still don't know much about computers. But once I saw the computer as the technology of literacy—not in abstract way, but in everyday practice—then I saw the computer differently. I was able then to incorporate the computer and all its potential and its problems into my vision of literacy.

One day on the WPA listserv, someone wrote that there is no evidence demonstrating that computers make people better writers. But in order to write at all in the future, this WPA said, the students we are teaching today are going to have to be able to use electronic technology. Consequently, we do our students a grave disservice if we don't help them become comfortable using this tool. This comment helped me see the computer as part of the always-changing-over-time definition of literacy. Yet this explanation did not require me to become a True Believer, one who would argue that the computer is about to bring the millennium—a position I clearly have a hard time with.

When my department chair wanted evidence that computers really do help people write better before he would request new computers for the writing center, I wrote a long memo reviewing the research on computers and composition but closing with a verbatim passage from this post. The computer may not make our students better writers, I concluded, but it probably will determine in the not too distant future who counts as literate and who does not.

Now that the computer is part of my vision of literacy, I find I am able to say with conviction and clarity to deans and provosts and humanities boards how necessary computers are for the writing program at Clemson. I've been able to write grant proposals for new computers for the TAs. I have argued to my dean and to my new chair that my successor as WPA needs more released time because the job must entail expanding the use of computers in our writing classes, and to accomplish that goal, he will have to spend time writing proposals.

As Audre Lorde has written, "When I dare to be powerful—to use my strength in the service of my vision—then it becomes less and less important whether I am afraid." Or uncomfortable. Or in total control.

This week the Composition Committee elected to exempt a 101 student whose work in the first few weeks of the semester shows mastery of our goals for that course. But I was concerned because all the student's papers were typed rather than word processed. Only after he assured me that he was learning to write on the computer did I agree to the exemption.

Works Cited

Berthoff, Ann E. 1990. "I. A. Richards and the Concept of Literacy." *The Sense of Learning,* 136–49. Portsmouth, NH: Boynton/Cook.

Ferganchick-Neufang, Julia K. 1996. "Breaking the Silence: A Study of Gender-Specific Problems in the Writing Classroom." *Composition Forum* 7 (Winter): 17–30.

Writing Program Administration and (Self)-Representation

Paradoxes, Anomalies, and Institutional Resistance

M. L. Tiernan

As I first began drafting this essay, something curious happened to me as a writer. Halfway or so through the piece, I realized that I had not yet spoken in the first person, though I had of course known all along that this volume was to be a collection of *personal* WPA stories. Deciding, then, to go back and "incorporate the personal" into my draft, I came to see that the problem was more substantive than I had thought, that I couldn't fix it by altering sentence subjects or adding occasional anecdotes, and that, indeed, "I" was having real trouble entering into a personal discussion of my WPA work.

Why was this? The easy answer was that I was simply not used to speaking or writing about this work as "mine." Since there are three of us who administer Lafayette College's writing program, along with one administrative assistant, it has always seemed more sensible, more true, to refer to *our* work, to *our* program, and even to *our* WPA stories—referential quirks that speak to the fundamentally collaborative nature of WPA work at Lafayette and, I would imagine, elsewhere. The more difficult answers came to me in rereading the story I had begun to write—a stammering, anxious story with heavily qualified prose, a story laden with themes of institutional power and professional illegitimacy, a story from which any narrator would be crazy not to distance herself.

Was it a true story? It revealed, at least, the extent to which I had come to depersonalize my WPA work, not just in writing, but in practice. As an untenured faculty member, how could I claim authority for work which might simply be revoked two or three years down the line? What would it mean, anyway, to claim ownership of work that is granted little disciplinary legitimacy, despite the fact that it is work I was hired to do? And how could I begin to make visible the legitimacy of this work within an institution—within, indeed, an entire professional culture—predisposed to see it merely as academic service?

These questions—which speak to some of the tangled and contradictory ways in which WPA work intersects with the personal and the institutional— have become the center of this essay. As they unfolded, one into the other, I recognized that the problem of personalizing my original draft gestured beyond writerly difficulty. To have cared enough to embrace WPA work as mine would

162

have meant investing too heavily in a process over which I seemed to have little personal control; it would have meant, also, running the risk of losing myself to more powerfully rooted institutional voices—voices with the capacity to energize at times, but also to distract and to deplete. Keeping my WPA work at a distance had become, in other words, a mechanism for personal (if not institutional) survival.

In revising, I have kept most of what seems to me real; I have tried, also, to make the story mine—whatever that can mean in the attempt to represent an endeavor that is not only cooperative, but also (necessarily) informed by a multiplicity of political, disciplinary, and institutional perspectives and voices. My strategy? To engage some of those powerfully rooted voices that we, or at least I, work by. I have found, after all, that I cannot tell this story, cannot "compose my self" for this essay, without recourse to those voices—departmental and cross-disciplinary, supportive and contentious—that both make possible and delimit what I do and who I am as an untenured writing program administrator both within and outside my department.

WPAs and the English Department

"But doesn't that mean we'd all have to teach more writing?"

"Oh God." *Voice indicating that he spoke for all who were present.*

"Well, we could split the writing course into two semesters—offer it to second-semester freshmen and first-semester sophomores. At least then we wouldn't have to teach more than one at a time."

"Still, something's gotta give." *Pencil tapping, impatience beginning to show.* "Even if we spread it over two semesters, upper division suffers."

"That won't work anyway. These students *need* writing in the freshman year, and we're simply the ones who have to do it, like it or not." *Tone asserting the authority of age-old experience, the drudgery of confronting the sameness of first-year papers. Betraying, also, a commendable, if paternal, fear: without us, students drift silently through the murky seas of inarticulation.*

"I don't know." *Somewhat defensively.* "That's an outmoded idea—Freshman writing, I mean. Some English departments have just given it up—spread it across the whole college."

"Fat chance."

"I hear that all the time, but I've never seen *evidence* that it works. Who's done that? Where?" *Besides, losing the writing course means giving up departmental clout, not to mention a number of tenure lines.*

"Let's just exempt more students."

"Great, and get stuck with a class full of slackers."

"At least then we could quit pretending, and teach what needs to be taught."
The nuts and bolts realist.

"Let's just exempt the *slackers.*"

Uncomfortable laughter, then silence.

"We'll consider this further at our next meeting."

Only the sounds of day's end: papers suffling, briefcases snapping shut, frustrations exhaling into air.

As I left a department meeting recently, I was reminded anew of the extent to which the teaching of writing remains on the periphery of academic pursuit—even among those of us whose very discipline supposes a love of reading and writing, a devotion to language itself. The reasons are familiar enough. Facing stacks of papers on a weekly basis steals precious time from a faculty possessed of precious little. Given, further, few resources for additional hiring, every teaching slot devoted to writing takes one away from literature, and course offerings for the major dwindle. But writing remains on the periphery for more complicated (and less practical) reasons, as well. I am asked on a regular basis by departmental colleagues how it is that I tolerate teaching so much writing, reading so many student papers, confronting, so often, classes so (presumably) bereft of intellectual substance and stimulation. Implicit in these questions is the lingering perception that since the teaching of writing is finally the teaching of discursive skills, its primary function is to service both the department and the college at large by preparing students for the demands of real college work.

For the untenured writing specialist who also administers a college-wide writing program, the idea of writing as service carries with it a number of implications and consequences, both personal and professional. If the *teaching* of writing is largely perceived as a service void of real intellectual work and real disciplinary content, then preparing other faculty to teach writing stands (like the illegitimate work of Plato's artist) suspiciously on the outskirts of academe, doubly removed from the substantive core of institutional and disciplinary "reality." In this context, it is no wonder that departmental colleagues continue to be baffled by what it is, exactly, that I "do" as a WPA.

As the assistant director of Lafayette's College Writing Program (CWP), what I do has changed substantially in the last five years, due largely to the implementation of a new core curriculum in which students must take a number of writing-intensive courses staffed by faculty from across the disciplines. These courses are required to affiliate with the CWP. In turn, the CWP provides each course with a trained student Writing Associate, who meets with each member of the class throughout the semester to discuss drafted work and to provide suggestions for revision; in addition, CWP administrators offer a variety of faculty-development workshops, sessions, panels, and in-house writing resource publications to facilitate the incorporation of writing into courses from across the disciplines.

Given the college-wide nature of these responsibilities, much that I do as a WPA remains inscrutable to the English department because it is not related—directly, at least—to the day-to-day concerns of the department itself; the department *is,* nonetheless, responsible for evaluating my WPA work. In attempts to resolve this paradox, I am asked to generate increasingly detailed documentation of my WPA activities: summative reports on the workshops I offer, reports on the composition conferences I attend (and on how such conferences bear on my CWP administration), self-defined job descriptions, daily journals (recording exactly how much time I spend doing exactly what), bibliographies of the reading I've done to "keep up to speed," and endlessly updated lists of my individual responsibilities in the CWP—a drastically abridged version of which looks something like this:

RESPONSIBILITIES, ASSISTANT DIRECTOR OF CWP

(Asterisks indicate work shared by two or more administrators)

1. *Writing Associate (WA) Training*
   - Design/Conduct full-day introductory WA workshop*
   - Interview and select new WAs*
   - Train WA mentors*

2. *Faculty Development*
   - Design/Conduct faculty workshops/brown bags/lunches/panels*
   - Bring in outside WAC specialists
   - Create/Update/Revise Writing Resource Book for affiliated faculty*
   - Field faculty questions/problems about the teaching of writing (individual conferences)*

3. *Professional Development*
   - Attend CCCC and submit report of sessions to program Director and Provost*
   - Review composition scholarship for possible inclusion in the program*

4. *Program Mechanics*
   - Solicit faculty affiliation with CWP
   - Collect/review faculty requests for WAs
   - Assign WAs to courses*
   - Prepare forms/procedures for use in interviewing WA candidates
   - Design evaluations for WAs, faculty, and students in affiliated courses. Compile results*
   - Mailers to announce upcoming CWP workshops and events
   - Schedule rooms/equipment/food for faculty development/WA activities

- Obtain from provost and keep updated record of new returning affiliated faculty

The more that I document, the more baffled my colleagues become; ironically, in fact, the documents themselves often serve as new sources of confusion. The issue of individual responsibility, for example, is an especially difficult one for my department to get at.

The problem is that the CWP administrators have a number of overlapping responsibilities. From where I stand, this could not be otherwise. For one thing, much of what I do in faculty development and Writing Associate training requires, or is at least enhanced by, the diverse perspectives and talents that come into play *only* by virtue of close and on-going collaboration. Beyond this, the CWP has become in recent years too enormous for even its discrete tasks to be undertaken singlehandedly; despite this, administering the program has been, for the most part, simply added on to the regular responsibilities of teaching and research. (Only in the last two years have I received a course release for my CWP responsibilities.) Further, the sudden expansion of the CWP to accommodate the needs of the new curriculum has rendered administrative tasks more complicated and unwieldy (both logistically and politically) than they were when I first became assistant director nearly five years ago. From my department's perspective, on the other hand, how can this shared work be evaluated? Whose work is this, anyway? Who is helping out (or stealing from, or riding on the tails of) whom?

Notwithstanding a number of recent publications in English and composition studies that have begun to identify the problematic institutional status of WPAs, there are still few models by which to categorize, let alone to evaluate, the nature of WPA work, collaborative or otherwise. As Edward White has noted,

> We don't have a guideline for evaluating WPAs because we lack a common definition of what a WPA does. At many campuses, the WPA is a temporary casual position, filled by a literature person slumming, who does relatively little and is less informed about composition than many of the part-timers. At the other end of the spectrum, we have WPAs who are full-time administrators, with assistants and staffs, running a major program that includes TA training, faculty development, writing across the curriculum, portfolio assessments, and the like. . . . How could a single document, of whatever scope, reflect such a diverse reality? (Gebhardt and Gebhardt, 52–3)

Aware of all this, I typically begin each semester with the firm resolution that I *will* be more meticulous about WPA documentation. By midterm or so—amidst the inevitable backlog of student papers, course preparations, advising, conferences, faculty development, committee meetings, and the rest—it is always the first thing to go. From what I can tell, it has little effect anyway. The question of what I do returns, predictably as the grey of Pennsylvania skies, again and again.

But *why* this ineffectuality, this stubborn interpretive impasse—amongst colleagues who are, after all, professionally trained readers? It is not only that we lack adequate evaluative models, but also that WPA work frustrates in a number of ways existing institutional paradigms and assumptions for evaluating academic success. At Lafayette, while I serve the college as a WPA, I do this primarily by teaching (both faculty from across the disciplines and student Writing Associates); pedagogy, furthermore, constitutes the primary subject matter for the research and scholarship that I do. In these ways, WPA work collapses the traditionally distinct evaluative categories of service, teaching, and scholarship—a collapsing which, though inherent to the work itself, brings with it personal, as well as institutional, consequences.

During my midterm tenure review, for example, my work as a WPA limped along behind teaching and scholarship (as it still does)—officially analogous to serving on a faculty committee, though demanding, simultaneously, at least fifty percent of my time, scholarly, pedagogical, and otherwise. Beyond this, the service designation assumes that WPA work requires no particular disciplinary or professional expertise, an assumption that, however persistent, is often undermined by the latent inconsistencies of daily institutional reality. I was, for example, hired as a writing specialist with the clear expectation that I would administer the CWP—suggesting an implicit awareness that WPA work requires at least *some* disciplinary specialization.

Similarly, while my senior colleagues evaluate my WPA work as service, they continue to ask that I account for it with increasing precision. With the exception of WPAs, I can think of no faculty who are required to document their academic service, apart from listing it on their vitae; still less are other faculty *hired* to serve on college committees. What this suggests is the extent to which we know at some level that something is out of kilter, that something in WPA work differs from mainstream kinds of academic work. In the midst, however, of a long-standing paradigm for academic evaluation that strikes us as commonsensical—so much so that it renders anomalous whatever it cannot account for—such knowledge remains hopelessly tacit and, hence, rarely acted upon.

At an undergraduate, liberal arts college, what I have come to think of as the limbo of writing program administration is especially problematic. Although WPAs at large research institutions certainly confront many of the same challenges and frustrations that I do, they often work, nevertheless, in departments in which composition and writing program administration are more visibly ensconced than at small colleges which tend not to have graduate programs. The presence of graduate students often ensures that WPAs function within a sphere of professional activity that is both familiar to and valued by the faculty at large: they attract prospective graduate students interested in becoming compositionists, they conduct graduate seminars in composition theory and pedagogy, they direct dissertations in rhetoric and composition, and so forth. Such activities make it relatively easy for departmental faculty outside composition to identify points of intersection between their own work and the work carried out by WPAs. More importantly, work with graduate students constitutes a fundamental (and highly visible) means of disciplinary self-reproduction. As WPAs at such institutions train new writing teachers and supervise graduate student research and scholarship, they also make visible to the English department composition's scholarly and pedagogical perimeters: the production of new specialists in the field, the perpetual extending and *deepening* of disciplinary knowledge. At Lafayette, on the other hand, the production and dissemination of disciplinary knowledge in composition and writing program administration occurs for the most part *horizontally*—across disciplines, at a distance from (and thus often invisible to) the English department.[1] I find myself often, then, in the awkward (and politically precarious) position of needing to educate departmental colleagues not only about *what* I do, but about the professional *worth* of what I do—about, that is, my own legitimacy as a scholar, a teacher, a colleague.

On good days, this educating occurs in informal conversations with department members, some of whom drop by my office on occasion to borrow handouts I've designed or to ask questions about their writing courses, their writing assignments, their thoughts about teaching the sentence, the thesis, the paragraph. I have learned to value such moments highly (even to seek them out), not primarily because they provide me with opportunities to speak some of what I believe about the teaching of writing (though they do that too), but because they represent to me rare gestures of faith in the disciplinary reality of what I do. More specifically, they represent to me small acknowledgments of my authority as a writing specialist and a WPA. In this, also, they begin to chip away at the long-standing assumption that the teaching of writing comes naturally to English professors, whatever their particular fields of expertise.

On days that are not so good, this educating takes more unseemly (and less pedagogically sound) forms. I think, for example, of my recent outburst at a colleague who referred to me once too often as the "Xerox Queen." "But you know I'm just teasing you," he insisted. "It's just that you're always sending off all these memos and handouts and announcements and things. I don't know how you get anything else done." As innocuous as such casual remarks are intended to be (this was, by the way, a friendly colleague), what is often not understood is the extent to which they feed all too smoothly into deep-rooted perceptions about the academic integrity of composition and writing program administration—traditionally gendered fields, both of which still retain blatant associations with "service," "nurture," "busywork."

Given the difficulties of WPA work within the English department, among colleagues who need *not* be persuaded about the value of students learning to write well, I should not wonder that faculty from across the curriculum are as well often wary of and resistant to my trespassing in their teaching and their disciplines.

WPAs and Faculty from Across the Disciplines

"What's so hard about teaching writing anyway?" *Meaning, What can you possibly have to teach me? Why do I have to be here?* "All you have to do is sit in your study at night with a cognac and a good cigar and underline topic sentences." *General laughter, signifying assent.*

"I agree. I have enough trouble getting students to *understand* the material, let alone trying to get them to write about it." *Content versus writing: again, again.*

"Not to mention *covering* the material—I have seventeen books in my course." *Emphasizing his uncommon rigor, his disciplinary standards, his contempt for having to teach what should have been taught in grammar school, in high school, in English.*

"Well my students won't even talk. If these courses are supposed to be seminars, why aren't we spending any time on how to generate good class discussion?" *Anything to avoid writing.*

"Mine talk enough; what they *need* is good manners." *Here we go.* "I've got one young man who does nothing but challenge me. He won't listen to a word I say—he's just . . . *prideful.* I'm scheduled for a writing conference with him this week, and I don't know *what* I can possibly do."

Ah, a potential segue: "Since our topic today is responding to student writing, this might be a good time to return to it and—" *But no.*

"To tell you the truth, the last thing I need to work on right now is how to teach writing." *It's lost.* "There are other problems with these courses that are just as important, and other ways besides writing to get at 'active learning.' Why do we have all this support just for writing, anyway? Why *not* for something like discussion?"

Because we all voted in this writing-intensive curriculum? Because I was charged by the provost, along with my WPA colleagues, to be the support for this curriculum that we all voted in? Because I am doing my job? Because there were supposed to be other people providing other kinds of support, but who and where are they?

When Lafayette adopted its new curriculum, few faculty faced the need for more immediate and large-scale change than those of us who administer the CWP. Since all who taught core courses were now *required* to affiliate with the writing program, the number of faculty we worked with rose from an average of fifteen to an average of sixty per semester, with a correspondent rise in the number of Writing Associates we needed to hire and train. As a relatively new faculty member, I found the prospect daunting. I was barely coming to know the members of my own department, let alone the rest of the campus community. Beyond this, though I came from a graduate institution where the teaching of writing was highly valued, and where I received as a teaching assistant rigorous and ongoing training in writing pedagogy from some of the most respected teachers and scholars in the field, I took my degree in Literature and Culture Studies—which is to say that in the few years prior to my being hired at Lafayette as a composition specialist, I had not done much scholarly work in composition. And I had certainly received no training that would prepare me for administrative work. This meant not only that I needed to reeducate myself in the field for which I had been hired but also that I needed to acquire, all too speedily, whatever knowledge I could about Lafayette's social, political, and academic culture.

Daunting, yes, but also exhilarating: the entire faculty—well, the majority anyway—had spoken up for writing, had said yes to its centrality in the learning process, and had seemed (in their speaking and saying) to be voicing, too, their confidence in the CWP, which would, along with other (as yet undefined) programs, provide whatever was necessary to ease the transition. I had not yet learned to read the politics of academic decision-making; even less had I anticipated the extent to which the support offered by the CWP would come to be viewed by many not only as suspect, but as professionally (sometimes personally) *adversarial.*

I am still frequently stymied, not so much by the fact that I encounter "resistance" to the teaching of writing or to suggestions about productive *ways* to teach writing (this is, after all, to be expected whenever faculty confront new pedagogical demands), but by the fact that the resistance often takes such vehement forms. I have been challenged publicly by a senior faculty member who asked me what sort of "credentials" one needed, anyway, to teach something like writing; I have been accused by administrative secretaries of misusing college funds for faculty development events, as if I had decided on some madcap whim to organize writing workshops for my own benefit and pleasure; I have been grilled repeatedly about why faculty from across the disciplines have been stuck with teaching writing, as if I were somehow responsible for imposing the new curriculum and for devising, further, a myriad of ways to enforce it.

If educating English department colleagues about what I do seems frustratingly repetitive at times, educating a larger, more diverse, and often less willing audience sometimes seems downright futile. One of the difficulties is that the resistance rarely springs from sources germane to the actual work that I do as a WPA. Partly because the CWP at Lafayette remains, essentially, the sole source of faculty development for the new curriculum, it also bears the brunt of whatever general dissatisfactions arise in relation to this new curriculum.[2] Indeed, the very idea of writing has come to function increasingly as a highly politicized nexus onto which are displaced a number of debates spilling beyond writing *per se* and into more variously inflected issues like active learning, critical thinking, the student-centered vs. the teacher-centered classroom, educational rigor—spilling, that is, into virtually all things *pedagogical.* What this means is that I am asked to teach (or to defend, as the case may be) not only the teaching of writing, but the value of pedagogical thinking, as well—and this to an audience predisposed (not just at Lafayette, but in higher education nationally) to view both writing and pedagogy as marginal academic fields which threaten to detract from the "real" business of disseminating disciplinary content or maintaining the rigors of the classroom.[3]

How is it possible to provide meaningful support in the face of such resistance? How, in particular, does an untenured person respond to such adversity from faculty (largely senior colleagues) any number of whom might be evaluating her case for tenure? When I think of these things, I am astonished that the CWP makes headway at all. And perhaps this is the place to say that although I have concentrated in this story on resistance and adversity (those gremlins inherent to any story worth telling), I have worked, also, in the midst of faculty from whom I have received endless support and goodwill, from whom I have learned immensely, and for whose presence I am daily thankful. Though the voices of these colleagues are not those that inhabit my thoughts on sleepless nights, they are the voices that sustain me.

On the other hand (and this may be the overarching paradox of writing program administration), my work is sustained by those very colleagues from whom I encounter resistance and adversity. They define (if often in stunningly deflected ways) the work that I do as a WPA and the work that remains to be done. And I speak here not only of the work of running a writing program, nor even the work of teaching the teaching of writing. I speak, most importantly, perhaps, of the more convoluted and self-reflexive work of learning how to *articulate* what it is that we do as WPAs in ways that are comprehensible to our departments, to our institutions, and to, indeed, the discipline of English studies generally.

WPAs and the Tenure Process

I referred earlier to some of the difficulties (and some of the reasons for them) that my colleagues have when it comes to reading my WPA work for purposes of evaluation and review. Some, by virtue of being neither composition specialists nor WPAs themselves, do not yet know how to read it; some are frozen in institutional paradigms for evaluation that render WPA work decipherable only in terms of its most menial components; and others, for reasons we may never understand, simply don't want to read it—or don't want to read it, anyway, in ways that ascribe to it any academic value or integrity. But that is only half of the story. The truth is that as WPAs, we are, ourselves, only beginning to understand how to document our work, how to "re-present" it publicly in ways that adequately (and persuasively) account for its scholarly and pedagogical dimensions.

The particular ramifications of this truth were driven home to me only last month, when I entered the early stages of my tenure review process. In preparing my materials to send out to external evaluators, I decided to include, along with my traditional scholarship, a section on my work as a CWP administrator. But how to manage this section? What to include? What representational structure to employ or (more likely) to create and make do? To submit everything from the last five years of my program administration would be to send on its way an "unreadable" monster, indeed—no matter how devisively sewn together; on the other hand, to pare the work down to two or three sample workshops would be to omit the complexities and scope of the work itself. Advice from departmental colleagues on the issue was diverse and (predictably) colored by the kinds of bureaucratic, political, and institutional double-binds with which WPAs have learned to live, if not always gracefully: "Since WPA work is service, it would be inappropriate to include it with your scholarly materials—it just isn't done"; or, "What a fascinating idea, but you'll need to find some 'other way' to represent it"; or, "It's not that I think you shouldn't *include* this material, it's just that no one will know how to read it"; or, "I'm afraid that your attempt to do this will ultimately backfire." After years of being asked to document my WPA work, doing so at the moment when it mattered (to me, anyway) the most was suddenly perceived by many as an act meant to challenge or undermine institutional procedure—suspect, disruptive, and likely, anyway, to be futile.

Things would no doubt be easier were we able to design a set of common guidelines for evaluating WPAs. As Edward White suggests, however, the range of WPA work (along with the even more dispersed range of institutional settings within which it is carried out) frustrates the very prospect of establishing such a "meta-paradigm"—which would be likely, at any rate, to present us in the last analysis with a new set of problems, a different order of paradoxes, anomalies, and resistances. Given this, it may be that what is needed is not so much a paradigm, as a number of smaller "articulations" of WPA work— articulations necessarily diversified and local, and, precisely because of this, accountable for the ways WPAs practice and know (and produce new ways of knowing) primarily in the contexts of the specific institutional communities of which they are a part.

If we do not know all of the reasons why some of our colleagues cannot or will not read us, we can at least find ways of more clearly representing to ourselves (and to any who are willing to listen) how it is that we might be more thoroughly and responsibly evaluated, and why it is that we might deserve to be read in the first place. It seems clear that current modes of academic self-representation continue to undermine the institutional value of WPA work, either by marginalizing it as campus service, or by rendering it inscrutable to those whose reading of it most matters to the professional lives of WPAs. In the absence of new models (or amidst the inevitable chaos of emergent ones),[4] it may be that the genre of the personal is in some ways an ideal vehicle for WPA self-representation. In its foregrounding of the quirky and the marginal, in its articulation of the exceptional and the unregistered, and in its embracing of many stories, many voices, it holds the capacity to begin to engage—if not to displace—those institutional paradigms by which WPA work remains, all too often, anomalous.

Notes

1. Though I am emphasizing in this section the problematic role of WPAs in the English department, it is relevant to note that the specific *nature* of much WPA work is perhaps most understood by and familiar to faculty outside the humanities. Faculty in engineering, economics, and business, for example, carry out something analogous to WPA work as they engage in the work of professional consultation; and faculty in biology and other sciences routinely *collaborate* in the production of research and scholarship. From this perspective, it may be that humanities faculty are among the most resistant to acknowledging writing program administration as legitimate intellectual work, since they traditionally define such work in terms of individual talent, originality, and publication.

2. This problem became so overwhelming that the director of CWP requested this year that the provost appoint an additional faculty member to act as a "pedagogical facilitator," providing faculty support in "non-writing" areas like class discussion and the coverage of course "content." While this additional support has been immensely useful both to faculty and to CWP administrators, it has also led to a new set of problems. It bolsters, for example, the already prevalent attitude that writing is an activity entirely discrete from course content, from course readings, from class discussions—an attitude that CWP administrators have persistently worked to dislodge.

3. Mariolina Salvatori's *Pedagogy: Disturbing History, 1819–1929* (Pittsburgh: University of Pittsburgh Press, 1996) provides a richly provocative account of the "devaluing" of pedagogy in American higher education.

4. Scholars like Ernest Boyer (*Scholarship Reconsidered*) have proposed shifts in the dominant categories for academic evaluation, from, for example, the disparate categories of "teaching/scholarship/service" to those that define the work of the professoriate in terms of more integrated or "overlapping" functions like "discovery, integration, application, and teaching."

Works Cited

Boyer, Ernest L. 1990. *Scholarship Reconsidered: Priorities of the Professoriate.* Princeton: Carnegie Foundation for the Advancement of Teaching.

Gebhardt, Richard C., and Barbara Genelle Smith Gebhardt, eds. 1997. *Academic Advancement in Composition Studies.* Mahwah, NJ: Lawrence Erlbaum Associates.

Hult, Christine, David Jolliffe, Kathleen Kelly, Dana Mead, and Charles Schuster. 1992. "The Portland Resolution." *Writing Program Administration* 16: 88–94.

Salvatori, Mariolina. 1996. *Pedagogy: Disturbing History, 1819–1929.* Pittsburgh: University of Pittsburgh Press.

Coda

Today I received a letter from a student I taught ten years ago or more. His is one of those letters that surprises teachers somewhere in the middle of their careers. In part, this is what he wrote:

> I'm writing this in the hopes that I can in some small way return the gift you have given me and so many students like me. You see, before I began my college career, I never considered myself (nor was I considered by anyone else) to be a particularly good writer. Not that it was something I ever focused on. I was able to communicate my ideas and that was enough. But that changed when I entered your class.
>
> Though a bit hazy, I can recall sitting in a 9 AM freshman humanities course, probably HU 101. I can't recall individual classes, but I can remember feeling a sense of belonging. I remember feeling safe in trying to express emotions with written words, like a young child that first time he picks out what clothes he'll wear for the day. It was new and felt risky, exposing part of myself, my emotions, making me vulnerable to criticism. But the vulnerability was never exploited. I remember your ability to make me feel comfortable in this new experience, your expressing enthusiasm, yet lacking surprise in seeing something come from me that to me was very surprising and foreign, like you knew it was there all along. It encouraged me to do more, explore more, express more.

Jeff was underestimating the effect of his words when he expressed the wish that his letter would return "in some small way" what he got from those classes. His letter reminded me what this business of running writing programs, this business of teaching others how to teach, is all about: It is about working with people until they find their own voices, their own strength. I remember Jeff, though not his individual papers. But I am not at all surprised that he describes my reaction to his work as seeming like I knew the good work was there all along. Of course, I did.

What's more, Jeff's letter reminds me how very much we, as friends, colleagues, and distant-but-connected scholars and teachers owe each other. Though we might sometimes feel singularly isolated in our positions, very few of the WPAs I know learned how to run programs and design curricula on their own. We had models and mentors. Some of those models came from the scholarship and research we continue to generate even as we work through the daily tasks of running writing programs.

My own first mentor was Win Horner whose office at the time was a cubicle two desks down from my own. Jeff should actually be thanking her because it was Win Horner who first taught me to treat students with such respect, to get real joy from teaching students to become independent of me. When I began running a writing center, I somehow discovered Mary Croft at the University of Wisconsin-Stevens Point and, later, Jeanette Harris whose work with teachers has always been informed by the kind of good sense and caring I wanted in my own work.

I asked Jeanette for her story, and she assured me several times that she didn't really have the sort of story that might fit a volume of essays like this one. Still, this is some of what she wrote.

On Being an Accidental Administrator

Jeanette Harris

I guess no one plans to become an administrator. It just happens to you gradually. Or, at least, that is the way it happened to me. I always thought of myself as a teacher—in fact, still do—but somewhere along the way I became an administrator. The process that resulted in this metamorphosis began when I was still in graduate school. Lil Brannon and I suggested to the chair of our department at East Texas State University (now Texas A&M-Commerce) that he allow us to start a writing center. Of course, neither of us really knew what a writing center was at that point. We had heard and read about these new tutorial programs but had never actually seen one. But in 1975 we set up shop in a tiny room on the third floor of the Hall of Literature and Languages, as the building that housed the English Department was grandly called. We had only a few student desks and some cast-off handbooks and dictionaries, and we were the only tutors; but students quickly discovered us, and in a few years the writing center had become a thriving program.

And that was how it all began. After we graduated, Lil left to take a faculty position on the East Coast, but I remained as director of the writing center at East Texas State until 1982, when I was hired by the English Department at Texas Tech University to establish a writing center there. Thus my initial administrative experience enabled me to find another administrative position, and the die was cast. I later became the director of composition at Texas Tech and then, in 1990, moved to the University of Mississippi to become director of composition there. After five years at USM, I was appointed Chair of the English Department and discovered just how challenging an administrative position can be. The first year was difficult because I was undergoing treatment for breast cancer, and the second because I was serving as director of composition as well as chair. At the end of my second year as chair and seventh year at USM, I again decided to move—this time back to Texas and also back to writing centers.

Today, I direct the William L. Adams Writing Center at Texas Christian University in Fort Worth. For the first time, my position is completely administrative: I teach no classes, do not have faculty status, and am not associated with an English department. Although I have always had administrative responsibilities and they have increasingly consumed larger amounts of my time, until now I have been able to think of myself primarily as a teacher. It is only now, at this point in my life, that I have to admit that I am, in fact, a full-time administrator.

And yet, I know that I have always viewed every administrative position I have held as opportunities to teach or to mentor. Rather than viewing myself as in charge, or directing, or managing, I think of what I do as a form of teaching. Assuming the role of mentor has enabled me to function as an administrator in ways that do not conflict with my sense of who I am.

There are likely two reasons why I view administration as mentoring rather than managing. First, I was a mother long before I was an administrator, and those nurturing instincts are much more deeply ingrained and basic than anything I learned in academia. Family systems theories encourage us to view all groups as surrogate families, and I believe, to an extent, this mindset is useful. I think we always assume roles of mother/father, wife/husband, daughter/ son, or sister/brother in relation to the people we work with on a daily basis. In fact, I suspect that one reason I did not enjoy the time I served as chair of one department was that it was difficult for me to think of myself as the father, which is what I felt was required in that traditionally male role. It was not that I couldn't do what was required of me of me as chair; it was that I didn't enjoy doing it. I believe other women, especially younger women, have very different feelings about such positions. But my family experiences did not prepare me to be comfortable in that role. By contrast, as a WPA I have always been quite comfortable because, in my mind at least, that is a maternal role.

The second reason I view administration as mentoring is that I was fortunate enough to have a wonderful mentor when I was a graduate student. JoAnn Cockelreas, one of my professors at East Texas State, taught me what it meant to be an academic. She literally forced me to begin submitting proposals for conferences and then insisted I attend the conferences when my proposals were accepted. She also forced me to begin writing my dissertation and dragged me through that dreadful process (remember, this was before PCs and word processing). Even though she was not officially my major professor, she spent countless hours editing my dissertation, talking with me about revisions, and listening to me complain about my lot in life.

More important perhaps than all of this was the fact that she served as a role model for me. Only slightly older than I was and having had, like me, a rather traditional life as a wife and mother before entering academia, JoAnn was someone I could imagine myself becoming. Although I stood in awe of her accomplishments, she demystified the whole process and reassured me that I could do what she had done. And because I could identify with her so easily, I was able to believe her.

My relationship with JoAnn convinced me that academics are supposed to support and encourage those who are less experienced. Thus, when I took the position at Texas Tech and discovered that one of the female graduate students assigned to the writing center was a nontraditional student returning to school, I almost immediately assumed the role of mentor to her. That student was Lady Falls Brown, who now directs the writing center I established at Texas Tech. The relationship that developed between us was very much like the one I enjoyed with JoAnn Cockelreas. I was several years older than she, but we had shared similar non-academic experiences, and it was easy and natural for me to assume the role of Lady's mentor.

Although Lady was the graduate student I took the most interest in, I discovered ways to mentor all of my tutors. That is, I did most of my teaching and supervising just by working in the center with the tutors. As they observed me working with students, the tutors quickly learned what they needed to do. I also spent time talking with them about their own professional development—helping and encouraging them to take those first tentative steps as scholars and researchers, just as JoAnn had helped and encouraged me years before.

Later, when I became a WPA, I mentored the TAs much as I had the tutors I supervised in the writing center. In addition to teaching them theories of pedagogy, holding staff meetings, and observing them as they taught, I tried to show the TAs what is involved in becoming an academic. This type of approach meant keeping my door open to encourage them to come by and talk with me whenever they needed or wanted to. It also meant encouraging them to think of themselves as professionals—to join professional organizations, attend conferences, write papers, and even submit articles for publication (which, of course, had to be read and critiqued).

As an administrative strategy, mentoring has several advantages for people like me who are not comfortable with a more authoritarian approach. First, it allows us to get to know the people we supervise or direct. This knowledge is valuable not only in establishing a good working relationship with people but also in determining their strengths and weaknesses—knowing what they do well and what they do less well. Second, encouraging people to develop professionally helps them to contribute more effectively to the program as well as to build a better resume. Thus, we are helping not just the people we mentor but the students they teach and, indirectly, ourselves. Finally, mentoring works because it is an invisible process. People, especially academics, often resent supervision and direction, not to mention outright orders. Mentoring allows us to achieve our goals through collaboration and consensus rather than an exercise of authority and thus to avoid at least some of the resentment that people often have toward administrators.

But mentoring is not at all a simple process. I have learned the hard way that it not only involves complications but also limitations. One of the complications is that it is a time-consuming process. It takes much more time to shape a program through mentoring than it does to issue orders and establish policies unilaterally. Results don't come quickly and sometimes don't come at all. Often the results occur years later, after people have joined different programs or departments or become administrators themselves. But the most serious limitation is that we cannot mentor everyone successfully—regardless of how much we may try.

Mentoring is essentially a process of identification. We tend to mentor those with whom we identify. In the past, academic mentoring was relatively simple. Male professors selected male students with whom they identified and helped them become even more like themselves. This is still the most natural form of mentoring. My mentor was a woman much like me in terms of age and life experiences. In turn, I have found it most natural to mentor women like myself who have returned to school late in life after raising a family. Like Lady, these women are people I like and understand—people I consider friends as well as students and colleagues.

As a WPA and even more as a chair, I have been faced with mentoring a variety of people—not just women like myself. It is easy, even rewarding, to mentor those who remind us of ourselves. But how do we mentor those in whom we do not see ourselves? Can we, in fact, effectively mentor those whose experiences, values, and lifestyles we do not share? The fact that we see so little diversity at our professional conferences suggests that we either cannot or do not mentor people unlike ourselves successfully. We continue to have generation after generation of WPAs who, in spite of their good intentions, simply do not represent the diverse populations we work with in classrooms. It is not that we actively discourage people who are unlike ourselves—on the contrary, most of us are eager for academia to become more diverse. However, without strong role models and mentors, it is difficult for people who are racially and ethnically diverse to enter the academic mainstream. Just as women were disadvantaged for decades because male professors usually chose to mentor other males, those who come from minority cultures are disadvantaged today because they have no one to convince them that their aspirations and dreams can become a reality.

The fact that mentoring is not always easy or even possible does not discourage me from believing it is worth the effort. It does mean that we need to increase our efforts—to move beyond the barriers to mentoring that are inherent in difference. If mentoring is, as I believe, an effective way to accomplish our goals as administrators, then we need to find ways to mentor students and colleagues in whom we do not readily see ourselves. As faculties and student bodies grow increasingly diverse, we need to change our familiar, comfortable pattern of mentoring only those with whom we identify, finding ways to offer those who are less like us the same support we offer those who are like us.

Even with the reservations I have about the fairness of the traditional process, I believe mentoring is one of the most effective ways to achieve our administrative goals. In my own case, there is simply no other way for me to approach the role I have accidentally assumed.

Jeanette's words provide a fitting conclusion to this collection, for if the individual's story can do anything for WPAs it is to make that mentoring connection for all of us. Perhaps because I have spent so much of my scholarship and my teaching calling for close attention to the politics of any given situation, I find myself thinking that, if he were still around to do it, this is probably where Jim Berlin would remind me that the personal may be political, but it isn't nearly as political as we wish it were. Sometimes it's just one person talking. It's only when we put the story together with patterns of action and institutional realities and cultural expectations that we can learn very much. That is why so many of the contributors to this collection tell their stories within the larger contexts of growing up, coming of age in a changing profession, learning to shape curricula within the constraints of entrenched bureaucracy. It is through such stories, tied to the scholarship, research, and teaching that continue to shape our profession that we mentor each other and see beyond self.

At least, that is how it's supposed to work.

Diana George
Michigan Technological University

Contributors

Patricia Bizzell is Professor of English at the College of Holy Cross in Worcester, Massachusetts. Her first full-time job was directing the remedial writing program at Rutgers. In 1978, she moved to the College of Holy Cross where she began a peer-tutoring workshop and a writing-across-the-curriculum program, which she directed until 1994 when she became director of the College Honors Program. Her long list of contributions to the field of composition and rhetoric include *Academic Discourse for Critical Consciousness* (Pittsburgh Press), *The Rhetorical Tradition* (with Bruce Herzberg) now in its second edition (Bedford), and *The Bedford Bibliography for Teachers of Writing* (also with Bruce Herzberg), now in its fourth edition with a new on-line version and the fifth edition in the works. She has also served as a member of WPA's Executive Board.

Johanna Atwood Brown is finishing up her Ph.D. at the University of Wisconsin–Milwaukee. She is currently taking a break from administrative work by teaching English full-time at a private college prep school in Flint, Michigan.

Beth Daniell is an associate professor of English at Clemson University where she was Director of Composition and Rhetoric for three and a half years, from 1994 to 1997. She studied rhetoric and composition at the University of Texas at Austin (Ph.D. 1986). The focus of her research is literacy, and she has published on this topic as well as on rhetoric and composition theory and pedagogy in a number of journals and collections including *PRE/TEXT*, *CCC*, and *Rhetoric Society Quarterly*. She is currently writing a book on the intersections of literacy and spirituality and is serving on the WPA Executive Committee.

Sue Dinitz teaches writing, trains the Graduate Teaching Fellows, and codirects the Writing Center (along with Jean Kiedaisch) at the University of Vermont.

Christina Doykos Breen teaches writing at the University of Vermont where she serves on the department Writing Committee.

Paul Eschholz, professor of English, came to The University of Vermont in 1969. A graduate of Wesleyan University, Eschholz earned his doctorate in American Studies at The University of Minnesota. While at UVM he has published with his colleague Alfred Rosa eight textbooks for linguistics and writing classes, including *Models for Writers* (6th ed., 1997), *Language: Readings in Language and Culture* (6th ed., 1998), and *The Writer's Brief Handbook* (3d ed., 1998). From 1977 to 1982 Eschholz directed the NEH-funded Vermont Writing Program, a project that has had far-reaching influence on the teaching of writing throughout Vermont and the country. Currently, he is codirector of The National Writing Project in Vermont and serves as director of the Center for Research on Vermont at the University of Vermont.

Toby Fulwiler is Professor of English at at the University of Vermont where he has directed the writing program since 1983. Before that he taught at Michigan Tech and the University of Wisconsin where, in 1973, he also received his Ph.D. in American Literature. At Vermont he teaches introductory and advanced writing classes. Recent books include *When Writing Teachers Teach Literature,* coedited with Art Young (1996), *College Writing* (1997), and *The Working Writer* (1998).

Diana George is Associate Professor of Composition and Cultural Theory at Michigan Technological University where she has coordinated the writing center, directed first-year writing, and served as Director of GTA Education. She is author, with John Trimbur, of *Reading Culture* currently in its third edition with Longman, is a recipient of the 1998 CCC Braddock Award, has coedited *Writing Center Journal,* and has served on the executive boards of National Writing Centers Association and the Council of Writing Program Administrators.

Alice Gillam directs the First-Year Writing Program at the University of Wisconsin–Milwaukee and teaches undergraduate and graduate courses in rhetoric and writing. Her essays on writing centers and pedagogy have appeared in *Writing Center Journal, Composition Studies, Journal of Teaching Writing,* and in various anthologies.

Nancy Grimm is director of the MTU Writing Center and Assistant Professor in the Humanities Department at Michigan Technological University. She also holds an adjunct position in the Department of Education at MTU. She is the 1998 recipient of the National Writing Centers Association Outstanding Article of the Year. Grimm has served as Executive Secretary of the National Writing Centers Association and as coeditor of *Writing Center Journal.* She is currently preparing a book-length manuscript on re-theorizing writing center practice.

Jeanette Harris is Director of the William L. Adams Writing Center at Texas Christian University. She was formerly chair of the English Department at the University of Southern Mississippi and Director of Composition at Texas Tech University and the University of Southern Mississippi. Her publications include *Expressive Discourse* (SMU, 1990), *Interactions* (Houghton Mifflin, 1991, 1994, 1997; with Ann Moseley), *Writing Centers in Context* (NCTE, 1993; with Joyce Kinkead), and *The Simon and Schuster Guide to Writing* (1994, 1997; with Donald H. Cunningham).

Marguerite Helmers teaches criticism, cultural studies, and writing courses at the University of Wisconsin–Oshkosh, where she directs the writing program and the common intellectual experience for new students. Published articles include interpretations of the nature writings of American author John Muir and an introduction to the travel writings of British essayist Stephen Graham. Her 1995 book *Writing Students* explores the metaphors that describe students in the professional writings of English teachers; an earlier version of the book won the 1993 CCCC Outstanding Dissertation Award. In addition to teaching and writing, she performs on the Celtic harp in the Milwaukee area.

Doug Hesse is Professor of English and Director of Graduate Studies at Illinois State University, where he previously served ten years as Director of Writing Programs. He edited *WPA: Writing Program Administration* from 1994 to 1998 and is currently Vice President of the Council of Writing Program Administrators. He publishes on rhetorical theory, narrative theory, and creative nonfiction, including chapters in a dozen books, most recently *Passions, Politics, and 21st Century Technologies*, and articles in numerous journals, including *CCC, JAC, Rhetoric Review*, and *Writing on the Edge*.

Mara Holt is the Director of Composition in the English Deptartment at Ohio University in Athens. She currently serves on the CCCC Executive Board, and is doing research on academic labor.

Stephen Jukuri is currently working on his dissertation for a Ph.D. in Rhetoric and Technical Communications from Michigan Technological University where he served as Assistant Director of Graduate Teacher Education. His most recent work will appear in *Rhetoric Review*, an article coauthored with Dennis Lynch.

Jean Kiedaisch has taught composition courses at the University of Vermont since 1980. For the past eight years, she has directed the Writing Center. She has published in the *Writing Lab Newsletter*, the *Writing Center Journal*, and the *Journal of Teaching Writing*.

Tony Magistrale is Professor of English at the Unviersity of Vermont. He has published widely in the areas of writing and American literature. One of his more recent books is entitled *Writing Across Culture*. It is an application of writing-across-the-curriculum philosophy to the intercultural experience.

Richard E. Miller is Associate Director of the Writing Program and an Associate Professor in the English Department at Rutgers University. His most recent work, *As If Learning Mattered: Reforming Higher Education* (Cornell UP, 1998), is concerned with providing an historical account of the business of administration and reform in the academy.

Mary Pinard is an assistant professor of English at Babson College in Wellesley, MA. She directs and teaches in the Undergraduate Writing Program and coordinates the Babson College Writing Center. She has taught literature and writing for many years at a number of institutions, including Wright State University, the Katharine Gibbs Secretarial School, Bay State Community College, and Emerson College. She is also a poet whose work has appeared in *Harvard Review, Indiana Review,* and *Prairie Schooner.*

Keith Rhodes is now in his fourth year of coordinating composition at Northwest Missouri State University. His publications and conference presentations have concerned ethnography, liberatory pedagogy, the early history (and even prehistory) of rhetoric, neurobiology, and about anything else that can give us an external perspective on the work of composition.

Monette Tiernan is currently Director of Writing Programs at Lafayette College in Easton, Pennsylvania.

Ralph Wahlstrom is an Assistant Professor of Rhetoric and Technical Communication and the Coordinator of the Writing Center at Buffalo State College of New York. His interest in literacy and disenfranchised students began in 1980 when he taught college English at the Marquette Branch Prison in Northern Michigan. He later taught at the Daqing Petroleum Institute in the People's Republic of China and designed and directed Student Support Services for Disadvantaged Students projects for thirteen years before joining the faculty at Buffalo State College where he is currently involved in research on liberatory practices in the college writing center. Dr. Wahlstrom received his Ph.D. from Michigan Technological University in 1996.

Bill Williamson is a Ph.D. student at Michigan Technological University. He served as the Assistant Director of GTA Education from 1993 to 1995, and has continued to work closely with GTAs and faculty on teaching concerns since.

Kathleen Blake Yancey is Associate Professor of English at the University of North Carolina at Charlotte, where she teaches courses in writing, in rhetoric, and in the teaching and tutoring of English. On her own campus and across the country, she works with faculty across the curriculum on portfolios, on reflective reading and writing, and on ways to enhance pedagogy. She cofounded and coedits the journal *Assessing Writing,* and she has edited or coedited five collections of essays. Her most recent project is *Reflection in the Writing Classroom,* a monograph that both theorizes and demonstrates reflection as a means of learning to write.